The Big Questions
in Science and Religion

The Big Questions
in Science and Religion

Keith Ward

TEMPLETON FOUNDATION PRESS

WEST CONSHOHOCKEN, PENNSYLVANIA

Templeton Foundation Press
300 Conshohocken State Road, Suite 670
West Conshohocken, PA 19428
www.templetonpress.org

Parts of this book were delivered as the Hensley Henson Lectures at the University of Oxford in 2008.

*Templeton Foundation Press helps intellectual leaders and others learn about science
research on aspects of realities, invisible and intangible. Spiritual realities include
unlimited love, accelerating creativity, worship, and the benefits of purpose in persons and in the cosmos.*

Designed and typeset by Gopa and Ted2, Inc.

Library of Congress Cataloging-in-Publication Data

Ward, Keith, 1938-
  The big questions in science and religion / Keith Ward.
      p. cm.
  Includes bibliographical references and index.
  ISBN-13: 978-1-59947-135-8 (pbk. : alk. paper)
  ISBN-10: 1-59947-135-3 (pbk. : alk. paper) 1. Religion and science. I. Title.
  BL240.3.W37 2008
  201'.65—dc22

                              2007045201

Printed in the United States of America
08 09 10 11 12 13 10 9 8 7 6 5 4 3 2 1

Contents

The Big Questions
in Science and Religion

Introduction

OUR VIEW OF the nature of the universe and of the place of humans within it has changed completely within the last century from anything that could have been imagined in the past. Discoveries in cosmology and evolutionary biology, in computer science and solid-state physics have revolutionized human thinking in fundamental ways.

This book assumes that these new scientific discoveries are basically correct. Scientists' findings are, of course, always revisable, and many of them will almost certainly need to be revised in the light of further research. But they provide the best information we have about the nature of things, and the view they present is wondrous and astonishing.

All past science has had to be rethought in the twenty-first century. That process of rethinking carries important implications for philosophy, morality, and religion. Religious beliefs cannot remain what they were before the rise of modern science any more than ancient scientific beliefs can. It would be absurd to insist that ancient religious beliefs should remain unchanged when our whole view of the universe has changed radically.

But that thought raises the question of whether religious beliefs can survive at all in the scientific age. Have they been resoundingly outdated? Or is there in them something of great importance, even though the way they are expressed will have to change in the new scientific context?

I have spent my academic life in the study of religions, especially of the intellectual beliefs of religions—beliefs about God or the ultimate nature of reality, about the soul and the possibility of immortality, about different ideas of revelation and religious experience.

One result of this study has been to see that religious beliefs have usually been formulated in the light of the best available knowledge about the universe that existed at the time. This leads to the conclusion that the unprecedented and revolutionary changes in scientific knowledge of our age will involve a new formulation of ancient religious beliefs.

But my study has also led me to believe that there is a distinctive central core of religious belief that has something to contribute to human knowledge and understanding, and that is quite different from scientific knowledge. To put it very briefly, there is a nonphysical reality (or realities) that is of supreme value and that humans can become aware of it through various forms of prayer or meditation. In the great religious traditions, this supreme value is said to have the nature of consciousness, intelligence, compassion, and bliss. Human awareness of it is meant to lead to the realization of those qualities in the human world and to the cessation of all forms of egoism and selfish desire.

Religious views usually stress, however, that as human life is in bondage to egoism, to hatred, greed, and ignorance, the way to union with Supreme Value is hard to find and even harder to pursue successfully. Religious life is, thus, often a matter of intense personal struggle and even conflict, as hatred, greed, and ignorance continually threaten to undermine the highest human aims and ambitions.

Science will not resolve these deep existential struggles. But science can help to dispel ignorance about the universe and bring some clarity about the relation of the objective Supreme Value postulated by religion to the observed nature of the physical universe. It may even help to clarify the nature and possible purposes of a being of supreme value.

Many of the greatest natural scientists have been religious believers and have seen their investigations as ways of seeking to understand the wisdom and glory of God in nature. But some scientists and philosophers have argued that only the methods of science can reveal truth about the universe and that religion is intrinsically antiscientific and superstitious. So science has been used both as a support for religion and as a way of undermining religion. That ambiguity remains and must be reflected in any fair treatment of science and religion.

In this book, I have selected what I think are the ten most basic questions about the nature of the universe and about human life, questions that involve both science and religion and the relationship between them. I have attached a subquestion to each main question, appearing in parentheses below the big question that introduces each chapter, to emphasize an important issue to which the main question is of primary relevance. Thus, the problem of the prevalence of suffering in the world—a major problem for any religious view—is a subquestion to which an understanding of evolution is most relevant. And the question of what it means for humans to have free will—a major problem in religion, philosophy, and jurisprudence—I have put as a subquestion to an analysis of the nature of space/time. I hope the relation of subquestions to the major questions will be fairly clear in each case.

Since my own expertise is in the study of world religions, I have tried to describe religious views in as global and comprehensive a way as possible. I try to show the relation between diverse religious views and how new scientific knowledge may have an impact upon them. It is a fairly unusual feature of the book that the world's religious traditions are considered seriously across a wide range, and this may have its own interest as an analysis of the nature of religious belief.

It has been my great privilege, largely thanks to the Templeton Foundation, to meet some of the world's most eminent scientists and to discuss these topics with them. I think I should mention that I have met more atheists at Templeton-sponsored conferences than anywhere else, so the accusation sometimes made that the foundation is biased in favor of religion is quite incorrect and grossly unfair.

Nevertheless, since such conferences are usually about science and religion and since quite a lot of scientists are religious, it is not surprising that there are attempts by religious believers to portray the relation of religion and science in a positive way. I myself am an Anglican minister, and so I am rather unlikely to conclude that religion is outdated superstition. But that does not mean I have a closed mind—I was once an atheist and only became a believer after I opened my mind to things I had not previously considered with proper attention. But I remember what it was like to be an atheist and have tried to present the antireligious case in an unprejudiced way.

So, while putting a case for a positive and healthy relation between religion and science, I have also presented the problematic points and the main opposing views as fairly as I can. I am not a professional scientist but an enthusiastic, even zealous, lover of science and "overhearer" of scientists. I have done my best to get the science right—I have checked it in every case with experts—but the views I express about the nature and limits of science are my own. I believe that the questions with which this book deals are the greatest intellectual and existential questions facing any thoughtful person in the modern scientific age, whether such persons are religious or not. So, the main purpose of the book is to convey the depth, difficulty, intellectual excitement, and importance of these big questions. My hope is that it may also convey an understanding of the nature of science and of religion. As such, it is a brief record of some of the most impressive achievements of the human mind and of some of the deepest unresolved questions that continue to confront all who agree with Plato that "the unexamined life is not worth living."

1. How Did the Universe Begin?

Two Ancient Stories of the Origin of All Things

THERE HAS RECENTLY BEEN a marked growth in the number of firms that offer to trace people's ancestry and genealogy. It seems that many people are interested in knowing their past histories. Knowing where you come from and how you got to where you are tells you something important about yourself. Perhaps knowing your origin will tell you what you really are, your true nature.

Many ancient religions share this interest in how things began and how humans came to be. The oldest surviving written religious account of origins comes from Babylonia (roughly, modern Iraq). The *Enuma Elish* (the words mean "when above" and are the first two words of the epic) exists in fragmentary form and has been dated to somewhere between 1000 and 1800 BCE. Representative of a number of Middle Eastern stories of origin, it clearly influenced the account of origins to be found in the Bible (which was written down much later, perhaps in the sixth century BCE).

In the Babylonian story, the gods arise from a primal deep or chaos, what the book of Genesis calls *tohu-wa-bohu*, the "great deep," though the compiler of Genesis implies that this sea was itself created by one supreme God. In Babylon, however, all the gods arise from the deep, and there is conflict among them that culminates in a great battle between Marduk, god of the city of Babylon, and Tiamat, the great dragon or serpent of the sea. Not surprisingly, given that the Babylonians wrote the story, Marduk wins and becomes the greatest of the gods. The dragon is defeated, and, from her body, earth and sky are fashioned. Humans are made from the blood of Kingu, general of her armies, and they are given the job of tilling the earth to provide food for the gods.

As an account of the ultimate origin of all things, this is rather disappointing. All forms arise out of the formless deep, but why they should do so or why they should have the nature they have is left unexplained. The writer of Genesis accepts the existence of primal chaos and even of a mysterious "dragon of the deep," called variously Leviathan or Rahab. Later in the Bible, Psalm 89:9–10 says, "You [Lord God] rule the raging of the sea; when its waves rise, you still them. You crushed Rahab like a carcass." Rahab is crushed but still lives. But at "the last day," "the Lord with his cruel and great and strong sword will punish Leviathan the fleeing serpent, Leviathan the twisting serpent, and he will kill the dragon that is in the sea" (Isa. 27:1).

The serpent and the saltwater sea remain symbols of a chaotic and destructive force that God needs to limit and order and that God will finally destroy—so, the writer of the book of Revelation, looking ahead to God's new creation, is finally able to say, "[T]he sea was no more" (Rev. 21:1).

For the Bible, this is no longer a war of the gods, but there is still the thought that chaos, the threat of the formless, is somehow part of creation. There is also the thought that human nature is somehow corrupted by the chaos-dragon (the snake in the garden, before he lost his legs?). In the Babylon story, humans are made of demon's blood. They have something of chaos within them, and only the power of Marduk can keep that chaos at bay.

In the Babylonian epic, the origins of humanity tell us something about human life. They suggest that it is compounded of destructive chaos and cosmic order. They suggest that humans are part of a constant cosmic conflict, in which goodness is hard to find. They suggest that human destiny is governed by the gods and that the proper human role is to work hard to make the earth fruitful and thereby to serve the greatest of the gods and win his approval.

The biblical account reflects many of these themes, but it replaces the gods with one supreme God. And it finds the ultimate origin of the universe not in chaos, but in a personal God who creates because the universe is good or beautiful (in Hebrew, *Tob*; Gen. 1:31). This does provide a reason for the existence of the universe.

To be good is to be an object of rational desire, to be something that is desirable for its own sake. In that sense, goodness requires a being that wants and enjoys the objects of desire, and it requires objects that satisfy rational desires. Consciousness of a beautiful object is a paradigm of goodness, for such consciousness is desirable simply for itself. So, to be truly good, there must be an object that is worthy of contemplation and a consciousness capable of such contemplation. It is always a reason for the existence of something that it is such a consciously apprehended object. God can create the universe as an object of divine contemplation. It would be good for God to do so, and the creation of good is a reason for creating anything.

According to the book of Genesis, out of the formless and infinite ocean of possibility, God fashions light. Or rather, God "lets light be," as though God were releasing a possible form of being into existence, allowing it to come into existence from the shapeless realm of mere possibility. Then, God created, on the planet earth, the atmosphere, the land and its vegetation, sea creatures and birds, animals, and, finally, human beings, made in the "image and likeness" of God (1:26).

There have been many interpretations of this phrase, "the image of God." But most scholars agree that it implies that humans, like God, have knowledge and creative freedom and share to some degree a responsibility for the care and cultivation of the earth. Most created things are good because they are beautiful, elegant, amazing in form and structure. Humans are good in a special sense because they are fully conscious of that beauty and they can themselves create beauty in new forms. They can appreciate beauty, the beauty of creation and the beauty of the Creator. They realize and are conscious of the goodness and beauty of the world. And that realization, the contemplative and sensitive awareness of beauty, is itself a new and distinctive form of goodness.

The Biblical Story As the Origin of the Scientific Outlook

I have looked at two Middle Eastern stories of origin. One, the Babylonian, belongs to an extinct religion. The other, the biblical, is still with us. One roots all things in primal chaos and sees humans as playthings of the gods, implicated in the conflicts of spiritual forces that are continually at work in the natural world, in storms and earthquakes, in fertility and human warfare. The other carries many echoes of that view; but, in its final form, probably compiled in the sixth century BCE, it roots all things in one God who envisages and actualizes creation because it is good. Humans, made in the image of that one God, must do the same— envisage, actualize, and enjoy the good things of creation and keep the mysterious threat of the unbounded deep at bay.

Between these two stories of origin, there is a division that continues to exist in the most sophisticated contemporary scientific accounts of the universe: the divide between chance and purpose. In the Babylonian account, the gods arise from the formless without any conscious intention. Human lives are determined by the conflicts of the gods, which, again, depend on chance outcomes of a perpetual supernatural contest for power. In such a worldview, there are religious practices—devotion to gods, for the sake of avoiding harm and gaining good. There may be a strong sense of spiritual presences, both beneficial and dangerous. But there is little or no incentive to see the natural world as rational or intelligible or to see religion as in any way connected with a rational or scientific view of the world. The gods are as petty and capricious as human beings—but they live longer and are infinitely more dangerous.

In the biblical story, the whole universe arises by a conscious intention to bring many forms of goodness—of beauty, elegance, and intelligibility—into being. So, there is a reason for the existence of the universe. The basic reason is that it is worthy of contemplation and understanding for its own sake. Creatures exist who recognize and appreciate beauty and goodness, and they thereby increase the sum of goodness in existence. The universe is an intelligible, rational order that can be understood and appreciated by creatures who are made in the image of the rational Creator. Events in the universe are not capricious or truly random. They are parts of an ordered structure and can, in principle, be explained and understood.

The biblical view of origins makes religious practice much more compatible with a scientific study of nature—a study that presupposes that nature is intelligible and comprehensible by the human mind. Of course, the Bible was written long before modern science existed, so we should not expect it to include any strictly scientific content. What we get, however, is the intellectual foundation for future science, in the idea of one rational Orderer of the whole of nature, who desires the universe to exemplify intellectual beauty and creates human beings (and perhaps other intelligent creatures too) to appreciate and understand it.

Three Problems with the Biblical Story

Things seem to be going rather well for the biblical account of origins. But there are some problems, which many skeptical modern scientists are not slow to point out. I shall mention three major problems. One is that this account assumes that the existence of the universe is good. Because of the amount of suffering and pain in the world, some people doubt whether this universe could have been created for the sake of goodness. The hypothesis does not seem to fit the facts.

A second problem is that the account assumes the universe has a purpose. But given the vast amount of empty space, the tiny amount of time for which humans have existed, and the fact that the whole thing will run out of energy sooner or later, some people doubt that any purpose can be seen in the universe at all.

A third problem is that introducing God does not solve the problem of origins. It just puts it one stage further back. For how did God come into being? Is God not even more complicated and mysterious than the universe—and if so, how can God really explain anything?

This is a bit of a blow to those who accept the biblical account of creation. Is there any way in which believers could respond?

The first problem is that the universe is not really good. Many writers have thought that it would be better for the universe not to exist. There is so much suffering and destruction in the universe that it is a pity it is there at all. And maybe it is not quite so intellectually beautiful after all. It may be rather messy and chaotic, and we are just lucky that some of our scientific theories have worked rather well so far. It may all go wrong quite soon, and we will discover that we cannot get any coherent scientific explanations for the universe after all. Perhaps, some cosmologists think, this orderly part of the universe is just a tiny part of a much larger megauniverse, most of which is chaotic.

Part of what this shows is that many scientists do have a lot of faith, quite as much faith as religious believers. The scientists' faith is that the universe is really comprehensible through and through; it does have intellectual beauty. As the Cambridge quantum physicist Paul Dirac (1958) remarked, the fundamental equations of quantum theory were selected largely because of their mathematical beauty.

Perhaps that faith is misplaced. Already (at the time of this writing) there are basic problems about making relativity theory and quantum theory consistent, and perhaps the basic principles of nature are quite beyond us. If you think the universe is an anarchical mess, beyond the grasp of science, you will probably not favor the hypothesis of a rational Creator. On this point at least, some scientists and some religious believers can make common cause and affirm their common faith that the universe is intelligible, a rational and comprehensible whole.

The other part of this problem is the age-old problem of why there is so much suffering in the universe. This is such a major problem that I will be returning to it when dealing with some of the other "big questions." For the moment, I will just admit that, if you think it really would be better if the universe did not exist, that is a good reason for thinking there is no Creator God. A believer in creation must assert that, in some way, suffering, or the possibility of suffering, is necessary to this universe and that it can be sufficiently compensated for or overcome.

The Babylonian postulation of a "primeval deep" is perhaps meant to assert this, and possibly science can show that chaos and destruction are necessary to the structure of the universe. For instance, without the immensely destructive explosions of stars, heavy elements like carbon, essential to life, could not form. And without the extinction of dinosaurs, humans could never have come to exist. It is possible that a greater understanding of the complex interplay between the fundamental laws and forces of the universe will show how destruction and creation are necessarily bound together in the universe and how no universe with beings like humans in it could otherwise exist. But, of course, it may not. And for many the question of whether an all-powerful God could have created a better universe without all this suffering remains unanswerable. The existence of suffering is a major objection to the hypothesis of a God who creates for the sake of goodness.

The second problem is that many people cannot see that there is any purpose in the universe. Some even think that modern science shows there cannot be a purpose in the universe, for it shows that the role of chance and randomness is much too great for there to be any consciously designed purpose.

The question of whether there is purpose in the universe is another "big question," and I will deal with it in chapters two and three. So, for the moment, I will put it aside, while accepting that, if the universe really is without purpose or design, it would be very difficult to believe that it is the result of creation by a God.

Can God Be an Ultimate Explanation?

The third problem, with which this chapter is mainly concerned, is that many people do not accept that God could be an ultimate explanation of the universe. If the universe is good or even if there are sufficient good things in the universe, the existence of a God who envisages good and decides to make it actual would explain why the universe exists. But what would explain the existence of God? Would such a God not be even more complex and problematic than the universe itself? So how does the fact of God help to explain the universe?

This is a variant of Bertrand Russell's question, allegedly addressed to his nanny when he was five: "Who made God?" The traditional answer is that God, like mathematics, is not the sort of thing that can be made, that can come into being or pass away. God is, in fact more like the "formless deep" than it may have seemed. Boethius (1969) described God as the "infinite ocean of being." God is a sort of limitless reservoir of all possibilities and is beyond all finite names and forms. From that ocean of possibility, particular things do arise, as in the Babylonian story. But they arise by conscious knowledge and choice.

Who knows and chooses? Not a particular disembodied person, with a particular personality and prejudices. That is much too anthropomorphic a view. Possibilities are stored in an unlimited consciousness. Each possible state of affairs has a value attached to it as part of what it is. The Infinite Consciousness is aware of each value, and if a possible state has a relatively high value (is "good"), that is a reason for bringing it into actuality.

The "ocean of possibility," thus, contains its own reason for existence. Possibilities, it may be said, can only exist in an actual being, and an actual being that contains possibilities sounds as if it has something very much like consciousness. That consciousness has good reasons for bringing some possible states into being, not by arbitrary whim but by simply attending to the nature of all possible states.

We might say, then, that the universe comes into existence because there is a good reason for it to exist (because it is good or contains overwhelmingly great goods). And the set of all possible states necessarily exists in an Infinite Consciousness in which alone possibilities are capable of existing.

The reason God cannot be brought into being is that God is the necessary condition of anything being brought into being. There is something like what mathematicians call a "phase space," a space of logical possibility that contains all possible states and that, therefore, cannot be other than it is (because the set of all possible things is exhaustive and cannot be added to or subtracted from). It is necessarily actual and is unique in being self-existent, in not deriving its existence from another. Being both actual and conscious, it knows what possible states are good and can be the source of their actuality.

This can be called a "choice" because it is a selection of some possible states for actualization. But it is not a purely random choice or a choice without reasons. It is a wholly rational choice, for the sake of goodness. Thus, the ultimate explanation of the existence of the universe is a combination of necessity and value. The unlimited ocean of possibility and the consciousness in which alone it can be contained is necessary. The coming into being of some possibilities is for the sake of their value. There can be no more complete an explanation for the universe than this.

There are two main versions of such an explanation in the history of philosophy. G. F. W. Leibniz held that there is only one possible world that can exist or that there is one *best* possible world that can exist. But Thomas Aquinas, holding that there is no such thing as "one best possible world," believed rather that any universe that contains overwhelmingly great goods can be created. Some modern physicists would add that all such universes do, as a matter of fact, exist, and the more depressive among them hold that all *possible* universes exist. That is depressing because many of these worlds will be very bad indeed. Even the worst possible world will exist. If that is not depressing, it is hard to know what is.

What are we to make of arguments like these? I think all will agree that we are arguing at the edge of the capacity of the human intellect. How could finite minds be expected fully to understand the inner nature of necessity and value? Yet, if we are made in the image of the Creator (as Genesis says we are), we may have at least a hint of what an ultimate explanation would be like, even if we could not ourselves obtain the final explanation.

These arguments, or arguments very much like them, have been used by Plato, Aristotle, Aquinas, Anselm, Descartes, Leibniz, Kant, Hegel, and by many other philosophers—quite an impressive list. But some people still feel that this is all just playing with words. It is nonsense to talk of something existing by necessity. Anything at all can either exist or not, and that is that. Talk of possibilities somehow existing, or even worse, existing in some disembodied consciousness, is nonsense. We know that consciousness is caused by very complex physical brains and cannot exist without them.

Worst of all, this is metaphysics in the old, bad sense. It is not verifiable or falsifiable by observation; it has no theoretical consequences. And so it is vacuous. It does not explain anything, since an explanation has to tell us exactly how and why something happened. But this alleged theory does not actually explain why anything in particular happens—why the sky is blue, why elephants have large ears, or why dogs bark. It has no consequences. It is, therefore, not even a proper theory.

These are certainly powerful points, enough to make many people feel that ultimate questions about the origin of everything are meaningless or useless. All explanations, it may be said, must stop somewhere. The best we can hope for is to find the simplest set of laws of nature and the simplest set of physical states, and then say that they just exist and that is that. No further explanation is possible. Nothing can explain itself, so there must be a final "brute state" that is beyond explanation.

Indian Religious Stories of the Origin of All Things

Some religious views, most notably Buddhism and Chinese religions like Confucianism and Taoism, accept such a view. It is not for us, they say, to address such ultimate questions, which are irrelevant to the practical problem of eliminating suffering where we can and finding a way of living in harmony with the balance of the universe, freed from suffering, hatred, greed, self-delusion, and attachment.

Still, even such religious views do make claims about the nature of ultimate reality. For instance, Buddhists generally believe in rebirth and think that humans have had many past lives in different forms. We may not know what our first origin was, but, according to Buddhists, we do know that we have had many lives and that what we are now is a result of what we did then.

Confucians believe in a Way of Heaven, a moral order that is built into the universe. In other words, these religions deny a purely material-istic view of the universe, a view that the universe is morally indifferent and purely random or accidental. There is a spiritual or mental reality, whether it is called "the will of heaven" or "nirvana," the state of liberated existence. And there is a moral law, a set of rewards and punishments for conduct, built into the universe.

It might be said to be the most general and basic religious belief that there is a moral causal order in the universe and that there is a nonphysi-cal or spiritual aspect to the universe. The point of human life is to live in conformity with the moral order and in union with spiritual reality. This is far removed from a materialist philosophy. Yet it is a philosophy, a belief about what sorts of things ultimately exist and about how human beings ought to live. But no attempt is made at an ultimate explanation of origins, of how things came to be as they are or of how they began.

In fact, the whole idea of a "beginning" of the universe is often denied, especially in the Indian religious traditions from which Buddhism sprang. These traditions are set out in the Upanishads, a major part of the scriptures of orthodox Hinduism, thought by traditional believers to have been dictated by the gods to ancient seers.

The Upanishads are both complex and diverse in the approaches they take, but their central doctrine is that the whole universe is the mani-festation or expression of *Brahman*, the Absolute Reality. *Brahman* is not a reality separate from the universe. It is the inner nature of the uni-verse itself. *Brahman* "is the life that shimmers through all contingent beings" (*Hindu Scriptures* 1966, Mundaka Upanishad 3:1.). "It consists of all things" (*Hindu Scriptures* 1966, Brihadaranyaka Upanishad 4:3). It is the reality of which all physical things are appearances.

That reality is certainly not physical—"*Brahman* is understanding, bliss" (Brihadaranyaka Upanishad 3:9). It has the nature of consciousness and enjoyment. As such it could well be termed the "Supreme Good," since it finds complete satisfaction in the contemplation of all possi-bilities in its own self. It is, as Aristotle put it in the *Metaphysics* (book 12), *noesis noeseos*, literally, "thought that thinks itself," a reality that is supremely happy in the contemplation of its own perfection.

This is very similar to the classical Christian (and Jewish and Mus-lim) idea of God as a being of supreme perfection or goodness. But, in the Indian tradition, it is thought of not as a reality distinct from the universe but as the ultimately real nature of the universe itself. And so the key question is not about how the universe began (was it originated by a spiritual god?), but about what reality underlies the appearances of space and time.

It does not matter to Hindus whether the universe began or not. In fact, it is usually thought that this space/time is only one of an infinite series of space/times. This space/time may have had a beginning, and it may move through a set of phases or "ages" (usually from better to worse), until it ceases to exist. But if so, it was preceded by an infinite number of other space/times, and it will be succeeded by an infinite number after it.

All of them are manifestations of *Brahman*, the only ultimate reality. Yet each universe may be thought of as created by *Brahman*. "It was Being alone that was this in the beginning—one only, without a second" (*Hindu Scriptures* 1966, Chandogya Upanishad 6:2). This Being thought, "Would that I were many." "He knew that he was creation, for he had brought it all forth. Hence he became creation" (Brihadaranyaka Upanishad 1:4)

This points to what seems like a major difference between biblical and Indian views of creation. In the Bible, God creates a universe that is different from the divine being. But in the Upanishads, the creation is part of the divine being. The universe is, as the twelfth-century Indian sage Ramanuja put it, "the body of the Lord." So, whereas the prophets of Israel tend to advocate worship of God as a distinct and superior reality by worshippers who are unworthy sinners, the seers of India tend to teach that all of us really are parts of God and so divine.

At the heart of each finite self is the divine self. "This Self [*Atman*] is *Brahman* indeed" (Brihadaranyaka Upanishad 4:4). The spiritual path of Upanishadic Hinduism is to overcome the illusory self, enmeshed in desires and self-delusions, and discover the true Self (*Atman*) within, which is identical with the one Supreme Reality. The religious life is a journey "from the unreal to the real, from darkness to light, and from death to immortality" (Brihadaranyaka Upanishad 1:3, 28).

The Hindu doctrine of how humans originate is that we originate in and are parts of one supreme Self of all. We have somehow become ignorant of this because of our selfish and materialistic desires. But through meditation and discipline, we can achieve knowledge of our essential natures. Then, "to him who has freed himself from ignorance . . . this same world of pain presents itself as essentially blissful. . . . [He sees himself as] a plaything of *Brahman*, whose nature is supreme bliss," as Ramanuja writes (*The Vedanta Sutras* 1962, 306).

If we ask about the reason for creation, Ramanuja says, "The highest Self, desirous of providing himself with a variety of playthings . . . so modifies himself as to have those elements for his body" (*The Vedanta Sutras* 1962, 405). The word *plaything* is not a very happy translation, and we may prefer a term like *companion*, which I think renders the sense better.

It is important to be aware that Ramanuja's is only one interpretation. Other interpreters, most notably Sankara, would disagree on many points. For Sankara, there is not a conscious decision on the part of the Creator to generate the universe. Rather, all finite names and forms arise from the One through ignorance (*avidya*), and they have the nature of illusion. They are not willed. They arise by necessity and have no positive purpose or goal that is to be achieved by means of them.

The major differences in the Upanishadic traditions are about whether *Brahman* is more or less personal in nature (is a supreme Lord or an Absolute without qualities), about whether creation is positively willed or just occurs through a mysterious arising of ignorance, and about whether liberated souls merge into *Brahman* and cease to be individuals or will continue to exist in a liberated, more blissful realm. But most commentators on the Upanishads agree on the general explanatory scheme for the existence of the universe.

This scheme is that there is one Supreme Reality of intelligent and blissful consciousness. It emanates from itself many worlds, in which beings become ignorant of their true identity with the supreme Self. The law of karma, of moral cause and effect, causes souls to be reborn in many worlds. The spiritual goal is to be liberated from worlds of suffering, and to reestablish identity with the Self. But worlds (that is, universes) will continue to exist, to be continually created and destroyed, as souls work out their karma, and the supreme Self becomes manifold, generating from itself an infinity of names and forms, perhaps out of *lila*, the joy of creation, or perhaps out of a necessary fall into ignorance.

The Possibility of Religious Explanations of the Universe

This sort of religious explanation is not vacuous. It makes some quite specific claims about the sorts of things that exist and about the past and future of human lives. There can be, and are, arguments about whether these claims are true, and that in itself shows that the claims are meaningful and that their content can be understood fairly well.

But can they be verified or disproved? Not, it seems, by public observation and experiment. We cannot observe the coming into being of universes, and we certainly cannot observe a disembodied consciousness creating a universe. We can only publicly observe the physical. We may think a physical state is intelligently designed if it is amazingly complex, integrated, elegant, and beautiful and if it seems to accomplish some worthwhile purpose. But such things cannot be established beyond reasonable doubt.

The only real verification would be if we discovered in the future that we had been reborn many times or if we found ourselves as blissful companions of Krishna (for many Hindus, a finite embodiment of the Supreme Lord) or as one with the Supreme Self—in which case such intellectual puzzles would long ago have ceased to matter. As an old Buddhist saying puts it, "If you have not found enlightenment, you could not understand the answer to your question. If you have found enlightenment, you would not ask the question."

So, in proposing such a religious explanation for the universe, we are presupposing that there are meaningful questions that may be verifiable in principle but that there is, in this world, no conclusive way of verifying or proving them false. This situation is not, however, all that unusual. A somewhat similar example from science would be the question of whether there is life in other space/times—we know what the question means, but there is no definitive way of answering it.

In this situation, some would say that agnosticism is the only responsible attitude. That may be so. But a Hindu would say that the real question is not about things that happened millions of years ago. It is about the nature of reality *now* and about whether the forms of space and time are appearances of some deeper spiritual reality. It is about what the human self really is and about its origins and destiny, why it is as it is and what it may fear or hope for.

Religious explanations do not provide exact predictions of publicly testable processes, but they offer explanations. They explain what the nature of reality is (it is at least partly spiritual), how humans have come to be as they are, how humans should act, and what the final goal of human life is.

The trouble is that such explanations are very contentious, and none of them can be established beyond reasonable doubt. There are profound disagreements about whether Spiritual Reality exists at all, about how humans should act, and about whether there is any goal or purpose for human life. This does not mean they are not explanations. But it does mean that they are hypotheses that have not been definitively established and that always have to compete with other hypotheses. For some people, that lack of certainty and of conclusive evidence is enough to rule out all such explanations as moot, more like science-fiction fantasies than like anything else.

But others will think that we cannot avoid adopting some hypothesis about whether there is a spiritual origin and goal of human life—even if our favorite hypothesis is that there is not. We just have to do the best we can with very ambiguous evidence.

The Spectrum of Religious Claims about the Origin of the Universe

The most general religious hypothesis is that there is a spiritual basis and goal for human existence. Within the spectrum of world religions, this hypothesis divides into three main religious attitudes. One is *theism*, prominent in the Semitic traditions (Judaism, Christianity, Islam, and their derivatives). The universe originates in a conscious intention, and there is a good purpose for the existence of the universe. Religious believers should help to realize this purpose, in loving obedience to the Creator's will.

The second is *absolute idealism*, characteristic of some Indian traditions. According to this belief, the universe originates in one spiritual (intelligent or conscious) reality. There may be no positive purpose in the existence of the universe, but it arises by necessity from the essential nature of *Brahman*, the Absolute. Religious believers seek to become conscious of their own inner identity with the Self of all and to be liberated from the illusion of being a separate desiring ego.

The third is *dualism*, or double-aspect monism, found in some forms of Buddhism and East Asian religions. The origin of the universe is unknown. Perhaps it has just always existed as a fundamental "brute fact." But spirit exists in addition to matter or as an aspect of matter. Accordingly, the religious quest is either to seek liberation from matter in a realm of pure spirit (to achieve liberation from the wheel of rebirth and enter into nirvana) or to apprehend and live in harmony with the moral and spiritual aspect of the material world (the Way of *Tian*—"heaven").

The religious question of origins is not really about whether the universe had a beginning. It is about whether the whole of space/time and everything in it depends upon ("originates in") a superior Spiritual Reality—or, in the third religious view, whether there is a spiritual aspect to it that is vital for determining how humans should act. A supreme Spiritual Reality or a spiritual aspect of material reality could exist whether or not the physical universe has a beginning. So it might seem that the scientific question of whether the universe began is not relevant to the religious question.

What matters is the nature of the universe *now*. For religious views, all material things are creations of, appearances of, or aspects of, a spiritual state or being. The basic reason for believing this is not a purely speculative theory about the origin of the universe. It lies in claimed personal experience of liberation—freedom from egoism and union with a spiritual reality of supreme goodness. When this is the experience of another person, who claims to have achieved liberation or to have intense knowledge of God's will or of unity with the Self of all, it takes the form of "revelation"—a teaching accepted on the authority of someone we believe to be more closely related to Spiritual Reality than we are.

It is such claims to personal experience that make belief that the universe originates in something like a Supreme Consciousness more than an abstract hypothesis. No public testing of such claims is possible since they are claims to apprehend a reality that is not physical and that, therefore, usually has no publicly observable aspect. But personal experience, especially when widely corroborated by others who are not sick or insane and when accompanied by a positive transformation in the moral and affective quality of one's life, is a form of evidence, one that can be overwhelming to those who have it.

This is very unlikely to convince a skeptic, who will dismiss such claims to personal experience of a purely spiritual reality as unreliable and unverifiable or even as delusions. There are no such spiritual realities, the skeptic will say. The natural sciences provide an account of the origins of the universe that needs no appeal to spiritual considerations, and that makes them both superfluous and implausible.

The Scientific Search for a Final Theory

At this point, I will turn from religious explanations to scientific explanations of the beginning of the universe. Most competent scientists agree on the account of the origin of the universe that modern cosmology provides. There seems to be plenty of evidence to suggest that our universe began to exist about 13.7 thousand million (an American, but not a British, billion!) years ago. From a microscopically minute region of stupendous heat and energy, without any consciousness, without any stars or planets, without even any subatomic particles, the material universe exploded into being. As it expanded and cooled, the first wave-particles—photons, neutrinos, and positrons—came into being. Over the next few hundred thousand years, atoms formed, condensed to form stars and galaxies, and, in the nuclear furnaces of the stars, forged the heavy elements like carbon that were to become the basis of life.

Many cosmologists, however, are unhappy at the thought that the universe begins from an initial "singularity"—a one-time event that precedes all the laws of physics and, thus, does not fall under any of them. Stephen Hawking has proposed that, in the very early universe, the dimension of time becomes more and more space-like, so that there is no need for a "first moment of time" to be explained. Edward Tryon suggested in 1973 that, since positive (rest mass and kinetic energy) and negative (gravitational) energies precisely balance one another, the universe may have come into being as a random quantum fluctuation from a zero-energy state. Thus, the universe might be a "free lunch," and we could get the ultimate human dream—something for nothing.

In quantum theory, particles flash into and out of existence, and the early universe is small enough to act in accordance with quantum laws. So, the whole universe may have quantum-fluctuated into existence and "frozen," at least for a while (a few billion years, it turns out), into a physically enduring material system.

Such theories aim to show how something could come from nothing, but do they really do so? Quantum theory consists of a very complex set of laws, and it does not seem sensible to say that the counterbalancing of positive and negative forces is equivalent to nothing at all. This zero-energy state is full of forces that balance each other exactly, and it is a very dynamic and constantly changing state.

It may look as though the universe has progressed from a very simple initial state to its present complex structure. But it is doubtful whether the initial state was simple at all. True, it did not consist of complex and integrated physical structures. There were not huge numbers of particles organized in intricate arrays. So, it was simple in physical structure and complexity. Even then, however, we now believe that the early universe contained dark matter and dark energy, so things were not as simple as they might have been!

Quantum theory utilizes an extremely complex set of laws, dimensions, possibility states, and fluctuating energy fields of various sorts. It involves Hilbert spaces, operators, commutators, symmetry groups, the Dirac equation and interaction potentials, Lagrangians and Hamiltonians, broken symmetries and associated particles. That does not seem very simple. Can it really be said that, at the big bang, there were just a few simple laws and particles? No, because there were no particles at all. And without particles, how or where were the laws supposed to exist? Perhaps they did not exist but just suddenly came into being out of nothing.

But if something can come into being out of nothing—and I mean really *nothing*, not some sophisticated balance of physical energies—it does not really matter whether it is complex or simple. It is not easier for a simple state to come into being than for a complex state to do so.

In fact, since there are infinitely more complex states than simple states, it seems more probable that a complex state would come into being, if probability has any sense here at all.

The idea that a simple state is more likely to come into being possibly arises from the physical principle of minimal effort—nature uses minimal effort to do what it does. But when nature does not even exist yet, that principle cannot exist either. If absolutely nothing exists—no states and no principles or laws—then it is impossible to say what might come into existence and whether it will be simple or complex.

This seems to imply that there could be no reason for the first state of the universe. And that is deeply unsatisfying for a physicist since a fundamental belief of physics is that there is a reason for everything. So, if there is no reason for the big bang, physics seems to have met its nemesis.

Some would just say, "So what? You can't hope to explain everything. And there just is no reason for the existence of the universe. Once you have explained how all its parts interact, there is nothing left to do." As Karl Popper wrote, "There can be no explanation which is not in need of a further explanation" (1972, 195). So there can be no such thing as a final or ultimate explanation.

But others feel that there has to be a reason for the big bang, or the whole basis of science—a belief that we can explain the universe—is undermined. So some cosmologists look for laws and energy states that precede or lie outside of the physical universe, that just have to be what they are, to which there is no alternative. Such laws, like the basic axioms of number theory, would just have to be what they are. Sooner or later, they will generate a universe, or perhaps many universes, of which this is just one. Einstein made this point by saying, "The enterprise of physics is . . . to reach as far as possible the utopian and seemingly arrogant aim of knowing why nature is thus and not otherwise . . . thereby one experiences, so to speak, that God himself could not have arranged these connections in any other way" (1929, 126).

Steven Weinberg, in *Dreams of a Final Theory*, writes, "[I]t is possible that there is only one logically isolated theory [a theory so rigid that "there is no way to modify it by a small amount without the theory leading to logical absurdities"] . . . that is consistent with the existence of intelligent beings" (1993, 191).

All attempts to provide an explanation for the big bang, however, seem to end by saying that underlying our present universe there is something beyond our space and time, something very mysterious—sets of quantum laws (and where are they supposed to be?) and complex energy states (and what is energy really?). We are almost back to the Babylonian primal deep.

The Idea of Necessity

There is something very interesting about the modern cosmological quest. It is looking not just for a primal chaos but for a deep mathematical structure that has to be the way it is, that necessarily exists, and from which the physical universe arises.

And that brings us back to one of the big objections to God as an ultimate explanation—that all existence is contingent, that there is nothing that has to be the way it is. Perhaps modern cosmology is more concerned with necessity than we might think. And why, after all, does all existence have to be contingent? Is that a necessary truth?

The main reason seems to be the one proposed by the philosopher David Hume: that we can always imagine anything not existing. As for mathematics, some think that is simply a set of things that are true by definition, so it does not tell you anything about reality. In slightly more technical terms, if something, X, exists by necessity, then it must exist in every possible world. But we can always conceive of a world without X. So, such a world is possible, and it does not have X in it. Therefore, there can be nothing that exists by necessity.

This argument convinces many. The philosopher Richard Gale uses it in his book *On the Nature and Existence of God* (1991, chapter 6). But others might point out that, contrary to what David Hume thought, the fact we think we can conceive of a world without X does not show that such a world is possible. We can very easily imagine an impossibility (as when we imagine finding a square exactly equal in area to a given circle). Perhaps we cannot imagine what makes something necessary. But there is no contradiction in saying that there is an X that exists in every possible world. If there is such a possible X, while we might think we can imagine a world without X, in fact, there could be no such world. There is no obvious contradiction in saying either that there cannot be such a world or that there can. So we are stuck. We do not know whether a necessary being is impossible or not.

Has that got us any further forward? Well, it does imply that we are in no position to say that we know a necessary being is impossible, that all existence is contingent. We do not know what the conditions of necessity are, but, if there were some necessary laws, that would give a reason for their existence—the reason being that there is no alternative: they have to be!

The peculiar thing about such necessary ultimate laws is that, in many ways, they seem to be possibilities rather than actualities. That is, they say what would have to happen if there were a physical universe. They lay out a set of future possibilities—and some physicists think there is, in the end, just one such set, the set of all possible universes. If that were true, we might have hit upon something that would give us a reason for thinking that there is an ultimately necessary basis for the existence of the universe. It would be the exhaustive set of all possible universes, which could not possibly be other than it is.

The Primacy of Consciousness

At just this point, the religious hypothesis takes on a new and perhaps unexpected relevance: the hypothesis that consciousness is an ultimate element of reality, even perhaps the only ultimate reality. Physical science has not usually concerned itself with that claim, precisely because it is physical science, concerned with the physical, the publicly observable, measurable, and repeatable. Consciousness is not physical, publicly observable, precisely measurable, or controllable in laboratories. Moreover, scientists can usually ignore it, and when they talk about the origin of the universe, they are talking of its purely physical origin.

However, in physics these days, things are not so clear. Some quantum physicists (John Wheeler and Henry Stapp, for example) are impressed by the fact that electrons are probability waves that only collapse into locatable particles when a measurement is taken or when an observation is made. This leads them to say that consciousness is a fundamental aspect of physical reality after all. Perhaps consciousness cannot be considered just a by-product of the physical activity of the brain. Perhaps consciousness has to be present for there to be an actual physical world containing brains at all.

This is certainly a controversial view. All quantum physicists would agree that what we see is a function of what sort of interaction we have with the physical environment. We see things only as they appear to us as observers. But many would not go along with saying that, therefore, consciousness is necessary to the existence of the physical world as we see it. Maybe, they would say, the physical world is stranger than we thought. But it may still be purely physical in its constitution, even if the "physical" is very odd stuff indeed.

But, if you do think that consciousness is fundamental to the existence of physical reality, this raises the possibility that some sort of consciousness is needed to make the universe actual. This would be a cosmic consciousness, a consciousness without a body. But out of what would it make some states actual and in accordance with what laws? All consciousness requires objects, things of which it is conscious. One hypothesis is that the cosmic consciousness primordially consists of all possible states. Those are the primary objects of its consciousness.

It is indeed very odd to think of merely possible things as somehow actually existing. So quantum physicists are very puzzled about how electrons can exist as probability waves in Hilbert space when they are not being observed or measured. However, one way in which we know possibilities can exist is as conceived by some mind. We can all think of possible states of affairs, and those states exist (but only as possibilities) in our minds. So, in addition to being necessary for the actual existence of any physical states, the Cosmic Consciousness might be necessary for the set of all possible states to exist, for all the laws of nature that govern relations between possible future states to exist, and for merely potential realities to have some form of real (consciously conceived) existence.

According to this hypothesis, the real basis of the physical universe is conceptual or mathematical. Mathematical possibilities exist in a cosmic consciousness, and it is that consciousness which, being necessarily actual, can give actuality to some of those possible states and laws.

Some hard-headed mathematicians are impressed by this hypothesis. Roger Penrose wrote, "Although I had not explicitly asserted, in either *Emperor* [*The Emperor's New Mind*] or *Shadows* [*Shadows of the Mind*], the need for mentality to be 'ontologically fundamental in the universe,' I think that something of this nature is indeed necessary" (1997, 175).

From Consciousness to a Physical Universe

But why should some possible states be actualized? It may be that there is only one set of laws that can give rise to a physical universe like the one we have or to any enduring universe at all. Maybe it is just necessary for some universe to be actualized. Maybe there is, in fact, no difference between the possible and the actual, and every possible (conceived) universe is also actual. We are in just one of these universes. Or, if there is only one consistently enduring possible universe, we are in it. We have to be in it; we have no choice; it is all necessary.

However, there is another important consideration. Once consciousness has been introduced, it may occur to us that consciousness not only registers the existence of its objects. It normally has a reactive response to those objects—either of appreciation and pleasure or of dislike and avoidance. We are not usually neutral about the objects of our consciousness. We like some and dislike others. We enjoy some and shun others.

This is not just an arbitrary subjective reaction. Some objects (some possible states) just are more worthwhile, valuable, or desirable than others. Pleasure is more desirable than pain, happiness than sadness. Knowledge is more desirable than ignorance, understanding than misunderstanding. Beauty is more desirable than chaos, creativity than destructiveness. Love is more desirable than hate, cooperation than obstruction.

There might be arguments about details and much room for personal preferences and for selections of relative importance among these values. But, in general, there is little argument about some states being more desirable than others. We can, after Aristotle, call states that are objects of rational desire "good." Then, any conscious being has a reason to choose good states rather than bad ones. In general, that a state is good is a good reason for choosing it.

We now have a principle for the actualization of some possible states—which turns out to be very much like the biblical principle enunciated in the book of Genesis. A rational consciousness would choose them for their goodness. It follows that such a consciousness will choose the best set of possible states for itself. It will be supremely good and desirable, supremely wise, beautiful, and happy. It will be supreme objective goodness, the blissful contemplation of what is supremely worthwhile just for its own sake.

Perhaps *choice* is not quite the right word here, for that might give the impression that God first thinks about what is good and then chooses to be good (which God might not have done). But the "choice" that a being of supreme goodness should exist is a "choice" or selection that follows immediately from the nature of the set of all possible states. The supremely good follows from its own possibility just because it has, as John Leslie has put it, an "intrinsic ethical requiredness" (2001, vi). The supreme good is necessarily actualized, in the perfection of the Divine Being itself.

But there are other factors that do not quite have this element of absolute necessity. For instance, if love and cooperation are great goods, a Cosmic Consciousness will also have good reason to actualize other conscious beings whom it can love and cooperate with, though that reason may not be absolutely compelling. Perhaps the actual existence of a material universe can be an object of further appreciation and give scope for the exercise of fuller creativity. While there may (or may not) be a requirement that some such universe should exist, this introduces scope for creative choice, both in which universes to make actual and in how exactly to relate creatively to those universes.

We now have two reasons for the existence of a physical universe—a principle of necessity and a principle of selection for the sake of goodness. These two principles, necessity and value, form an intelligible reason (and, I think, the only intelligible reason) for the existence of the universe.

We are in no position to know precisely how far things exist by necessity and how far they are selected for value. We can only say that the

Primal Consciousness is necessary to the existence of the set of all possible states, which is necessarily what it is. And the universe arises from it partly by necessity and partly because it is evaluated as good. That is a truly ultimate explanation for the universe.

Are Quests for Ultimate Explanation Properly Scientific?

This seems like a rational hypothesis. But for some physicists, it goes too far beyond physical theories. It does not give rise to any specific testable predictions. It introduces the idea of a nonphysical consciousness, which is unnecessary and possibly incoherent. And it postulates a new and very complex "Cosmic Consciousness," which only complicates the original simplicity that scientists like.

It is true that this is not a hypothesis that can be tested by experiment. If it has a virtue, it lies in its theoretical elegance and comprehensiveness. That is, it says there is just one Consciousness whose nature has to be what it is and that accounts for the existence of all physical things. It does so by resorting to just two principles—necessity and value. That makes it an elegant and simple hypothesis.

It is a theory about what sorts of things there are and why they exist— a theory that has traditionally been called "metaphysical." It says that there are basically two sorts of things, material and spiritual; that the spiritual exists by necessity and produces the material by a combination of necessity and value.

There are considerations that count in favor of this hypothesis—the mathematical elegance, intelligibility, and beauty of the universe; the seeming necessity of the laws of nature; the feeling of objective moral obligation; and alleged apprehensions of a personal Presence or Consciousness greater than any finite consciousness but one present in and through many finite objects and events.

There are also considerations that count against the hypothesis—the existence of great suffering, what some feel to be the apparent pointlessness of existence, the role of chance in the evolution of organic life, and the difficulty of believing that consciousness can exist without any material basis.

In the end, one set of these considerations will prove decisive. The presence of God may become overwhelmingly apparent to all—or the universe will simply expire, and everything will cease to be, as randomly and inexplicably as it came into being. But we, living in the middle of this cosmic drama, cannot see either its ultimate origin or its end.

We can only speculate. From a scientific viewpoint, we can trace the universe back to its origin in the big bang. There the strictly scientific quest ends, with a basic set of laws and a physically noncomplex initial state. But to assert that these basics tell us the true nature of reality, and its ultimate origin, is to move beyond experimental science into metaphysics.

The God Hypothesis

The metaphysics of materialism claims that everything that exists is ultimately material. Consciousness, value, meaning, and purpose are either reducible to the material events in animal brains, or they somehow emerge from material events as epiphenomena, accidental by-products of material processes with no causal role to play in the way things are—and certainly with no part to play in the origin of the universe.

Materialism is one member of a set of logically possible theories about the nature of the universe. This set (I do not imply that it is the only possible set, but it is exhaustive within its stated limits) posits the following: either everything ultimately has the nature of spirit (idealism) or it is purely material (reductive materialism), or spirit and matter both exist more-or-less independently (dualism and double-aspect monism), or spirit emerges from matter (emergent materialism), or matter emerges from or wholly depends on spirit (theism).

The universe is so complex and our knowledge of it so limited, that all these theories have something to be said for them. Physical science is only concerned with the physical side of things, so we might think it is not committed to any of these theories. It does not have to deny the existence of Spirit. But there are some scientists who think that science on its own gives a completely adequate account of the universe, and it gives the only testable account, so they find in the success of science a reason for embracing materialism.

Yet this view is, in turn, hotly contested. Some scientists think that materialism gives an unduly restricted account of what science itself has discovered about the universe. Perhaps most practicing scientists think that science is in no position to come to a firm conclusion on such arcane matters.

Materialism is immensely counterintuitive. It conflicts with our common-sense view that all human knowledge begins from personal experience, that we have thoughts and feelings that no one else can observe, that we are free to plan the future, and that our intentions make a real difference to the world. In short, materialism has a major problem with consciousness. It is the problem of how something that seems so obviously nonmaterial (not located in public space and not observable by others) actually is material in some very subtle way.

But there are plenty of materialists who are confident they can solve the problem. The main basis for this confidence is the enormous success in modern study of the brain and the rise of computing and artificial intelligence. These matters will be dealt with in more detail in chapter six, where I will suggest that materialist accounts are more matters of faith than of established scientific fact. The materialist faith is that one day a complete materialistic account of all mental phenomena will be given, in which consciousness is explained in wholly material terms.

If, however, such materialist proposals are felt to be implausible and if consciousness is taken to be a fundamental and basic element of reality, then any account of the origins of the universe will have to include an account of the origin of consciousness as well as that of matter. Matter may have originated with the big bang; but, if we are trying to explain the origin of consciousness, we have to explain the capacity to understand, appreciate, and act creatively since these are the crucial capacities of a conscious being.

The simplest explanation posits just one being that unites all possible states in one consciousness and that actualizes states by the use of one most general principle of selection. This being, God, is not a tremendously complex being. God has no physical structure at all. God knows and does lots of things. But divine knowledge is the uniting of all possibilities in one consciousness, and the divine act of creation is the selection of states for one basic reason. This is a form of unity that includes many states and principles in one all-inclusive and elegant whole, the organizing principles of which are as rational, elegant, and simple as possible. The exclusion of such a possibility rests on a determination not to allow that a Pure Consciousness could exist and on an insistence that all consciousness must depend upon a physical structure that must be at least as complex as the physical reality of which it is conscious. The God hypothesis, however, is that consciousness can exist without any physical structure. Its simplicity consists in the uniting of all information in one consciousness and in the inclusion of all its actions under one governing intention—the creation of value.

The materialist will respond that we know of no consciousness that is not the result of very complex brain activity. It is extremely unconvincing to suggest that there could be a consciousness without such a material basis. So, is the denial of a pure, immaterial consciousness just due to lack of imagination? Or is the assertion of such a consciousness due to a failure to take seriously enough modern scientific accounts of how consciousness arises gradually from simpler purely material processes? That is another "big question" to which I shall return in chapter six.

Religious and Scientific Cosmologies

It may seem that we have moved a very long way from the Babylonian, Hindu, and Genesis stories of the beginning of the universe to a rather abstract hypothesis about a pure consciousness that acts on purely rational principles. Such a hypothesis would have been incomprehensible in early human history, and the religious accounts tell a picturesque story in a way that can convey a profound spiritual message. Acceptance of modern cosmology does mean that all the ancient religious stories of origin are literally false. Yet they may still point to the important truth of the primacy of Spirit and to the possibility of finding human fulfillment by appropriate relation to Spirit. Stories may be the best way of affirming such a truth, especially in a prescientific age. But they must now be complemented by our more accurate knowledge of the physical history of the cosmos, with which they were never primarily concerned.

It is time to draw some conclusions about what religions and the sciences have to say about the origin of the universe. As to the physical beginning of the universe, there is general (though not quite universal) scientific agreement that the universe began with a state of extreme physical simplicity—a minute state of infinite mass and density—but also of enormous complexity and mathematical elegance in the laws governing its expansion into the universe we see today.

In the light of this discovery—less than 150 years old—all ancient stories of the origin of the universe have been rendered obsolete as literal accounts. The book of Genesis, for example, which sees the earth as a disc floating on a great sea; the sky as a bowl on which the stars, sun, and moon are hung as lamps; and the first humans as living in a garden in which God takes an afternoon stroll and in which apples are forbidden fruit, can clearly be seen to be a prescientific story that is literally false but may still have a deep spiritual meaning. That spiritual meaning is well worth exploring in detail, for what it can tell about the relations of God, humanity, and the created order. But it does not compete with cosmology. It is not in the same ballgame.

Nevertheless, in science, the question remains of what, if anything, came before the big bang or of what, if anything, accounts for it. It is not clear that science can answer this question or if this question can have any answer at all. Some cosmologists seek a theory of everything, some ultimate mathematical system that is necessarily what it is and necessarily gives rise to this universe, and perhaps to other universes too. Among such mathematical physicists, some are materialists, perhaps better called naturalists, since we are no longer sure of what "matter" is. They see the universe as arising without any purpose or design. The universe may arise by some inner necessity, as a quantum fluctuation in a vacuum, perhaps. It then assembles structures of great integrated complexity by a quasicomputational process, pulling itself up gradually by its own bootstraps into complicated and interesting arrays of events.

Others find in the intricate order and integrated complexity of nature evidence of intelligence, though they rarely speculate further on this or see it as having any religious implications. Some mathematicians and quantum physicists, like John Wheeler, Roger Penrose, and Henry Stapp incline to such a view, and Einstein famously spoke of the "Old One" as the great Intelligence underlying the universe. But that intelligence, at least as far as physics goes, does not necessarily show any particular interest in human beings, who have just been thrown up inevitably in the cosmic process.

Many cosmologists refrain from indulging in such speculations. They think there just have to be some ultimate brute facts that cannot be explained. Such facts should be as simple as possible (though, to be honest, no one knows why they should be simple), but appeal to mathematical realities and objective necessity is much too Platonic, too metaphysical, for them. There is quite enough to do, without getting into all that. And there, scientifically, the matter rests.

Conclusion: The Question of Spiritual Reality

It is characteristic of religions to posit a Spiritual Reality or realities, of consciousness and value, in conscious relation to which humans can find their proper fulfillment. Some religions, like Buddhism, are not concerned with origins and just accept the existence of a spiritual realm as given. For them, consciousness is one of the ultimate "brute facts," and a theoretical desire for simplicity cannot be used to rule out things, like consciousness, that (to them) obviously exist.

Some religions, like Indian nondualism (*advaita*), see the physical universe as arising from a Supreme Consciousness by necessity and tend to think that some finite world has always existed or that a succession of finite universes exists, without beginning or end. The question of a beginning of the universe is not of great importance, but it is important that there is real mental or moral causality in the universe, so that souls can reap the consequences of their actions in accordance with the law of karma. Some physicists assert that appeal to such a spiritual law is not necessary to account for the universe and that there is no evidence for its existence anyway. But it is hard for a physicist to assert that there is definitely no such law because a complete and exhaustive account of all causes of events is not available and may even be unobtainable in principle. But a physicist can say that a purely naturalistic account gives a better explanation of how the universe began than would mysterious unmeasurable and untestable laws of moral influence.

The Semitic religions usually posit a beginning of the universe and say that our space/time originates by the creative act of a pure consciousness—God. Some, like Robert Russell, think that it is religiously significant that the universe had a beginning, for that points to an explanation in some reality beyond space/time, perhaps to a timeless intelligence. But, as Aquinas held, the universe can originate in (that is, be wholly dependent upon) God whether or not it had a beginning. So, the question of beginning is not really important. What matters is the dependence of the physical upon the spiritual, and that could well be without beginning. Creation, in other words, is not the beginning of the universe but the dependence of the whole of space and time, at every moment, upon God.

The really decisive split is between those who think the universe originates in consciousness or that at least consciousness has significant causal effects in the universe and those who think the universe originates in blind chance or blind necessity and that the basis of causality is purely natural.

Many scientists believe that cosmology has nothing in particular to say on this issue, though clearly cosmology is only concerned with the physical (nonconscious) aspects of the universe. Some are naturalists, asserting that science—and only science—can provide complete explanations for the existence of everything, explanations that are nonpurposeful and nonconscious in nature. This position is in conflict with virtually all religious belief systems. This is a major area of possible conflict, though whether the conflict is between science and religion or between a particular naturalist philosophy and religion remains to be decided. And some cosmologists, and some of the most able, find a place for consciousness and intelligence in explanations of the origin of the universe. This hypothesis is of great interest to religious believers. But it has to be said that such cosmologists do not very often connect their hypotheses of origin with any particular set of religious beliefs.

So, the answer to the question about the beginning of the universe is that this physical space/time began with a big bang. But there may be many other space/times as well as this one. The most important religious question is not really about the beginning of this universe but about whether it (and any other universe) originates in—and depends at every moment upon or relates to—a Spiritual Reality of consciousness and intelligence.

To this question, there are three main responses from cosmologists—

"that is none of our business"; "definitely not"; and "it's a pretty good hypothesis." It is the third response that is of most relevance to religious believers, as it offers the prospect of a fruitful interaction between those believers who want a rational foundation for religion and those scientists who seek an ultimate and truly comprehensive explanation for the universe. But while this is a dream for some, it is a nightmare for others, who find religion offensive and dangerous.

Is this question, after all, resolvable by cosmologists anyway? That is quite another question, and one I shall return to in chapter seven.

2. How Will the Universe End?

(DOES THE UNIVERSE HAVE A GOAL OR PURPOSE?)

Religious Attitudes about the End of the Universe

FEW WHO HAVE SEEN it can ever forget the ending of Richard Wagner's Ring, as Valhalla, the home of the gods, is consumed by fire, and the cursed ring of power achieved through the renunciation of love returns to the waters of the Rhine. The gods die, but the soaring music of the orchestra carries a hint of a purer world to come without the duplicity of the gods.

Wagner used Viking and Teutonic myths in writing his epic music–drama, and many of these myths are codified in the Norse Poetic Edda, perhaps written down in the late thirteenth century, and the Prose Edda, collected by Snorri Sturluson a little earlier. They speak of the end of the world, or at least of the world we know. Ragnarok is the doom of the gods and the destruction of the world in a last final battle between the gods and the frost giants, both of whom had arisen from the primal conflict of ice and fire in Ginnungagap, the yawning emptiness at the world's beginning.

Fenrir, the "gray wolf who is watching the abode of the gods," swallows sun and moon and kills Odin, king of the gods. Jormungand, the world serpent, bursts from the sea and destroys Thor, god of thunder. Hel arises with the pale armies of the unworthy dead and battles with the heroes of Valhalla on the Vigrid plain. Surt, the fire god, identified with Loki, father of the wolf-age monsters, sets the nine worlds ablaze, and the earth finally sinks into the primal ocean of chaos.

This Nordic vision of the end of time is about as far from a dream of gradual progress toward utopia as you can get. The world is born in conflict, and the earth is formed from the corpse of the murdered frost giant Ymir. Viking warriors hope to gain Valhalla after death, where they fight all day and feast each night. The alternative is the pale underworld ruled by Hel, half-woman and half-decomposing corpse. The world will end in conflict, when gods and frost giants mutually exterminate one another, and fire and water destroy the earth.

All this belongs to Norse mythology, to a religious view that has long since passed away. Or has it? There are remarkable echoes of the Sumerian mythology that passed into the Christian Bible, and when the northern peoples accepted Christianity, in the tenth century, they forged an unexpected alliance of their harsh warrior code with the Christian gospel.

In Christianity, too, there is talk of a cosmic battle between good and evil and a decisive battle at Armageddon that will bring the earth to ruin. But in the Christian scheme, the world was created by a basically good God, not out of a conflict between ice and fire. So, good triumphs in the end, and Armageddon is followed by the reign of Christ in glory and by the creation of "a new heaven and earth," the descent from heaven of the holy city of Jerusalem, and a world without tears or suffering. Possibly influenced by this, versions of the Norse myth speak of Balder, the gentle and wounded god, who after the destruction of Valhalla and earth, will rise from the domain of Hel into a green land risen from the sea. There may be a new race of humans there and gods more benign and a fair land free from the ancient conflict of fire and ice.

There may be an ultimate hope, but the outlook is depressing for most people. The Vikings reacted by adopting an attitude of tragic heroism, fighting to the end a battle that could not be won. Christians originally retreated from the world, the "vale of tears," to await the world's end and the return of the Messiah. But there are strands in Norse mythology that entered into Christianity—and there are more obviously strands in Islam—that call for heroic participation in the great battle of good and evil, a battle that will only end with the destruction of the old order and a dramatic new creation.

The Indian traditions are hardly more optimistic. The world passes through four great ages, or *yugas*, each one lasting many hundreds of thousands of years. The first age, the age of gold, lasts longest, and in it all are happy and good. Succeeding ages grow shorter and get worse. We live in the fourth age, the *Kali Yuga*, in which ignorance and evil grow ever greater. It will go on getting worse, until Kalkin, the tenth avatar of Vishnu, rides out on a white horse to put an end to evil and to usher in the twilight sleep of Brahma, when all is quiescent and nothing lives. Then the cycle begins again, and it will be repeated endlessly.

Only in China, among the great traditions, is there a fairly optimistic view of the future. In Confucian thought, humans are basically good, and if society is ruled in accordance with the Way of Heaven, it is possible to have a just and flourishing human world. However, the danger of imbalance and chaos is never far away, as the checkered history

of Chinese dynasties shows. So, the good life is precarious and probably rare, unless there is a form of immortality with the ancestors that is
beyond decay and conflict. But such hopes, though present, are muted
in East Asian religions and have never had the prominence they often
have in the other main religious traditions. In this respect, the Chinese
attitude is not unlike that of early Hebrew religion (represented in most
of the Hebrew Bible or Old Testament). There is little concern with a life
after death or a distant future, but there is a hope for the continuance of
one's family lineage and for a happy and prosperous society.

Religions do not, in general, have as much interest in the end of the
universe as in its beginning. That is probably because they consider that
things, once begun, will continue very much as they are. They do have
an interest, however, in the question of whether there is a purpose or
goal in human existence.

Religions have a strong awareness of the suffering and evil in human
existence and are largely concerned with identifying the causes of such
suffering and with ways to avoid or alleviate it. A major goal of religious
life is, therefore, to find liberation from suffering and evil and to find
lasting happiness and true goodness.

In theistic religions (see the typology in chapter one, "The Spectrum
of Religious Claims about the Origin of the Universe," 19–20), the universe exists for a purpose, and it seems likely that purpose would include
the happiness and virtue of conscious beings. At some time, that purpose
will be realized, and evil will be eliminated—whether in the future or
in another form of existence beyond this physical universe (perhaps in
a "new creation"). This allows for a final great battle between good and
evil, resulting in the destruction of evil and the emergence of a new and
more perfect world.

In idealist and dualist religions, there is often no positive purpose for
the universe, which emanates by necessity from Pure Consciousness.
The human goal tends to lie in escape from the illusion of plurality and
reunion with the One Real or (as in Jainism) in a disembodied, individual, desireless, and omniscient existence.

There are versions of idealism and dualism, however, that view the
finite universe more positively. For them, the goal is achieving a good
and happy life, free from suffering, either on this earth ("nirvana is sam-
sara"—liberated existence is identical with this suffering world, when
seen by the enlightened mind, free from passion, said the Buddhist sage
Nagarjuna) or in a "Pure Land" beyond the physical universe.

Just as the religious question about the beginning of the universe is
really about the ultimate nature of existence, so the religious question
about the end of the universe, when it arises, is really about the ultimate

goal of existence. The religious goal is variously conceived, from the realization of a divine purpose in or beyond this universe, to escape from the material universe to pure spiritual existence or to union with the Real, to achieving a good and happy life by living in accordance with spiritual principles and insights, either in or beyond this universe.

Ultimate Pessimism and Ultimate Optimism in Scientific Cosmology

Modern cosmology has developed a great interest in the question of the end of the universe, but the most obvious way in which it conflicts with literal interpretations of virtually all religious views is in its vastly expanded view of the size and age of the universe. The Semitic traditions tend to place humans and the earth at the center of the universe and allow the universe a very short time span of a few thousand years. Indian traditions have a more expansive view, but even the million-year *yugas* do not approach the billion-year range of modern cosmology, and even a *mahayuga*—one cycle of existence of a universe—is dwarfed into relative insignificance by the scientific prospect of billions of years of cosmic time yet to come and of billions of other galaxies and stars that seem to be forever beyond our reach.

The immediate implication of modern cosmology is that humans seem to be much less important in the scheme of things than traditional religions have thought. Out of the fourteen thousand million years for which the universe has existed, human beings have existed only for between five and ten million years. Art, literature, philosophy, and science as we know them have existed only for a few thousand years. We have had no intimations of intelligent life from anywhere beyond this one small planet. The sun will die in five thousand million years, making all life in our solar system impossible. It seems likely that we will exterminate ourselves long before that anyway.

Humans are a tiny, lonely, momentary flicker in a vast cosmos that seems to have no purpose or direction. In accordance with the laws of thermodynamics, all the stars and galaxies in the universe will eventually cease to exist, probably leaving a cold emptiness alleviated only by the occasional drifting of positrons though its vast solitude.

In this scenario of modern cosmology, if Armageddon were to come tomorrow and the planet earth were to end in a cataclysm of violence, that would have virtually no effect on the galaxy of which the earth is a tiny part, much less on the hundred billion other galaxies that exist in the universe. Intelligent life would have been a peripheral accident in a cosmos whose laws are completely indifferent to whether complex carbon molecules ever come into existence or endure for a brief instant of cosmic time, crawling about on the surface of small and isolated planets.

Peter Atkins, thinking of the laws of thermodynamics, which specify that all energy in the universe must ultimately decay, writes that "all change . . . arises from an underlying collapse into chaos. . . . everything is driven by decay. Everything is driven by motiveless, purposeless decay" (1994, 21). And Steven Weinberg (1993, 196) agrees: "All our experience throughout the history of science has tended . . . toward a chilling impersonality in the laws of nature." And again, "In the final laws of nature we will find no special status for life or intelligence. A fortiori, we will find no standards of value or morality" (Weinberg 1993, 200).

On the other hand, not all cosmologists share this gloomy vision. Freeman Dyson, Martin Rees, and Frank Tipler are among those who think that conscious intelligent life could expand to fill the whole cosmos and could, in a subjective sense, become immortal. Admittedly, there is no guarantee of this, but it depends on "fascinating physics, most of which is quite well understood" (Rees 2001, 119). As Freeman Dyson claimed, in a 1978 paper in the prestigious journal *Reviews of Modern Physics*, as the universe expands and cools, lower-energy quanta of energy would be needed to store and transmit information. So a virtually infinite amount of information could be processed in an objectively finite time toward the end of the life of the universe. Perhaps—and we are thinking billions of years into the future—thoughts and memories could be downloaded into magnetic fields that could exist in the darkness of interstellar space.

Frank Tipler, in his 1994 work *The Physics of Immortality*, supposes that the virtually infinite intelligences that might exist in the far-future universe would be able to recover all information from the past, and would choose to reconstitute all living beings who had ever existed. Thus, in the creation by advanced intergalactic intelligences of replicas of past humans, we have a scientific form of the hypothesis of the resurrection of the dead. It seems conceivable that intelligent life could thus cover the cosmos. It might even find a way to download itself through black holes or space/time warps into newly created universes. In a strange way, modern physics is able to translate some religious hopes of a "new creation" into a possible scientific scenario.

Of course, this is all fantastic, but it seems to be physically possible. And is this vision of a universe that culminates in a universal and final flourishing of intelligent life really any less plausible than the impersonal and value-free vision propounded by Atkins and Weinberg, of a universe that simply decays into unconscious chaos?

After all, intelligent life may not be an accident, and it may not be peripheral to the ultimate state of the universe. Atkins himself says, "elephants have turned out to be inevitable given molecules capable of competition and reproduction. . . . If you merely specify the elements . . . sooner or later there will be elephants" (1994, 5). We may or may not think that elephants are of great significance. But the same will go for human beings or for vast intergalactic intelligences. They are not, after all, accidental. Quite the reverse. They may be inevitable. If you think the laws of physics are absolute and universal, it will, in fact, be true that, given the complete set of physical laws and the initial state of the universe, nothing will be merely random or accidental. Whatever happens will inevitably happen—or, allowing for quantum fluctuations, at least the general course of things will inevitably go as it does.

So it could be the case that the universe will inevitably generate vast cosmic intelligences—and maybe, in the end, one vast cosmic intelligence that is virtually omniscient and omnipresent. In that case, intelligence will be far from peripheral to the universe. It will be the final all-encompassing state of the universe and its inevitable consequence. Such an intelligence may then have the power to create new universes in the laboratory of intergalactic space or in the crucibles of black holes. God may be the inevitable end point of this universe. And God may, in turn, be the Intelligent Creator of new universes—which strongly suggests that a God, the product of some previous, now extinct, universe, might have created this one as well.

Once we have got to the stage of postulating intelligences that can decant thoughts, memories, and intentions from one universe to another, we seem to have moved a long way from the idea that all consciousness has to be embedded in things like human brains, confined as they are to parts of small animals on the surfaces of planets within a particular space/time. If consciousness can be contained in magnetic fields or clouds of electrons and positrons, and if it can be transferred to a different space/time, the link to materiality becomes very tenuous.

So, a theist might think that much in modern cosmology actually points to a disconnection of consciousness from the forms of embodiment with which we are familiar. It points to the possibility that intelligent consciousness may actually be an inevitable and universal state of the far-future universe. This may lead us to doubt whether everything is driven by "purposeless decay," or whether it is quite so obvious that there is no special status for life or intelligence in the laws of nature. To some cosmologists, the universe looks as if it gives intelligent life the very special status of being the final, universal, and inevitable state of the physical universe. Is it a step too far to say that maybe this is the goal or purpose of the universe? Or, to take two steps while we are at it, to say that this goal is planned by a Consciousness that is not embodied within this universe or even at all?

Evolution and Transhumanism

There is strong disagreement among cosmologists, but it is important to stress that this is not a disagreement about the basic scientific facts, such as the age or size of the universe and its expansion from the big bang to a final state in which, in accordance with the laws of thermodynamics, its present ordered state will end, whether in a big collapse or, as seems more likely at present, in an infinite expansion into frozen emptiness. This universe, which at present manifests states of ordered complexity, will certainly come to an end, though it will take billions of years to do so.

Disagreements are about whether intelligent life is accidental or inevitable and whether it is a pointless by-product of the laws of nature or is destined to become the most important and universal feature of the evolution of the physical universe. These views involve very different predictions about the far future, but they are not experimentally testable now.

Scientists could well remain agnostic about such very speculative issues. It seems that they are not decisively settled one way or another by hard science. They involve different assessments of the value and point of life, of the presence of necessity, and of something very like purpose or at least direction in nature. Some might find human life fairly pointless even at best and think that billions of years of cosmic evolution is hardly worthwhile if it ends up with the unspeakable cruelties and suffering of Auschwitz and the thousands of other barbarities and trivialities of human existence.

Steven Weinberg says, "Remembrance of the Holocaust leaves me unsympathetic to attempts to justify the ways of God to man. If there is a God that has special plans for humans, then He has taken very great pains to hide His concern for us" (1993, 200). Others, however, or even the same people at different times, find in the practice of science itself a testament to the value and importance of the search for truth and understanding and beauty. As Weinberg has also stated, "There is a beauty in these laws that mirrors something that is built into the structure of the universe at a very deep level" (1993, 194).

Intellectual beauty is a great value. Appreciation of it and the search for truth, even at great personal cost, are great human goods. Science, at its best the search for truth and beauty in the physical universe, is very far from being value-free. But is this enough to outweigh the Holocaust and the pain that humans inflict on one another through violence and war? Perhaps that is where the issue really lies.

Those who hope for a continuance of intelligent life in the future universe usually think that suffering and ignorance can be eliminated, perhaps by genetic redesign, perhaps by transcending the human species altogether and by the formation of very different and vastly improved forms of information-processing systems (that is science-speak for what we call memories and thoughts).

In this respect, the cosmological optimists differ from almost all traditional religions and introduce a factor none of them ever envisaged. Human life is not the center of the universe, and it did not begin with a "golden age" that has degenerated ever since. Human life is a fairly early stage in the evolution of intelligences that will far transcend humanity. It has evolved from even simpler and more barbaric forms, and the progress of science and technology will enable it to evolve beyond recognition. The World Transhumanist Association, founded in 1998, is devoted to the development of "transhumans," forms of intelligent life superior to the human. The new paradise will not be the city of Jerusalem or a garden flowing with streams of water: it will be a virtual reality of pure knowledge and bliss, located in an intergalactic cloud far beyond the Milky Way.

But what are the chances of this actually happening? Even the most optimistic transhumanist must have moments of doubt. Though he is not, I think, a transhumanist, Martin Rees has written that "our remote descendants are likely to have an eternal future" (2002, 81). Yet, in the very same essay, he also writes, "Extreme pessimism seems to me the only rational stance" (83). For the technology of the twenty-first century, fairly small changes in climate or collisions with asteroids could destroy our species in a number of entirely feasible ways. The optimistic prediction of intelligent life's spreading throughout the cosmos turns out to be just hanging by a thin thread of possibility. It might happen, but we wouldn't want to bet on it.

Possible Religious Goals of an Evolutionary Universe

Such possibilities, however small, were not even conceivable when the Bible and the Upanishads were written. Human lives were, on the whole, short, hard, and violent. The cruelties of military empires, the ever-present threat of wars, the ravages of plagues and natural disasters, dashed any long-term optimism. The best hope was that military oppressors would be defeated in a final violent conflict and that nature itself might be renewed by a divine act that eliminated all causes of suffering and disease (including the adjustment of the stomachs of lions so that they could eat grass or the eating habits of mosquitoes so that they fed on nectar rather than blood).

If that was not going to happen, then the human goal had to be sought outside the physical universe. And, in truth, there is not a huge difference between reconstructing this universe so that lions eat grass and moving humans into another universe altogether. Both views require a radical change in physical nature.

But would the ultimate goal be physical at all? In religious traditions, there is a continuum of possibilities that have been proposed. At one end, there is the replication of the present universe, so that we would exist in the same bodies that we have now and in the same sort of environment. Next to it is the view that we shall live again, but with different, better bodies and in a more perfect environment. Further along the continuum is a view that gives up on bodies altogether, thinking they are altogether too restrictive and unsatisfactory. We shall only find a satisfactory existence when we are rid of the physical altogether and become pure spirits of intelligence and thought, without the need of material embodiment. And at the other end of the spiritual continuum is the belief that even a sense of individuality is a restriction. We shall not attain a fully worthwhile goal until our little finite selves are wholly merged with one Infinite Intelligence, and we realize that we are one with the Self of all or that the sense of a finite separate self is an illusion.

It does not seem that the first view in this continuum of possibilities is very convincing, that a satisfying spiritual goal lies in living in this universe or one just like it, even with an enlightened eye. For any universe very like this one would still be subject to natural disaster, disease, and death.

If our bodies were to be beyond physical disease and decay, the second law of thermodynamics, which ensures the decay and decomposition of all things, would have to be changed. The physical structure of earth, the stability of which depends upon volcanic and seismic activity, would have to be changed. The digestive system of all predators would have to be changed. As Thomas Aquinas put it, we might still have intestines, but we would not need to use them. We would still have toenails and hair, but they would never grow too long.

By the time we have made all the changes needed to eliminate causes of suffering and death from our world, we would find ourselves living in a very different sort of universe, whose laws were quite different from ours. So we move further along the continuum and find ourselves living in a universe like this in many ways but with a wholly different physical substructure. This would not be a replica universe but a different sort of universe in which lions really could lie down with lambs and humans would not need tear ducts since they would never cry.

This transformed universe could come into existence in the far future. That would be very like the Frank Tipler hypothesis, in which humans, and maybe other animals, will be reconstructed in new forms in a virtual world by some vast intergalactic intelligence. Is this so very different from the belief that God will one day eliminate evil and suffering and create the universe anew? Not really—except that, if there is a God, a vast but disembodied intelligence who created this universe, we could virtually guarantee that God would do this if God wanted to. Whereas there is only a small probability that Tipler's Cosmic Intelligence will ever actually exist. And perhaps we can only really speak of the universe's having a goal if there is an Intelligence there from the beginning, a mind who planned it that way. Otherwise, it is not really a goal to which the universe inevitably moves but only a debatable outcome, which may or may not happen.

If religious faith in life after death (a faith that we will live again in a better form, by the grace of a great Intelligence) was based on the Tipler hypothesis, we would be betting on an extreme hypothesis. Of course, we may think all religious faith is extreme and poorly evidenced anyway, so not much would be lost. But, at least if there was a God, a future better life would be a much better bet, and it might (if God is truly benevolent and good) even amount to a certainty.

Whether or not there is a God, I think we can see how the universe could have a goal and roughly what it would be—the existence of intelligent life with understanding, wisdom, and happiness, free of suffering, disease, and death. We can even see how the cosmic evolution of the universe up to this point could be seen as planting the seeds of such a future existence. Natural science cannot show that human life is just an accident or that the universe is indifferent to human life or that it is of little value anyway. Intelligent life could be built in as a natural or even inevitable outcome of the fundamental laws of the universe, and it could carry enormous potential value, at least in some future form.

Religious Views That Place the Goal of Life beyond the Universe

Many religious views, especially in the Indian traditions, live with the thought that the universe has no such future goal. For them, true human fulfillment lies in leaving all physical universes behind. The physical universe has had a part to play in the story of human souls. It provides a context in which desires can be explored and fulfilled and the futility of desires can be realized. So, human life is not an accident, and the universe is not indifferent to it. The universe is a necessary part of the journey of souls that have "fallen" into passion, ignorance, and selfish desire and that need to rise again to the spiritual realm from which they have come.

For such religious views, it does not matter much how the universe began or how it will end. Yet, the universe does in a sense have a purpose. That purpose does not lie in its final state but simply in the fact that it provides a place in which souls can work out their karma, the consequences of their actions in past lives, and perhaps develop toward a greater spiritual maturity that can be completed in future lives.

According to these views, human life in this cosmos is only a part of a larger series of lives in other worlds. Traditionally in Indian thought, there are six hells (places of even greater suffering than in this world) and six heavens. But there could be an infinite number of other worlds, in which souls could be embodied. The end of this universe is just the end of one particular world, which will begin again anyway. It is not the final destination of any human soul, but it can be a good jumping-off point toward a more enlightened spiritual existence (whether that is union with the One Self, as in Advaita Vedanta, or entrance into nirvana, as in some forms of Buddhism, or into a Pure Land of wisdom and bliss, as in other forms of Buddhism, or becoming a liberated soul, as in Jainism).

To many people, such an idea of many embodiments is both irrational and immoral. It is irrational because there is no evidence of past or future lives and because souls cannot jump into different bodies. It is immoral because it makes people think that, if they suffer, it is because they deserve it. They must have done great evil in past lives, so there is little incentive to relieve their suffering, which is a just judgment anyway.

These objections are not insuperable. If memories and thoughts can be downloaded into different forms of neural network, as some scientists suppose, it is not a great leap from that hypothesis to the view that they can be downloaded into completely different bodies. Some people do claim to remember past lives, so there is some evidence to support the theory. Admittedly, however, the evidence is not strongly established, and the evidence that we have remains a puzzle rather than a proof.

As for the moral point, we can still have compassion for those who suffer, even if they in some sense deserve it. Compassion is still an obligation, and we might be able to help others to face up to and overcome the pain they feel. We should look to the future and to what embodied souls may become, not to the past and what they may have been.

These arguments are not likely to be definitively settled by science. They are more likely to be settled, if they can be settled at all, by trying to decide whether consciousness is a product of complex material processes or can have independent existence, whether it does look as though people's human lives seem to be appropriate in terms of what we can see of their characters, and whether a worthwhile ultimate goal of human existence is complete liberation from embodied existence. Science and close observation may be relevant to such discussions. But they will rarely be decisive, and wider considerations—our judgments about the nature of the human self, about the meaning or pattern of human life stories, and about what we hold to be ultimate values—will be very important.

It can always be held that these are just subjective choices and that, if we were really concerned about the facts, we would rely solely on what the sciences can establish. But the fact is that speculations about the end of the universe, whether pessimistic or optimistic about the existence of intelligent life, will not be very relevant for those who hold religious views that the goal of human life lies wholly beyond the universe. Scientific disputes about such topics may suggest that at least hard science cannot disprove religious beliefs on these matters. Maybe believers and unbelievers alike will have to be content with that.

The Self-Unfolding Nature of an Evolutionary Cosmos

The Semitic religions, which are theistic, have more interest in the question of whether the universe has a goal. They think that human lives begin with physical birth in this universe and that the personalities we have in this life on earth are much more central to our natures than they would be if we all had lived thousands or millions of times before, in many different forms.

For some Indian traditions, human bodies are like sets of clothes that we wear for a while but will then discard and, it is hoped, find something better. But for Judaism, Christianity, and Islam, our body is an essential part of what we are. It is not like clothes; it is more like skin. If there is an ultimate goal for such beings as us, it will have to be a more perfect form of what we now are, an embodied life of knowledge and freedom and friendship but one without pain and suffering.

A natural question that arises is, if such valuable intelligent life without suffering could exist and if there is a God who can make it exist, why did God not simply create life in the first place as obviously valuable and intelligent? Why did God create, instead, the messy and dangerous, wasteful and painful process of gradual evolution toward a future more valuable intelligent life?

One reason that can be suggested is the consideration that human life is not only properly embodied, but it is embodied in an evolutionary universe. I am thinking primarily here not just of the Darwinian evolution of life on earth but of the cosmic evolution of the universe over billions of years from an initial simple state, the big bang, to the complex system of galaxies and stars, planets, and incredibly organized organisms that now exist.

This process of cosmic evolution was quite unknown before modern times, and yet it has an interesting resonance with some of Aristotle's ideas. Aristotle saw change as a movement from potentiality to actuality. Substances realize their potential, striving to reach a state in which that potential is fully actualized. Aristotle was not thinking of evolution. Indeed, he held that each substance has an essential nature that cannot change, even if it can be realized more or less fully. One essential nature cannot change into another.

But if the whole cosmos is regarded as one substance, the development of matter into complex integrated forms can readily be seen as a realization of potentialities implicit in it from the first. The first state of the universe was too simple even to contain elementary particles. But as the universe began to cool, particles like photons or quarks formed. Then there were simple atoms of hydrogen and helium, forming large gaseous clouds that became stars. Within the nuclear furnaces of stars, heavier atoms formed and built up a range of chemical elements. Some of these formed large molecules, which came to replicate themselves and build organic bodies, with primitive sense organs. Central nervous systems came to be and brains that gave rise to consciousness, sensation, and thought.

There has been a gradual development from quarks to consciousness. Each stage has been more complex and structured than the one before. The cosmic process shows increasing differentiation and the cumulative construction of complex unities. The parts of these unities interact with one another so that they have a capacity to respond to their environment in increasingly complex ways. Plants have a more complex set of responses than rocks, using and seeking out influences from the environment to grow and reproduce. Animals are more active and exploratory than plants, and humans are able to recognize their environment consciously, think about its nature, and react to it in creative ways.

Humans do not seem to be a sudden, unexpected intrusion into what was previously a purely mechanical process—that was Descartes' error. Humans have a highly developed way of receiving influences from the environment and responding to them actively. But that is a natural development from much earlier, more basic and unconscious stimulus-response processes that exist in simple form even in subatomic particles.

Theologians like Augustine have suggested that a creator God might act in accordance with a principle of plenitude—the principle that every sort of good that could exist should exist, as long as it does not give rise to an unacceptable level of evil. So, a Creative Intelligence might wish there to be stars and galaxies, objects possessing awesome beauty and intellectual interest. Even if finite consciousnesses never came to exist, the cosmos would have value for a God who delights in its beauty. But God might also wish there to be plants, which would blossom and flourish in the light of the stars, and animals that would act largely by instinct but would be capable of pleasure and friendship in increasing degrees. And God might wish there to be animal intelligences that could share in the appreciation of all these kinds of beauty and goodness.

Though Augustine did not think of it, all these things could develop in accordance with simple and elegant principles of differentiation and organic formation from the simplest to the most complex over millions of years, just as fertilized cells develop into babies and human beings in a much shorter time. Evolution is a very natural and familiar process. We see it in the growth of every plant from seeds and of every adult animal from a tiny cell. On the cosmic scale, this would be a realization of the potentiality of the physical world to become fully personal and to realize a multitude of intermediate forms of developing life in the process.

Would this not be a beautiful and elegant creation? Not everyone would think so. For some, there is still too much suffering and wastefulness, too much randomness and accident, for the process to be truly valuable. And for some, human consciousness is so pointless and unhappy that it is not worth having. But these are value judgments, not scientific judgments. At least a stress on the intricacy, beauty, and intellectual elegance of the evolutionary process is a counterbalance to presentations of evolution as nothing but a blind and ruthless struggle for survival.

It is possible to think of the cosmos as manifesting the principle of plenitude, as a gradual and continuous unfolding of potentialities tending toward the increase of consciousness, intelligence, creative freedom, and personal cooperation, as a whole whose parts are interconnected in subtle and highly integrated ways. Then, the Aristotelian theory of "Forms" or essential natures and the Aristotelian belief in final causality can be restated, so that the cosmos can be seen not as a set of changeless fixed essences that strive to be themselves but as one integrated process of cosmic autopoiesis—self-unfolding—that moves toward greater consciousness and self-direction.

This process may possess distinctive sorts of value that could not exist in a static universe, however perfect it might be. It might even be that there is a deep necessity in the evolution of complex intelligent life forms from simpler physical structures, in accordance with basic physical laws. Such a universe, even if it is only one possibility out of many possible forms of finite existence, may, nevertheless, exist as a necessary expression of values potential in the divine ground of all possibilities. There may be a necessity inherent in the Divine Being to realize this possibility, which may be said to be "chosen" for the sake of the great goods it contains, despite the destructive elements that an evolutionary universe inevitably carries with it.

The Goal of the Far-Future Universe

If we could accept such a picture of the cosmos, then we could see it as having a goal, in the flourishing of personal consciousness. But this may be a goal, a possibility to be aimed at, not something that will inevitably exist without effort or striving. The process would then be part of the purpose. To achieve something by effort, through hard self-discipline and application, is a distinctive form of personal excellence. Such excellences are traditionally called "virtues," and the cultivation of virtue, of intellectual and moral excellence, might be seen as one of the main goals of human life.

For billions of years, there would not be a conscious striving for excellence. That comes only with the genesis of rational consciousness. But there would have to be, in the long development that leads to consciousness, the laying-down of physical structures that prepare the ground for such striving and for the existence of consciousness. That means the laying-down of flexible physical structures that allow for the choice of alternative futures, for both success and failure, and for a nexus that gives conscious decisions a causal role to play in the physical world. There would have to be an openness and freedom in the structure that might, for many observers, be indistinguishable from chance. Thus, an element of "randomness" or "chance" might be built into a goal-oriented universe whose goal involves the cooperation of finite intelligences generated within the universe itself.

This is the core of the "free process defense" used by the physicist John Polkinghorne (1989, 66–67) to explain how great natural evils can exist in a world created by a good God. Randomness necessarily means that the destructive possibilities of the cosmos, entailed by the basic laws of physics, will often happen by chance. They are not directly intended by anyone, much less God. But those laws, and that element of randomness, may be necessary to lay the foundation for the moral freedom that will later characterize intelligent life.

Then, when intelligent moral agency appears on the scene, it may actually increase the evil in the world, rather than (as it should) gradually eliminate it. If the intended goal is to be achieved only by discipline and striving, then it is entirely possible that conscious beings may strive and fail. Or they may just refuse to strive.

As we gaze around the human world, it looks as though very few people succeed in getting anywhere near a goal of understanding, wisdom, creative freedom, and joy. Many try but are deterred by hardship or by the attractions of more easily obtainable pleasures. Some fail, are embittered by their failure, and actively seek to destroy such virtues wherever they are found. If we have to characterize human lives in general, we may be tempted to say that willful misunderstanding, ignorance, destructiveness, addiction, and misery are more obvious features of human beings than anything else.

The outlook seems bleak. It may be that we just have to live with what we have got and that even in this ambiguous world it is possible and desirable to cultivate dispassion and mindfulness, inner calm and joy. But that would be to renounce the idea that there is a desirable goal for the whole cosmos, and it would involve denying that there is a Cosmic Intelligence who has created the universe for the sake of its goodness. That is an intelligible religious view. It is the view of some forms of Buddhism, but it is not characteristic of most theistic forms of religious belief. So can the view that there is a positive and achievable goal for the universe be sustained?

One possibility is the "Omega hypothesis." Within Christianity, this has found its main proponent in the Jesuit paleontologist Pierre Teilhard de Chardin. According to this view, the evolution of life will continue beyond the present forms of human existence and culminate in an "Omega point," a "hyper-personal" reality in which all particular consciousnesses are united (Teilhard 1959, 257–72): "The universe is a collector and conservator . . . of persons . . . the noosphere [the collective realm of thought] . . . will reach collectively its point of convergence—at the 'end of the world'" (1959, 272).

No one has ever claimed that Teilhard's thought was clear, but it has immense poetic power, and his book, *The Phenomenon of Man*, earned a long and enthusiastic introduction from the biologist and humanist Julian Huxley. The key point is that present humanity will be transcended in a more unified superconsciousness, a convergent reality that will finally transcend even material embodiment, and become something like pure information.

At that point, the goal of ontogenesis will be achieved, and the material universe will be fully personalized—and more! In *The Phenomenon of Man*, Teilhard proposes two ways in which this may happen. The first is by the gradual conquest of disease and hunger, so that "the final convergence will take place in peace" (288). But the second is that "evil may go on growing alongside good, and it too may attain its paroxysm at the end." Then, there will be a great divide between that part of the universe that refuses unity in omega, disintegrating with the death of the physical universe, and that part that experiences "an ecstasy transcending the dimensions and the framework of the visible universe."

For both views, humanity is part of a process that transcends humanity. And that seems to fit the pattern of evolutionary thinking. The typical lifetime for a complex species is about ten million years, but astronomer Owen Gingerich puts a much lower limit on the existence of the human species. "To me," he says, "it is unimaginable that *Homo sapiens* will still exist on earth ten million years from now, except perhaps by some remote chance in zoos" (2002, 231).

Humans, as we know them, may become extinct. It will then be our remote descendents who will inherit the omega point. We humans will have played our part in the cosmic process and passed away. Or, if we have no descendents, if we wipe ourselves out in the near future, then the cosmic goal may be achieved elsewhere. It is possible that the earth is a failed experiment in striving for the cosmic goal. All life on earth will become extinct; but on some other faraway planet, in another galaxy, far, far away, a more successful attempt is already under way and will be the source of the seeding of the whole universe with intelligent and benevolent life that never will be and never was human. In any case, it seems as though the human species will not play any part in the evolutionary goal of the cosmos.

The Theistic Hope for a New Creation

Theistic religions have rarely been happy to believe that present humans will simply be eliminated, leaving the future to some superior life form. Yet early forms of Christianity, especially, have accepted the pessimistic view that evil cannot be eliminated from human life, which makes the achievement of an omega point that includes humans in the future universe questionable. Some other solution that can include present human lives and yet that is not unduly optimistic about the human future seems called for.

Optimistic scenarios of continuous human progress received a sharp blow when the first half of the twentieth century saw more people violently exterminated in war than in the whole of the rest of human history. And those wars were conducted by the most cultured and progressive humans on the planet. It does not fill one with unqualified hope for the future.

Those who believe in a Cosmic Intelligence who creates the universe for the sake of its goodness seem committed to thinking that the goal of a good society of finite persons must in the long run be achieved. It would also be natural for them to think that good will overwhelmingly outweigh any evils that have existed in the cosmic process and that those evils will not simply be unredeemable and pointless, without any worthwhile outcomes or consequences. It is morally important that such outweighing of evil by good, and such possible redemption of evil, must be possible for every being who has suffered. One person's suffering cannot morally be outweighed by another person's flourishing. It is those who have suffered who must share in the ultimate goodness of creation.

But if much terrible evil arises from the freedom of finite persons not to enter into "the convergence of love" and if such freedom cannot be eliminated from human existence, then the ultimate goal will not be attainable while human life exists in its present form.

It follows that the ultimate goal can only be attainable beyond this space/time. Yet, because it is a goal of beings in this space/time, it must be a credible fulfillment of potentialities that existed in this space/time. As the theologian Jurgen Moltmann says, "The future, new eternal world is therefore to be the new creation of this world we know" (2002, 261). It is not a quite different form of existence. It is to be the re-creation of this universe in a more perfect, a transfigured, form.

What this scenario adds to the scientific speculation of intelligent life's existing (at least virtually) forever in transhuman form is that it is a goal for all who have ever existed and not just for the final generation of thinking galactic clouds. As Moltmann says, this is "the only model that perceives a future for what is past and expresses hope for the dead" (2002, 262). Or, if Frank Tipler rises up and says that he can provide that too, with his virtual replicants, it is worth pointing out that his prediction looks like a very improbable and always insecure future, while the God hypothesis (provided, of course, that there is a God) gives us an intended, assured, and perfectly just future for all.

It is at this point that the phrase *wishful thinking* will occur to those who are skeptical about the existence of God. Is the believer not just inventing an invisible "sky" in which nutritious (if spiritual) pies can be eaten, because all the pies on earth proved unsatisfactory? Isn't this just the biggest piece of wish fulfillment in the history of thought?

Maybe so. And yet it is modern science that suggests that this space/time may not be the only one there is and that even this space/time may be nothing more than the appearance of some "veiled and mysterious reality" that lies beyond it. If—and this is a very big "if"—consciousness is the basis of reality and if the universe can plausibly be seen as the product of a great Intelligence, is it not also plausible to think that there must be some point into the existence of the universe? Further, would that point not lie in the existence of valuable and worthwhile conscious states—apprehensions of truth, beauty, and goodness—in many finite personal agents? And would an Intelligent Creator not then ensure that such a valuable goal were actualized?

It is from such considerations, rather than simply from some personal desire to go on forever, that belief arises in a world beyond this in which the goals faintly discerned and ambiguously pursued in this world could be realized.

Can this universe exist in transfigured form? The Qur'an is typically forthright: "One day the earth will be changed to a different earth, and so will be the heavens" (14:48). "Even as we produced the first creation, so shall we produce a new one" (21:104). "We are not to be frustrated from changing your forms and creating you in [forms] that you know not" (56:60–61).

In Christianity also, there will be "a new heaven and a new earth; for the first heaven and the first earth had passed away, and the sea was no more" (Rev. 21:1). Chaos and destruction, for which the saltwater sea is a common biblical symbol, are eliminated. And "this perishable body must put on imperishability, and this mortal body must put on immortality" (1 Cor. 15:53). The new creation is imperishable, beyond the range of the laws of thermodynamics, and immortal, beyond the reach of death and decay. Yet it is "this" body that will exist.

Humans will not be exact replicas, and they will not be totally new sorts of individuals. They will be beings who are what they are in that universe because of what in this universe they were and made of themselves. Moreover, it is not just humans who will exist in the new world. Trees, plants, animals, insects, clouds, and mountains will exist there—everything but sea, apparently, though very big lakes may be allowed. But all is transfigured by the glory of God, to whom all things are transparent and who permits nothing to remain in being that has not learned to love or that has no place in a world of interwoven love.

This means that what we do in and to this universe has lasting consequences for the world to come. What we create and shape will be present, though transfigured by glory. What we destroy and frustrate will fail to be present as it could and should have been. In that sense, the future world will perhaps always bear the marks of the tragic, of a failure to be what should have been, of absence where there should have been presence, of pain never quite forgotten, even though transfigured by present joy. Nevertheless, the goodness of that world will be overwhelming, and it will be the result of what took place in the ontogenesis of this world.

If such things are possible, then this cosmos may have and may achieve an ultimate goal, even as it passes into the long silent darkness in which even the last star has ceased to be.

Three Scientific Views of the End of the Universe

What, then, have science and religion to say about the end of the universe? Some scientists find in the size of the universe, the impersonality of its laws, the huge improbability of any organic life forms ever existing, and the very brief period during which such life forms have a window for existing, signs of the pointlessness and lack of purpose in the universe. The darkness between the stars dwarfs human life into insignificance. There may be beauty and mathematical structure in the cosmos, but it will end as it began, in unconscious emptiness.

Other scientists take a much more optimistic view. Intelligent life may be inevitable, given the basic laws and constants of the natural world. It may spread throughout the galaxies and achieve virtual immortality. Human life will be left behind in this march toward Cosmic Consciousness, but life itself will expand and progress, until a reality very much like the traditional God—virtually omniscient and omnipotent—will come to be and may, in turn, create other universes beyond this one.

I think that most scientists, however, may find the first of these views more an expression of subjective tendencies toward depression than an objective assessment of the facts. And the second view, while within the realm of physical possibility, is subject to too many unknown variables and accidents to be the object of a realistic hope. For them, human life will end—but it may have a few thousand million years yet to go, which is not bad. The fact that its total span of existence will be short in cosmic terms does not deprive it of significance. Individual human lives grow, flourish, and celebrate many moments of value and pleasure before, inevitably, they die. So the life of humanity itself can flourish before it fades. The values of scientific understanding, of artistic creation, of moral heroism, and of shared friendship are worthwhile in themselves. The fact that they do not last forever makes them, if anything, more to be treasured and valued. Human life may indeed be cut short by war or natural disaster—all the more reason to seek peace and to preserve the ecosystem within which we live. Human existence is almost unimaginably rare in our universe, and it will inevitably end. But we can still seek worthwhile goals of activity now, goals that we choose and pursue while we live, as the Viking warriors of the Norse sagas fought and feasted and rejoiced, even as their world ended in the final conflagration of ice and fire.

Modern Religious Views about the End of the Universe

Most religions were originally formulated before anything was known about the size and destiny of the physical cosmos. Such knowledge necessitates a revision of all the physical data involved in religious beliefs about the end or goal of the universe. But it is characteristic of most religious beliefs that they do posit a goal or purpose for the existence of the universe.

For some religions, mostly those in originally Indian traditions like Buddhism, the purpose of the universe is to be a place in which human souls can work out their own destiny or karma. The ultimate aim of human life lies beyond the physical cosmos, perhaps in a liberated existence of pure consciousness, or perhaps in a "Pure Land" free from suffering and pain. A variant on this general view places little or no emphasis on a continuing life beyond the cosmos and stresses the possibility of a liberated or enlightened human life in the present. Religion is about the search for enlightenment, or *samadhi*. That is basically a higher blissful and concentrated state of consciousness in present life and may have no implications for the possibility of a "life after death."

According to these views, the physical end of this universe, like its physical beginning, is of no particular religious relevance. What matters is that the laws of the universe allow the process of moral self-making (or unmaking) to play an important causal role in the way things go. Scientific views about the nature of causality may make that a highly debatable belief—but that is another question, and I will consider it later.

Theistic traditions tend to have a greater interest in the end of the cosmos because they see the whole physical universe as the expression or manifestation of an underlying spiritual or conscious reality of supreme value—usually called "God." It, therefore, seems plausible that there should be some reason for physical existence. This is sometimes envisaged (usually in Indian Hindu traditions) as a "fall" of souls into a world of desire and pleasure. But it can also be seen as the creation of new souls to form communities of personal agents and enjoyers of the beauty and goodness of created existence.

Hindu cosmologies envisage infinite universes. This one will end but will be repeated an infinite number of times. So the goal, insofar as there is one, is progression to a happier universe and return to God beyond this specific universe. Again, it does not matter much what happens to this universe as it dies, its job done.

It is the Semitic traditions that most strongly imply the realization of a positive goal for the universe. God creates the universe for its goodness, and that goodness must, therefore, we might well think, be realized. However things are not very clear-cut. It could be that goodness could be realized in the emergence of societies of intelligent, virtuous, and happy persons, whether on earth or throughout the whole universe. The religion of the Hebrew scriptures seems to express such a hope for the world, though the arrival of the "kingdom of God," when peace and righteousness will rule, has to be preceded by a "great and terrible Day of the Lord," eliminating all the oppressive and militaristic forces in the world.

In the development of Jewish theological thought, the notion arose that the arrival of a final perfect society would not be enough to justify all the evil that had occurred on the way to it, especially the deaths of the martyrs and the heroes of faith. So the idea of resurrection arose (possibly influenced by Persian Zoroastrian religion), as a belief that all the dead would rise to a life that would compensate them for the evil they had suffered.

Further reflection on what would be needed for a perfectly good society led, in the thought of Second Isaiah, in the sixth century BCE, to a realization that the laws of nature themselves would have to be changed if all destruction and suffering were to be eliminated. So the idea of a new and transfigured creation arose—not just another universe than this, but this universe (or at least this earth) transformed into an incorruptible and timeless or everlasting reality.

All these ideas are incorporated into the Christian book of Revelation, written under the influence of the basic belief that, in Jesus, the nature and purpose of God had been normatively disclosed. In a riotous array of images and dramatic narratives, Revelation foretells a cataclysmic destruction of evil, as the forces of "God and Magog," the militaristic empires of earth, destroy themselves in war. It foretells the triumph of goodness and a recompense for the suffering of the innocent victims of history, symbolized by the return of the martyrs of faith and goodness, with Christ as their king, to rule the earth "for a thousand years." Then, all the dead rise to judgment, and the new Jerusalem descends from the sky to usher in a new heaven and earth, in which God will be present and clearly known by all.

No one can take the book of Revelation literally—lambs do not go about with swords in their mouths, destroying armies. Unfortunately, many have tried to make the symbols correspond to specific events and people in human history. All such attempts have yielded false predictions, and one might have thought they would have been given up by now. It is true that "Babylon," the city of earthly power doomed to destruction, almost certainly referred to the Roman Empire. But it referred more widely to powers of military oppression in general and, thus, to such powers in any age.

The book of Revelation does not give an exact timetable for the future, which some sort of secret knowledge can enable us to decode, so that the gnostics, the initiates of secret knowledge, can tell us exactly what is going to happen. Like the Norse myths and like the creation stories in Genesis, Revelation gives sets of symbolic images that are meant to express spiritual truths, truths not about what will happen in the next few years on earth but truths about how God stands in relation to human life, and assurances that the goal of human life will be realized.

The spiritual meaning is that evil will be wholly eliminated because it is inherently self-destructive—"If you kill with the sword, with the sword you must be killed" (Rev. 13:10). Those throughout history who have given their lives for the sake of goodness will receive an overwhelming recompense (that is the meaning of "first resurrection and the millennium"). No one will escape judgment for what he or she has done in his or her life. Yet all will be offered a place in a new and transfigured earth, which will exist timelessly or forever (these are alternatives, each selected by different theologians). Christ will be seen as the eternal Wisdom of God, who was embodied on earth in and through the person of Jesus of Nazareth. So, in the end, all the good that has ever been will be gathered into the mind of God, and all the conscious creatures that have ever been will share in appropriate fashion their delight in that goodness.

The Relation of Religious and Scientific Claims about the End of the Universe

These truths (or claims) are embodied in a wholly prescientific cosmology. Earth is the center of the cosmos, and the stars are lamps hung on the dome of the sky. Earth has only existed for a few thousand years, and it will cease to exist in its present form within a generation or so. Jesus will return in glory at any moment. And the new creation will, in an instant, in "the twinkling of an eye," totally change the nature of the whole universe, after the stars have fallen from the sky, and the sun, the moon, the and saltwater sea have been expunged.

The disparity between the biblical cosmology and modern cosmology is enough to make some people simply reject the Bible as a form of primitive ignorance, compounded by hallucinatory fantasy. The movement of "creationism," arguing for the literal truth of Genesis, pales into insignificance before "millenarianism," arguing for a secret interpretation of Revelation that tells the initiated literally what is going to happen soon. I think all we can say here is that millenarianism is in total conflict with scientific cosmology. If millenarianism is part of Christianity, then Christianity and modern cosmology cannot be reconciled.

Millenarianism, however, has never been part of the teaching of any mainstream Christian church. It does keep popping up in the most surprising places, and it will probably never wholly die out, but most mainstream Christian churches accept the sort of "spiritualized" account I have offered (which agrees, for example, with the general commentary given by Richard Bauckham in the *Oxford Bible Commentary*).

This is a matter of hermeneutics, or biblical interpretation. If it is accepted that spiritual meanings can be expressed in symbolic forms and can be distinguished from literal facts about the physical cosmos, then we can assign spiritual meaning to religion and literal meaning to cosmology. It is scientific cosmologists who have the authority to tell us what will probably happen in the far future of the universe.

Religious thinkers will be concerned with the existence of God, as the supreme spiritual consciousness underlying the physical universe. Their claim is that the physical universe is not all there is and that its end does not annihilate all there is. Yet, for theists, the universe has existed for a purpose, which is to generate many forms of goodness and many beings who can appreciate and create such forms of goodness. In the end, in a transfigured cosmos, when this cosmos has passed away, all the good this universe has produced will be realized in perfected form in God. All evil and imperfection will pass away, and finite agents can be re-created to know the good as it truly is, its causes and its consummation.

For some, such a separation of spiritual meaning from literal meaning is unacceptable. There is only one real world, and we have to live with that, not invent some more tenuous and wispy world in which our fondest dreams can be realized. But religion is founded on the claim that the spiritual world is the real one. The physical world is its transient and temporary manifestation. That the universe has a purpose and that its goal will be realized are integral parts of the hypothesis of the ontological primacy of God.

Scientific cosmology cannot resolve this deep dispute. But it can give us much more, and much more reliable, knowledge of what the physical manifestation of a supposed spiritual world is. It can do religion a service by forcing it to consider what spiritual truths religion does seek to express and to refrain from making unsubstantiated claims about literal facts, future or otherwise.

At that point, the skeptic will reply that all the claims religions make, whether about literal or spiritual facts, are unsubstantiated. This reply is hardly surprising, since the skeptic will say, there are no spiritual facts anyway. But now the argument is not about cosmology. It is, much more broadly, about whether there is a God or a spiritual realm of being.

So will the universe end? Probably, but it does not much matter to most religions. Has the universe a goal? Science does not usually ask that question. But for many, not all, cosmologists, it may have, and if so, the goal has to do with the increase of knowledge, freedom, and intelligent life. Will the goal be realized? Not literally forever, in this universe, it seems. But it may be realized for a while, or it may be realized more fully if there are universes of an appropriate sort beyond this. Perhaps surprisingly, some strictly cosmological thought would not rule this out as a possibility. For much religious thought, the goal will be realized, in another universe, which may be a transfigured form of this one. If this is to be more than a bare speculative possibility, it must be founded on a firm belief in the reality of God, or spiritual being. And that seems to be a matter that takes us beyond science, though not beyond the possibility of reasoned debate.

3. Is Evolution Compatible with Creation?

(HOW CAN THE "CRUELTY AND WASTE" OF EVOLUTION BE RECONCILED WITH CREATION BY A GOOD GOD?)

Degeneration or Progress in History?

THERE IS CERTAINLY A conflict between science and religion if the texts of most religions are taken literally because most religions originated long before the idea of evolution was taken seriously. Many of them present the history of the world as a degeneration from a golden age. Far from evolving or improving, in their view things are progressively getting worse.

Traditional Hindu texts speak of this as the age of Kali, the worst of the four ages of the cosmos, which is destined to end in degradation and chaos. Traditional Buddhism predicts a slide into ignorance, until Buddhism itself disappears, only to be renewed by the appearance of some future Buddha. Judaism and Christianity speak of Adam and Eve in a "garden of bliss," not having to work, surrounded by fruit and vegetables, beyond the reach of disease and death. Things have certainly gotten worse since then. Even the site of the garden has been lost; its gates are guarded by angels with flaming swords; and death, pain, and labor are parts of the human lot, punishments for the sins of our first parents.

Philosophers in all these traditions know how to read the scriptures metaphorically and are rarely committed to such literal readings. Nevertheless, they often have a more sophisticated reading of the degeneration thesis. For Thomas Aquinas, the best-known medieval Catholic philosopher and theologian, all efficient causes must contain as much reality as their effects: "[A]ny perfection found in an effect must be found also in the cause. . . . [E]ffects obviously preexist potentially in their causes" (*Summa Theologiae*, 1a, question 4, article 2).

It is the word *obviously* in this quotation that brings out the difference between the medieval view that the greater cannot come from the less and the modern evolutionary view that it obviously does. For a modern evolutionist, more complex and organized things "obviously" have developed from simpler and less organized things. So, the best explanation of the integrated complexity of things in our universe is given in terms of very simple initial states and a few laws of nature. The simple explains the complex, as a long cumulative build-up of simple and transitory elements produces more complex and enduring entities.

To a medieval philosopher, this argument is not at all obvious. In the first of his "Five Ways for Demonstrating the Existence of God," Aquinas says that "to cause change is to bring into being what was previously only able to be, and this can only be done by something that already is" (*Summa*, 1a, question 2, article 3). Something can only become hot, he says, if it is caused to do so by something that is already at least as hot.

If this is accepted, it seems to follow that complex things can only be caused by even more complex things and that God, the first cause, will have to be more perfect and real than anything God causes. It may also seem that stupid people can only be caused by even more stupid people and that God must be the most stupid, as well as the cleverest, being there is. To get around this, Aquinas has to argue that stupidity is not a positive quality. It is just an absence of cleverness. But God should also be the reddest and bluest and greenest of all things or perhaps the most brightly colored thing there is. To a modern mind the argument sounds very fishy (perhaps God is also the fishiest thing there is?).

What is interesting to a historian of ideas, however, is the contrast between a medieval and ancient Greek view that all good things must spring from a reality of greater goodness or perfection and the evolutionary, post-nineteenth century view that very complex and good things can develop from simpler and less perfect forms of being.

The German Idealist Roots of Evolutionary Thought

A good test case is the question, "Can conscious mind develop from unconscious subatomic particles?" For an evolutionist, it is just obvious that it does, and that is that. But many people feel that mind cannot be wholly caused by matter. This feeling is a remnant of the premodern view that things cannot be caused by things that seem quite different in kind or that are of lesser value.

According to this view, there is a deep unintelligibility about something quite new originating out of nothing and nowhere. If it did, there would seem to be no reason that it should come into being and no reason that it should be one sort of thing rather than another. The key thought is that, if the universe is rational, there must be a reason that things come into being and have the natures they have. In our discussion of the "first big question," the suggestion was that the reason for things having the natures they have is that a total array of all possible states necessarily exists, from which actual states are a selection connected with a "choice" of goodness. And a reason for things coming into being when they do is that they are brought about by something that, being necessarily actual, has the power of being in itself.

These reasons may or may not appeal today. But their basis is the postulate that the universe is wholly intelligible. The postulate of God, far from being an arbitrary assertion of *blind* faith, is indeed faith, but it is faith in the ultimate rationality of the universe. For the medieval mind, it seemed that ultimate reason must be purely actual, without any potentiality unrealized, and changeless. For only then, it was thought, could there be an uncaused cause of all, beyond the reach of decay and dissolution.

There was a great change in human thought that came to clear expression in the eighteenth century. It is a change from seeing all finite things as lesser imperfect reflections of some primally perfect being, so that the world is a fall from perfection toward nothingness and is only held in being at all by the remote influence of its original source. And it is a change toward seeing finite things as "a progressive, gradually self-disclosing revelation of the Absolute."

This phrase comes from the German philosopher and Christian pastor Johann Gottfried Herder (1744–1803). It still speaks of an "Absolute," a perfect and supremely intelligible being as the source of all. But now part of the perfection of that being lies in its self-expression in history, its entrance into the flow of the temporal process. And in that process it discloses, or even shapes, itself progressively. Progress, development, and time become positive goods rather than regrettable necessities.

Such a possibility had always been present in Christianity, which has as a central tenet that God, the supreme changeless and perfect reality, became incarnate in time and suffered. That should have suggested that time might be important for the Supreme Being, not just some sort of unfortunate overflow of the divine perfection into finite forms that could never properly express it. For Christians, God was perfectly expressed in time, and that idea gives a much more positive role to the temporal and historical.

There were also elements in Christianity that might suggest progressive revelation—Jesus apparently revised many earlier religious views and promised to send the Spirit to lead further into all truth. The church was seen as "the body of Christ," the vehicle of Christ's continuing presence in the world, and that symbolism might imply a positive role for the church in the world.

But there were strong elements that blocked such progressive interpretations—Jesus was the final revelation of God, and the church came to see itself as the guardian of an unchangeable and complete revelation. Further, Jesus was often seen as "the end of history," so that history might end at any time. And the influence of Greek eternalism—the assumption of the primacy of the timeless over the temporal—dominated intellectual thought.

German thinkers like Kant, Herder, Schelling, and Hegel, however, were Protestants who saw the Reformation as a new and positive reformulation of Christian faith, no longer constrained by an authoritarian tradition. The growth of scientific innovation was also an important factor, giving rise to a feeling that progress in knowledge and in the mastery of nature was possible. The Greeks were impressive intellectual ancestors, but the new European discovery of a progressive accumulation of knowledge of and power over nature gave Enlightenment thinkers the courage to move beyond the ancients in many ways.

So, evolutionary thought, the thought of change and progress in history and in the development of life on earth itself, developed as a religiously imbued intellectual movement in eighteenth-century Germany. Of course, belief in evolution and in creation are compatible since evolutionism originated in the context of a revised view of creation as the progressive self-revelation of God, of Absolute Spirit, in the genesis and development of intelligent life forms.

The price of such compatibility, however, is that literal readings of ancient religious scriptures must be abandoned, and we must accept the German idealist metaphysical vision of human history as the progressive self-expression of Absolute Spirit. Many religious believers will not accept the former possibility, and many scientists—who often have an aversion to abstract speculative philosophy—will not accept the latter. In fact, reading a few pages of Hegel is sometimes enough to put people off philosophy forever.

So quite a number of people, whether philosophers or antiphilosophers, do what Karl Marx did, and drop all reference to Absolute Spirit (*Geist*), as an unwanted relic of the medieval mind-set that still insists that the cause of the universe must be more perfect than any events within the universe. Once we drop that relic, we can rest comfortably with the thought that the universe may be progressive, without supposing that there is some hidden intelligent mind that is directing the process. And once the directing intelligence goes, we can see evolution as not even necessarily progressive. The word *evolution* might be a misnomer since it suggests progress. We might do better to speak simply of adaptive change, which does not necessarily lead anywhere in particular. The way has been prepared for Charles Darwin and his successors and for the modern creed of neo-Darwinism.

The Mechanisms of Evolution

It was Charles Darwin who established evolution as a properly scientific theory, based on close and extensive observation. The publication of *On the Origin of Species*, in 1859, moved the theory from philosophical speculation to scientific hypothesis. Although it was not until the 1930s that Darwinism was subjected to rigorous experimental testing and not until the 1950s that the molecular basis of heredity (the structure of DNA) was known, the two basic mechanisms that Darwin proposed for biological evolution are generally accepted by biologists as correct.

These mechanisms are random mutation and natural selection. As we would now put it, as DNA replicates, there are copying differences (often called "errors") in the transcription process—about one hundred in each human generation, for example. Since DNA codes for the construction of proteins, which build the bodies of plants and animals, this sometimes results in slightly different recipes for body building. Most of these differences have little or no significance. Some are very harmful to organisms, causing deformation or death. And some may cause positive gains like better eyesight or stronger teeth.

These mutations are random, in the sense that they do not all move in a positive direction of improvement. They seem to occur without specific intelligent guidance since they cause good and harm indiscriminantly. This gives rise to a widely held view among biologists that there is no direction in evolution. Mutations of all sorts occur, scattering changes at random, blind and indifferent to what those changes are.

The second mechanism, however, selects from these mutations, eliminating some and choosing others. Such selection is natural, in that it proceeds in accordance with ordinary laws of nature and not by some form of intelligent or intentional action. Many mutations are eliminated because they cannot survive in their natural environment. Some are better able to survive because they are better adapted to the environment. So, mice that grow more fur in cold climates survive better and, therefore, reproduce better than bald mice, which rarely live long enough to reproduce at all. The climate selects for furry mice, not because furry mice are better or more progressive but because they happen, by chance, to be better adapted to the cold.

The role of chance in this process is very strong. Evolutionary biologists are keenly aware of the great suffering that genetic mutations can cause and of the millions of extinctions of species that have occurred and that continue to occur in nature. As Darwin wrote in a letter to Asa Gray, dated May 22, 1860, "I own that I cannot see, as plainly as others do, and as I should wish to do, evidence of design and beneficence on all sides of us. There seems to me too much misery in the world" (Darwin 1985, 275).

The theory of evolution, as often presented, counts against evidence of design in the universe. As the biologist Francisco Ayala (who is, incidentally, a Catholic) says, the world is "so full of dysfunctions, wastes, and cruelties as to unwarrant its attribution to any being endowed with superior intelligence, wisdom, and benevolence" (2004, 56).

Awareness of the sufferings of animals, including humans, is hardly original with the theory of evolution. But perhaps evolution makes us more aware of how necessary waste and pain are to the process that gives rise to the existence of complex life forms. And it does not allow us to attribute suffering to some primal sin of Adam and Eve, by which death came into the world. Suffering and death existed long before the first humans did, and they seem to be essential factors in the ascent of humans to dominance on the planet earth. They are not just imperfections that might have been avoided, if Adam had not sinned. Without them, Adam, or the first member of the species *homo sapiens*, would never even have existed.

Suffering and Randomness in Evolution

Paradoxically, this insight into the necessity of suffering and death may actually help to alleviate the problem of suffering, which at first it seems to exacerbate. If suffering is attributed to the sin of some first human being, it seems grossly unfair that all animals should now suffer for something for which they are not responsible. Augustine's theory of "original guilt," according to which all are guilty for that original sin, which they did not, of course, commit personally, seems morally perverse. It is not, incidentally, in the Bible and is not accepted by Jews or Eastern Orthodox Christians or most Protestants.

But if suffering and death are necessary elements of the evolutionary process, then, without them, humans and other conscious animals would never have come to exist. Perhaps, then, they are regrettable but necessary conditions or consequences of the existence of evolved intelligent life on earth.

The obvious response to this is to say that a benevolent and powerful God could surely have devised some other way of creating humans. An Intelligent Designer could have prevented all harmful mutations and encouraged all adaptive and progressive mutations, so that intelligent beings could have evolved without any mischances or defects.

This is, in effect, suggesting that the basic laws of nature, from which the occurrence of genetic mutations derive, could have been quite different or perhaps that nature need not have proceeded in accordance with general laws at all. If either of these things were the case, then humans as we know them would not exist. There might have been physically and mentally perfect intelligent beings—and some theologians used to think that Adam and Eve were precisely that.

Humans are complex organisms that carry their evolutionary history with them, coded in their DNA. They have tendencies toward lust and aggression, toward kinship altruism and sympathy, tendencies to strive for truth and beauty and to compete with others for fame and power. If some sort of perfection is possible for them, it is a perfection achieved through effort and discipline, through a process of overcoming egoism and learning altruism, through an endeavor to discover truth and attain selfless understanding, through a struggle to overcome despair and disappointment and learn wisdom and mindfulness.

Is such an animal worth having? Opinions may differ. But if it is, perhaps it could only exist as a result of a basically Darwinian process of evolution. Some biologists would go further and claim that the apparently random nature of the biological processes of replication and mutation is entailed by the basic laws of physics and chemistry. Given the structure of carbon atoms, the chemical composition of nucleic acids and proteins, and the exactly correlated relationship between the electromagnetic and nuclear forces within the atom, carbon-based replication with genetic variation had to take place more-or-less exactly as it does.

In other words, the Darwinian process of "descent with modification" is not at all random, in the sense that it might have been quite different or that anything at all might have happened in the history of the universe. What happens follows strictly from the laws of physics, and the basic laws of physics, in turn, are, to use Steven Weinberg's term, "final"—that is, there is no other possible mathematically consistent set of laws that could produce a universe of the sort of integrated complexity that is required for the existence of intelligent life.

This is a highly contentious issue. Biologists like Stephen J. Gould maintain that evolution could have proceeded in a very different way. He uses the fossils retrieved from the Burgess Shale, in Canada, to demonstrate his point. Those fossils are of types of organisms that failed to survive, from which fact he infers that they might easily have done so—in which case humans would never have evolved. So, he sees life not as a tree with humans at the top, as a sort of predestined summit of evolution (so far). Life is more like a straggly bush, upon which humans are one twig alongside many others. All the twigs are dispensable, all got there by a series of accidents or copying errors in the replication of DNA, and none is more important than the others. There is no direction in evolution at all, as the continued and unevolveding existence of some of the most successfully adapted organisms—bacteria and beetles, for instance—shows.

But Gould's opinion, that the whole process of evolution is a freak accident, is one that he revised in his late essays, and that is strongly contested by other biologists. Simon Conway Morris, who personally worked on the Burgess Shale, draws a very different conclusion from their failure to survive. They did not survive because they were not well adapted to their environment. That environment is what it is because of the laws of physics and chemistry. Those laws inevitably favor certain sorts of development. They constrain the sorts of organism that will flourish within rather narrow limits. In fact, the laws of physics will ensure that carbon atoms, formed in the supernovae of stars, will find conditions in which they form long molecules capable of replication. Further physical constraints ensure that, sooner or later, those molecules will build bodies sensitive to light and heat, capable of moving around their environment with their sensitive organs placed toward the front (in the direction they are moving in) rather than in the back (where they have just been). Animals will mostly have eyes in or near their heads, not in their rear ends, where they would be much less use (much less adaptive, that is).

So, the poor old Burgess rejects, now on display in a most attractive museum near Calgary, Canada, just had their eyes and other relevant bits in the wrong place. They were, indeed, predestined for extinction. Their disappearance was not an accident. Nor is the emergence of intelligent life an accident. The laws of physics, the nature of the physical environment, and the physical constraints of replication and mutation ensure that, in a universe with the basic physical constants and laws of this one, carbon-based life forms with opposable digits, eyes in their heads, and large brains are bound to come into existence.

From such a view as stated by Conway Morris, evolution can be seen as a "walk through protein hyper-space." Such a hyperspace is the logical space of all possible states of physical protein assemblies. It may seem to be infinitely large, and our evolutionary walk through it on earth may seem like a drunken, uncoordinated, and unrepeatable stumble through hyperspace. But Conway Morris argues that "the 'landscape' of biological form, be it at the level of proteins, organisms, or social systems, may in principle be almost infinitely rich, but in reality the number of 'roads' through it may be much, much more restricted" (2003, 11). There are only some feasible roads through protein hyperspace because of physical constraints that force a convergence of paths upon mutating organisms. There may be many paths to take, but they will converge on a number of solutions that are likely to be repeated wherever life evolves.

Conway Morris' view is quite subtle. Even though, he says, the possibility of intelligent life is already laid down in the basic structure of the universe—"the deep structure of the universe indicates life's inevitability" (2002, 159)—nevertheless, life may be very rare or even unique to this planet. That is because conditions for its existence need to be just right—we would need planets of the right size and distance from their local stars, with large satellites, some protection against stray comets, and an atmosphere to ensure just the right amount of safe radiation from the nearest star, which also needs to be just at the right stage not to fry or freeze the planets in question. These conditions are so various and so precise and need to be so exactly correlated that, says Conway Morris, they may occur only once even in this vast universe. So he proposes that "the universe has to be this sort of size with that sort of history for us to happen. We are inherent in the fabric of the universe, but the sentient reality is only here" (172).

In a remarkable reversal of perspective, the vast size of the universe becomes not a threat to the significance of human life but a necessary means to the existence of humans, who seem to have returned to centrality in the cosmic story.

There are quite a lot of ambitious conjectures in this account. But there are just as many in Gould's account. The hard facts established by scientific observation are not in doubt. Humans have evolved over millions of years from simple cells oozing about in primeval planetary slime. The process has been one of replication, mutation, and adaptation to environment. The process has involved much destruction, conflict, and, at least at later stages, suffering. But it is hard to see how that could have been avoided, given the general nature of the process. It has also involved much cooperation and coordination between various physical entities to form cells and functioning organic bodies, so it is not purely a story of struggle and conflict. Given all the alternative possibilities, it does seem fantastically improbable that it should ever have happened at all. On the other hand, it seems like a natural development inherent in the basic structure of the physical universe.

Those are the facts. Do they lead us to the conclusion that it all happened by blind chance or to the conclusion that it shows intelligent design? Do they suggest that intelligent life is inevitable in the universe or that it is a freak accident? Do they show that there is a progress in evolution or that the strongest will survive, regardless of moral considerations? Do they show that humans are at the top of the evolutionary tree or that they are dangling precariously on a side branch? Do they suggest that there will be life elsewhere in the universe or that we are unique and alone?

I think that biological science does not answer any of these questions. It brings forward considerations that are relevant to finding an answer, and it rules out some answers—such as the traditional Christian theory that God created a perfect human being before there was any suffering or death on earth. But it leaves the big questions unanswered. It is not surprising that should be the case: why should science answer every question?

Creation and Creationism

As I write this, there is a good deal of argument and a good deal of confusion about creationism, intelligent design, and broadly Darwinian evolution. It is important to distinguish among them clearly. Creationism is the theory that the world was created literally as the book of Genesis describes it. Creationists are divided into "young earth" and "old earth" theorists, who differ about how long the first days of creation were. The motivation for this view is to defend the literal inerrancy of the Bible, and it clearly conflicts with evolutionary theory since it denies that humans, like all other animals, evolved from other, simpler species.

Creationism should be sharply distinguished from belief in Creation, which is the belief that the whole universe depends upon an intelligent conscious being beyond it. Evolution is wholly compatible with belief in Creation, even in a strictly neo-Darwinian form. For such a strict Darwinian view, the mechanisms of random mutation and natural selection are sufficient to explain the course of evolution, and no other causal factors understood are at work. Yet the whole causal structure may itself depend upon the existence of a creator God. That God would, nevertheless, have no specific causal input into the evolutionary process.

Darwin himself did not rule out other mechanisms of evolution, such as sexual selection. Given the fact that the properly scientific study of evolution has only been going on for about eighty years and that it is extremely difficult to be sure that one has identified every causal influence at work in any natural process, it is a leap of faith to say that mutation and natural selection are the only factors at work in evolution. But it does seem that they are sufficient in practice to give a plausible, if not absolutely exhaustive, explanation of how evolution works. In any case, there is general agreement that they are the main discernible factors at work.

Even if the only role God has is to set up the causal system, Stephen Gould's view that what happens is wholly accidental would have to be rejected by a theist, as it is quite implausible to think that God set up the universe but would be taken by surprise if anything good happened and never envisioned human beings coming into existence at all.

If the laws of nature do, as Conway Morris suggests, make the existence of intelligent life virtually inevitable, then God would not be surprised when human beings begin to exist, since they, or something very much like them, are possibilities that are bound to come into existence sooner or later. God can set up the process so that what God wants will eventually happen, though there may be many ways in which it can happen and many routes to its happening.

This appears to have been Charles Darwin's own view. He wrote, "I cannot persuade myself that electricity acts, that the tree grows, that man aspires to the loftiest conceptions, all from blind, brute force" (1985, 275). The laws of nature are designed, but God plays no further role in how they operate. They are totally autonomous.

It may still seem rather odd that God sits there and does nothing, having put the laws of nature in place. Most things that really exist have causal influences on at least some other things. So, if God, a supremely wise consciousness, really exists, would that not have some continuing causal influence on a universe God had designed?

Intelligent Design

This is the consideration that has led to the thesis of intelligent design. The intelligent design movement is not a form of creationism, and most of its adherents (certainly, William Dembski and Michael Behe) have no difficulty in accepting the facts of evolution. But they hold that God is a causal factor in evolution. Moreover, divine causality—or at least some form of intelligent design—can be empirically established by the existence of certain objects possessing what Michael Behe calls "irreducible complexity." They could not have eventuated through purely Darwinian mechanisms, and they entail some sort of intelligent design.

Behe gives as an example the bacterial flagellum. Some bacteria—microscopic bugs—have tiny propellers—flagella—on their backs, that spin at thousands of revolutions a minute and propel the bacteria. Around forty proteins are needed to construct them, and they must be organized and coordinated in an amazingly complex way.

This organism, say intelligent design proponents, could not have evolved by small incremental steps, as Darwinian evolution requires, because if any of its parts were lacking, then a working flagellum would not exist. The flagellum is "irreducibly complex" in that all the parts must be coordinated at once if it is to function. A Darwinian account would require that there were thousands of stages, each of which would produce some survival or adaptive advantage, and they would finally, and accidentally, result in some bacteria having tiny propellers. But if any parts of the propeller were missing, it could not work as a propeller at all. The flagellum is irreducibly complex. And that means it could not have been gradually assembled by chance. It must have been intelligently designed.

Kenneth Miller (2004) has responded to this argument caustically, by pointing out that the flagellum does have functioning parts, one of which is a protein secretory system that allows bacteria to transport proteins from the inside of a cell to the outside through a membrane. This is, in effect, a subsystem of the bacterial flagellum and shows that the flagellum could have been assembled from smaller component parts, which had some survival advantage of their own. It is not, therefore, irreducibly complex.

Many biologists also find it implausible to introduce a Designer at specific stages in evolution, a being who will construct a complex organism by direct manipulation of available material, when the Designer leaves untouched all the genetic malfunctions and deformities that occur in evolution. Francisco Ayala argues forcefully that such dysfunctions point to the "opportunistic, tinkerlike character of natural selection, rather than intelligent design" (2004, 70). And Kenneth Miller objects to views that require the laws of nature to be abrogated by direct outside intervention, whereas, he thinks, what we have is "a universe in which the beauty and harmony of natural law has brought a world of vibrant and fruitful life into existence" (2004, 94).

The arguments of the intelligent design theorists are of some theoretical importance, since Darwin said that, if one could find a structure that could not have been formed by numerous, successive, slight modifications, his theory would "absolutely break down" (1972, 191). But the intelligent design arguments have found few supporters in the biological community.

Nobody claims that the total sequence of such successive steps has been elucidated for all complex life forms. But many steps have been demonstrated in many cases, and it is part of the working methodology of evolutionary biology, part of many research programs, to find further steps. To most biologists, it looks as though intelligent design theorists are just appealing to ignorance and finding intelligent design in the gaps not yet filled by science.

But intelligent design theorists see themselves as finding deficiencies in the methodology of a purely naturalistic approach to science, so they try to drive a wedge between the proper empirical activities of science and an assertion of methodological naturalism—that is, the view that all investigation of the physical world must assume that there are no discoverable supernatural causal factors at work in nature. Philip Johnson wrote a book called The *Wedge of Truth* (2000) that explicitly set out to distinguish the empirical methodology of science from a commitment to naturalism (to the view that there is no supernatural reality like God).

Perhaps, however, Johnson's wedge is in the wrong place. It should be between methodological naturalism and philosophical naturalism. Philosophical naturalism is the view that there are no supernatural causal factors at work in nature. But methodological naturalism only asserts that, if there are such causes, they may not be discoverable at all or their discovery may not be part of proper scientific method.

Biologists, like other scientists, only deal with empirically discoverable aspects of nature. They need not deny that there may be other aspects that are not discoverable by public observation and so are not parts of science. This seems to be the position of those like Francisco Ayala and Kenneth Miller, who strongly defend naturalistic methodology but who also think there is a God, whose being and acts are not discoverable by science.

There is a tension in the assertion that there is a God who presumably acts, taken together with the view that those acts are not discoverable by observation. What is the difference between saying that and saying that there is no God at all? Ayala has suggested that religions deal with questions of "value and meaning," with aesthetic and moral perceptions "that are forever beyond science's scope" (2004, 73). And, in *Rock of Ages* (1999), Stephen Gould has spoken of "two non-overlapping magisteria" of science and religion, which speak of quite different and nonconflicting realms of inquiry.

That may be so. But if God is supposed to be the Creator—the ultimate cause of absolutely everything—we might think that the existence of God must make some difference to how things are. The problem is that we can never be in a position to compare a universe that we know to be without God with a universe with God, to see just what the difference is. The theist will say that, without God, there would be no universe—which is the biggest difference there could ever be! But the atheist will simply reply that there is a universe without God, and we are in it.

Would it follow that, if there is a God, we could detect specific instances of designing activity? Or at least that random mutation and natural selection are not sufficient causes for the complex world of living things? We do not, after all, expect God to make a difference to car mechanics. Why should we expect God to make a difference to biology? Maybe all we can say is that, if there is a God, the evolutionary process will be efficiently designed to produce an intended result. If what we have is intelligent life, then intelligent life could be an intended result. Evolution has brought us here, by processes that are amazingly elegant, integrated, and complex. Two quotations from Darwin make the point: "How infinitely complex and close-fitting are the mutual relations of all organic beings," and "from so simple a beginning endless forms, most beautiful and most wonderful, have been, and are being, evolved" (1859, 80 and 490).

I think there is force in the argument that the existence of an Intelligent Designer who could ensure that intelligent life would come to exist would make the process much less improbable than if the process happened "by chance." A hypothesis that makes a process much more probable must be rated as a probable hypothesis, given the available evidence. So, the evolution of intelligent life makes the hypothesis of an Intelligent Designer probable. In that sense, the intelligent design hypothesis is a good one—but this is intelligent design in a general sense and does not entail the existence of empirically identifiable and special cases of design within the process.

The "Indifference" of Evolutionary Laws

Why, then, should the evolutionary process be seen as "blind, pitiless, or indifferent" as it undoubtedly is by some biologists like Richard Dawkins? Partly, it is because Dawkins thinks the hypothesis of God is itself highly improbable or even self-contradictory. The existence of an Intelligent Designer may make the emergence of intelligent life in a physical universe more probable. But if that Intelligent Designer is more improbable than the process it seeks to explain, it is pointless to rely on it. That argument leads back to the first of our "big questions" and far beyond the limits of evolutionary biology.

But Richard Dawkins is also impressed by the fact that the laws of nature work impersonally. They do not change to protect the innocent from harm or to punish only the guilty. And they produce pain and death as well as pleasure, beauty, and vitality.

What is at issue here is the character of God, the ultimate designer. For some people, God is a benevolent person who would not willingly bring harm to anyone. If God is a "heavenly Father," then God will not do less than a terrestrial loving father would do. God would protect creatures from harm and not let them be stricken down by disease or killed by natural disasters, if God could possibly help it.

Knowledge of biology will cast serious doubt on this oversimple idea of God. But millions of people died in plagues and disasters before anything was known about evolution, so this problem has not really gotten any worse since Darwin. In fact, Darwinism could be said to help ease the problem considerably. Those who believe that disease is a punishment for sin have to think that everyone who gets measles has done something wrong, while those who escape are morally better. Further, if you are really good, you will never get ill at all.

The problem of the suffering of the innocent is made much worse by such beliefs. You have to think those who are afflicted are not really innocent—and that idea compounds the injustice of their situation. If you think that God is personally supervising and arranging every detail of a person's life, then God seems to act in very unjust ways.

Aristotle said that the rule of impersonal law is better than the rule of whimsical tyrants. So, the rule of impersonal laws of physics may actually be better than the changing whims of a continually interfering God. In fact, if God arranged for perfect moral justice in human affairs, there could be no laws of nature at all. Good people would float gently to earth when they fell from high mountains, while the evil would be crushed by meteorites directed upon their heads with perfect accuracy. We would all, of course, be directly aware that such a God existed. But, in such a world, could morality be more than self-interested prudence in the face of a God known to be all-powerful? Or would God detect hypocrites and direct meteorites upon their heads too? Then we would know with certainty just who was good and who was bad. And that might not be altogether a good thing. This would be life in the ultimate police state.

But, it may be protested, would not heaven be like that anyway? It would be a world without unjust suffering and in which virtue had its due reward. So, is heaven ultimately undesirable, full of self-satisfied and self-righteous people who don't have to care much about their actions since they can never come to any harm?

I suppose what this suggests is that heaven cannot really be like a continuation of life on earth, only better for the lucky few. In this life, we work out our freedom as well as we can. In the next, if there is one, there is a wholly different form of existence that springs causally from this one but does not have the same spatiotemporal structure. This world is vitally important because, in it, each one of us shapes our character by facing up to many moral and intellectual challenges. In heaven—that is, in the clear presence of God—what we have made of our lives is eternalized, reconciled, and validated in a quite different form of experience.

Without our striving after virtue in this world, heaven would not be a possibility for us. Heaven is not a continuation of such striving but its consummation and its ending. Fortunately, too, according to most religions, God will forgive our wrongdoing and grant more than we deserve—it is a gift that does not depend solely on our own virtues but on the mercy and love of God. It is chiefly in that sense that God will ultimately prove to be indeed a loving Father.

But the details of life in heaven are not of immediate concern. The fact is that human existence is lived out in an arena of impersonal laws of nature. Such laws may be "blind," but they result in the possibility of purposeful and intelligent life. They may be "pitiless," but they permit the possibility of human compassion and mutual care. They may be "indifferent," but they seem inherently fitted to generate life in all its variety and wonder.

There is a similar ambiguity here to that noted when thinking about cosmology. Space can be seen as empty and dispiriting, but it can also be seen as awe-inspiringly beautiful and a necessary condition of our existence. The evolution of life on earth can be seen as the workings of blind and indifferent laws without meaning or purpose, but it can also be seen as a fantastically complex, organized, cumulative process that inevitably results in the emergence of intelligent life.

Theistic Evolution

The pessimistic view of nature as "red in tooth and claw" is not universally shared by biologists. Alfred Lord Tennyson himself, who penned that famous quotation, ends the poem from which it comes, *In Memoriam*, by referring to "One God, one law, one element, / And one far-off divine event, / To which the whole creation moves." After his moments of despair at the death of his friend, he comes to see the whole universe as purposeful and ultimately good.

Among biologists, there are counterbalancing views of evolution, like those of Frans de Waal, Erik Parens, and Steven Rose; they see the neo-Darwinian stress on competition, selfishness, and survival as one-sided. Brian Goodwin writes, "We are every bit as co-operative as we are competitive; as altruistic as we are selfish; as creative and playful as we are destructive and repetitive. And we are . . . agents of creative evolutionary emergence, a property we share with all other species" (1994, xiv). It is possible to see the evolutionary process as one of creative emergence and dynamic interrelationship, rather than as one of ruthless competition for mere replication. There is competition and destruction. But there is also what seems to many biologists to be a holistic, emergent, and self-organizing propensity to complexity, order, and consciousness. If that is so, there may be positive value in the evolutionary process, as a process that makes possible a partly self-shaping creative advance toward intelligent consciousness.

Science will not decide the issue. Intelligent design is a reaction against reductionist views that claim that "science shows" human life to be an accidental by-product of purely mechanical and purposeless processes. But its claim that specific instances of personal purpose and design, not even in principle explicable in Darwinian terms, can be identified by science has not been generally accepted by the scientific community, whether religious or not.

What science shows is that evolution happened. Whether it is accidental or inevitable, blind or goal-directed, is not conclusively decided by science. There seems little reason that the original "optimistic" nineteenth-century German evolutionary theories should not be broadly true and be compatible with a generally Darwinian approach. Evolution may be the progressive self-manifestation of the nature of Absolute Spirit, and the mechanisms it uses may be those of replication with modification and preferential selection by the total environment of the cosmos.

If such a "spiritually directed" view is taken, then genetic mutations will inevitably produce some of greater complexity, tending eventually to the emergence of consciousness, and the cosmic environment will inevitably favor the selection of intelligent life forms. There will be a predetermined goal, though its specific nature and the way to achieve it may be left open. The existence of such a goal in the Divine Mind will have some form of causal influence on evolutionary development—it will ensure that this will be an evolution toward a goal, not just random change without any particular direction.

But such a general influence may not be empirically detectable by reference to specifically identifiable and otherwise inexplicable occurrences. There is no visible person to announce the goal and no visible material body that can be observed to be ensuring that it comes about. We would not expect the influence of a Cosmic (i.e., completely omnipresent but disembodied) Mind to be detectable by specific physical observations or to be confirmed by specific predictions.

The physical biochemist Arthur Peacocke characterizes the evolutionary process as one of "unfolding the divinely endowed potentialities of the universe through a process in which its creative possibilities and propensities become actualized" (2001, 77). God, he suggests, is "an Improvisor of unsurpassed ingenuity," setting up a system in which chance and necessity interweave so that "the full gamut of the potentialities of living matter could be explored."

Peacocke does not think there is any need for "a kind of special guidance . . . whereby God pushes or pulls evolution in a direction it would not otherwise have taken" (2001, 75). On the other hand, he is a leading proponent of "top-down causation," or "whole-part influence," by which the nature of whole systems helps to determine the behavior of their parts in a distinctive way. If God is a totality that includes this universe, then "God could affect holistically the state of the world-system" (110). The system as a whole is what it is because God is its ultimate source, and God does have a general causal influence on the evolutionary process. But there are no gaps in the system in which God intervenes, and so there are no gaps in a purely naturalistic account of the process.

There will, nevertheless, be some empirical consequences of the existence of God. The postulated goal of evolution will have to be of value, and it will have to be achieved by a process efficient for its purpose. Evolution seems to fit these conditions sufficiently. The process as a whole would have to be good. This is really where atheists part company with theists. The theist is bound to affirm that the creation is good. But the theist could argue that evolutionary history, by some internal necessity, has to play out generally the way it does—accomplished by mutations only some of which are beneficial, limited by necessities that even God cannot change, yet leading overall to good outcomes. Part of the reason for this necessity is that natural selection takes place in an environment governed by impersonal laws of physics, whose final nature is in some sense necessary and whose ultimate outcomes are in broad strokes, though not in detail, predictable.

What Can an Omnipotent Being Do?

An atheist might well object that the God who creates this evolutionary history, being bound by some sort of internal necessity, is not strictly omnipotent and so does not count as the traditional God of religion. Moreover, such a God does not act in particularly providential ways to protect all creatures from harm. So, God is not benevolent either. Perhaps there is some sort of "Absolute Spirit," but it is not omnipotent or benevolent, and so it is not God after all.

However, at this point, we need to be aware that the idea of God has not been fixed for all time by some philosopher or religious text a thousand years or more ago. Like ideas in science, ideas of God change, and they are capable of changing again, if developments in knowledge require it. There are, of course, popular ideas of God as a male father figure who can do absolutely anything and wants to help everybody to be happy. But such ideas are neither typical of those who actually worship God in churches, synagogues, and mosques, nor do they represent at all accurately what the major thinkers of religious traditions have said about God.

The basic philosophical idea of God, espoused by religious thinkers like Sankara, Ramanuja (Hindus), Anselm, Aquinas (Christians), Maimonides (a Jew), and Al Gazzali (a Muslim) is that God is the one ultimately self-existent reality, of supreme and unsurpassable value, and beyond the capacity of the human intellect to understand fully in an analytical way. Our ideas of God will, thus, always be provisional and inadequate, but they will reflect our ideas of what supreme value is and of what we speculate to be the nature of a self-existent Source of the world, as we see that world in the light of the best available scientific knowledge. It will not be surprising if modern knowledge of evolution prompts us to make some revisions to our idea of God.

Even the classical theologians have never held that God's goodness primarily consists in wanting to preserve creatures from all harm. In the classical traditions, to call God good is primarily to say that God's own being is perfect. God's being consists of a set of states that are of supreme intrinsic value. An intrinsic value is a state that is preferred for its own sake alone and not as a means to some other state. A supreme intrinsic value is a state that is more valuable than any other state of the same sort. Thus, supreme happiness would be a quality of happiness that was more valuable than any other available happiness.

Given these simple definitions, God's being contains more supreme intrinsic values that any other possible being. God is, for instance, supremely happy, wise, knowledgeable, and powerful. That is what it means to say that God is perfect. God is happier, has greater knowledge, and is more powerful than any other being could possibly be.

Given this definition, we still cannot tell just how happy, knowledgeable, and powerful God is. God may be the most powerful possible being, but there may still be limits on the power of such a being, though we cannot tell what they are. Part of the traditional "problem of evil" arises from an overambitious definition of omnipotence. It is said that omnipotence means that God can do anything that is logically possible—that is, anything that we can describe without self-contradiction. But we can describe things without apparent or discoverable self-contradiction that cannot exist. For instance, we can describe time travel without apparent self-contradiction. But time travel may, nevertheless, be impossible. We do not know. The fact that we can describe it consistently does not mean that it is possible. There may be reasons unknown to us that make it impossible—many physicists think there are. Some physicists disagree. But there is no way of deciding who is right. We certainly cannot settle the issue by simply saying that some description of a state seems consistent to us. As David Hume put it, how could the imaginations of a petty brain like ours become the criterion of what is possible or impossible? Hume was right about that, but he was wrong to suggest that anything we can imagine must be possible. In fact, his latter statement is undermined by his former one.

The point here is basically simple and very important. The human mind is in no position to know what is really possible or impossible in reality. The fact that we can imagine states of affairs does not mean that they are possible. So, the fact that we can imagine, or think we can imagine, God's creating a universe without suffering does not mean that such a thing is possible.

This statement is, like most philosophical assertions, controversial. Some would insist that, if we can imagine something, it is possible, and God could do it. I am just pointing out that this is a highly disputable opinion. "Possible worlds theory" is a very complicated philosophical topic, on which a huge amount of literature exists and upon which many doctorates are even now being written.

If we take the view that we cannot tell, just by imagination, what is really possible even for the most powerful possible being there could be, then we could, and perhaps should, take *omnipotence* to mean simply that an Omnipotent Being is more powerful than any other being could possibly be. Perhaps we might want to add that an Omnipotent Being will also be the source of all other powers that could ever exist.

How much more powerful than that could you want to be? Well, you might want to be powerful enough to do anything that is logically possible. But such a thing might be impossible for any possible being. Why? We do not know. But let us have a little humility and admit that we do not know everything. God may be omnipotent, meaning that God is the source of all other powers and is more powerful than any other possible being. Yet there may be limits to divine power, limits that will be inherent in the divine nature itself, and we can never know precisely what they are. In that case, God, as the most perfect and powerful being there could possibly be, could still be "limited" by internal necessities. That would be no defect because no being could evade what is truly necessary.

God, Necessity, and the Problem of Evil

Necessity is not an alien idea for classical theology. Indeed, classical theologians usually agreed that the divine nature is necessarily what it is. It could not be otherwise. Most states in the universe are contingent—they could have been other than they actually are. God is different. God, the ultimate source of all beings, has to be the way God is. There is simply no alternative to the way God is. Even God cannot do anything about it.

This is not such a strange remark as it might seem. After all, most people would agree that God cannot lie or commit sin or commit suicide. But that *cannot* is not an external limitation on God. It follows from the divine nature, of being perfectly good. God is necessarily perfectly good. God necessarily exists. God is necessarily the most powerful possible being. And whatever limits there are on God's power, they are necessarily part of the divine nature itself. They cannot be changed, and they could never have been otherwise.

So, it may be that God necessarily creates this universe and perhaps others. If so, then the answer to the question, "Why did God create this universe?" will be that God had to, not because some other being compelled God to do it, but out of an inner necessity of the divine nature.

It is not very easy for us to decide exactly what a perfect God would be like. But it seems reasonable to think that a perfect God might wish to share happiness, creativity, and understanding with other beings. To put it bluntly, goodness shared might be more perfect than goodness confined to itself. Thomas Aquinas said, "A thing has a natural tendency . . . to spread its own good to others" (*Summa Theologiae*, 1a, question 19, article 2). So, a good reason for creation would be the creation of a universe in which other personal beings, capable of happiness, creativity, and understanding, could exist. There could well be a very large number of different universes that could realize this aim. A perfect God might well create a huge number of universes containing personal beings of different sorts. Or God might just create one of them—again, we must be careful not to claim to know too much about what God might do. At any rate, it seems it would be a good thing to create a universe in which persons would exist who could relate to one another and to God in shared creativity and understanding.

In some possible universes, including this one, it could well be that some suffering is inevitable. Modern science helps us to see this. If humans have evolved in our universe from a primeval big bang, then that process of evolution necessarily involves suffering and destruction. Stars had to explode to form the heavier elements of which life is composed. Millions of organisms had to die in order for human life to evolve on this planet. Even now, humans have to destroy plant or animal life in order to survive. The physical laws of this universe depend upon destruction, mutation, conflict, and, therefore, destruction and death, if intelligent persons are to evolve in it. If we understood the laws of nature fully, we would see that such destruction and the suffering conscious beings feel when involved in it are inevitable consequences of having a universe like this.

Human beings are essentially parts of an evolving physical universe, with general laws that have to be exactly what they are in order to produce human persons. Those laws will produce earthquakes, stellar explosions, periodic extinctions of life, and volcanic eruptions as an essential part of having a universe like this. If beings like human persons are going to exist, they have to exist in a universe in which suffering and death are necessary. The choice is, then, either no human persons or some suffering. We cannot have human persons and a universe without suffering. That is one of the limitations on God's power—if God is going to create human persons, God will have to create a universe in which some suffering necessarily exists.

If these arguments are accepted, it is possible to see how a God who is omnipotent and perfectly good, in the senses defined, could—and may even have to—create a universe like this. You may reject these defined senses, but they seem coherent and defensible. Or you may say, as Ivan does in Fyodor Dostoyevsky's novel *The Brothers Karamazov*, that you are still repelled by the amount of suffering in the universe and you would rather reject the whole idea of God than pay the price of the ticket for human existence.

In a sense, most religious believers agree. They worship—admire and revere—the perfection of the Divine Being. But they stand perplexed and bitter at the amount of suffering, however necessary, in the world. Partly for that reason, rather than out of any selfish desire for further personal existence, most religions have posited an afterlife, in which overwhelming good becomes possible for everyone. Almost all religions that believe in God believe in an afterlife, recognizing that divine justice and mercy are not properly worked out in this world.

A perfect God who chooses to create this universe, accepting that suffering is necessary in it, must offer to all conscious beings who suffer, if it is possible to do so, an overwhelming personal good. That personal good is a life after death. Maybe anyone (including Dostoyevsky) who truly sees the possibility of overwhelming happiness, understanding, and creativity in a life of perfect consciousness of God beyond this world, for everyone without exception, and who accepts the necessity of suffering if there are to be any humans at all, will accept that the creation of this universe is ultimately good and worthwhile.

Original Sin and Evolution

Whether or not that is the case, it does seem clear that human selfishness, greed, and hatred have immeasurably increased the amount of suffering in the world. That excess suffering is caused by the misuse of human freedom and is an unavoidable consequence of human moral freedom and of that solidarity of humans in community, which involves the innocent in the sins of the guilty. This is what is usually known as "the free-will defense," and I think it is an important part of an explanation of why there is so much suffering in the world.

What some Christians call "original sin" can be seen, from an evolutionary perspective, as the decision by groups of early humans or even prehominids to realize their genetically inherent tendencies toward lust and aggression, at the expense of similarly inherent tendencies toward kinship bonding and altruism. Over generations, those destructive tendencies have "switched on" the relevant genetic mechanisms, until it has now become "human nature" to be selfish and aggressive.

Original sin, from an evolutionary point of view, consists in a natural inclination toward self-centered and destructive behavior, rooted in the genetic code of humans, switched on by repeated inculturation. Humans are essentially related to one another as parts of social communities and given responsible moral freedom. But the repeatedly reinforced behavior of past generations has repressed our altruistic genes, alienated us from a sense of the presence of God, and vastly increased the amount of human and animal suffering.

Humans may not, as the Genesis account suggests, have brought suffering and death into the world. But they have immeasurably increased the sum of suffering, and they have brought spiritual death, the death of the sense of God, into the world.

Religions do not take an easy and optimistic view of suffering in the world. They begin from the problem of suffering and from the features of human personality and society that make that suffering worse. Thus, Buddhism finds a major root of suffering in attachment to selfish desire and recommends a way to overcoming that desire. Hinduism sees humans as trapped in ignorance *(avidya)* of their true nature and seeks ways of discerning the true self of divine goodness hidden within. Christianity sees humans as bound by the power of sin and needing liberation by the divine power of love. Judaism and Islam seek to overcome principles of self-centeredness by devotion to a God of compassion and mercy. The East Asian traditions seek to discipline the self by meditation or devotion to ancestors and to the Way of Heaven.

The "golden age" myths of these traditions are ways of saying that the true nature of humans, what they are made for, is a life of compassion, wisdom, and love. But humans have "fallen" into desire, ignorance, and self-centeredness, and they need to find a way to return to primal innocence. We know there was no historical golden age or fall and that there is no return to primal innocence. But wisdom, creativity, and love can still be seen as the essential goals of human life. Humans have taken a moral path that leads away from those things, and that path was laid down as a possibility in the evolutionary structure of developing life on earth. It is the task of religions, and of all humane thought, to return to the way that was not taken and to provide at least a road map for the journey.

All of this may still be rejected. These notions of divine omnipotence and goodness may seem like the construction of epicycles to save a doomed hypothesis, and they do not, it may be said, leave us with a God worthy of unqualified worship. The idea of divine necessity may seem like an empty notion, without real substance. The universe may be judged to be bad on the whole, and human freedom may not be considered worth the suffering that is held to be inseparable from it. The idea of an afterlife may seem like a lame and untestable fantasy to compensate for the very real evils we see in the universe around us. And religions are never going to escape from literal interpretations of the myths they propagate, so they will always be a barrier to real scientific understanding of the world.

It is worth noting that none of these objections is directly based on the scientific facts of evolutionary biology. They are philosophical objections to the idea of God, moral objections to an assertion of the goodness of creation, and cultural objections to the fantastic and obscurantist nature of religion. These issues will remain disputed for the foreseeable future. As far as the facts of evolution are concerned, they are compatible with belief in the creation of the universe by God, on condition that literalist interpretations of scientifically relevant parts of ancient scriptures are given up and that the naturalistic methodology of evolutionary biology is not claimed to provide a complete, exhaustive account of the nature of reality.

Claims on both the religious and scientific sides to give an all-encompassing and exclusive view of truth will bring religion and science into conflict. A more tentative search for the spiritual meaning of ancient scriptures and for the methodological fruitfulness of biological research programs offers the prospect of a more positive and creative interaction, the results of which cannot be laid down in advance.

In an evolutionary universe, any plausible religious vision must be rather different from anything envisaged before the eighteenth century. How far and how deeply such revisions will need to go is for particular religions to explore. Is this a disaster for all preevolutionist beliefs, or is it an exciting and creative expansion of vision? To answer that question, we must first engage in the inquiry. And it has only just begun.

4. Do the Laws of Nature Exclude Miracles?

Miracles in the World Religions

MIRACLES ARE PREVALENT FEATURES of religions. In the Indian traditions, Krishna lifted up a mountain to protect the world against rain sent by the god Indra. Modern-day gurus like Sai Baba regularly work miracles, producing rings and even statuettes out of thin air and healing devotees of various ailments. The Buddha, according to the Jataka tales in the Pali canon, emerged from his mother's side, stood up, began to walk, and declared that he would not be born again. In the Semitic traditions, the series of ten miraculous plagues and the drying up of the Sea of Reeds to enable the Hebrews to escape from Egypt (the Exodus) are commemorated each year in Jewish Passover ceremonies. The canonical Gospels record thirty-five miracles that Jesus performed, twenty-three of them miraculous healings and nine nature miracles, like walking on water, stilling a storm, producing food out of nothing, and turning water into wine. Three times he is said to have brought the dead back to life. And, of course, the virgin birth and Jesus' own Resurrection from death are integral parts of the Christian creed.

In Islam, many miracles are recorded in the Qur'an, and the Qur'an itself is said to be the greatest of miracles, being such than no ordinary human poet could have created a text of such beauty and power—"This Qur'an is not such as can be produced by other than God" (10:37). Miracles are less important in the East Asian traditions, but even there the lives of the great religious teachers are surrounded by stories of their extraordinary powers and more-than-human wisdom.

The creation and end-of-the-world stories in ancient scriptures have been relegated to the realm of mythology—of literally false accounts with spiritual meaning—by the discoveries of modern science. Can we, or must we, do the same thing with the miracle stories that are such a prominent feature of most religions? Some, like the stories of Krishna, do seem mythological in this sense. The central story of Krishna and the milkmaids (*gopis*), for instance, could easily be taken as a symbol of the deep emotional love between Krishna and his devotees, rather than a genuinely historical account. And the story of the Buddha's miraculous birth, probably not written down until four hundred years after it occurred, sounds like a common mythological motif, found in many cultures throughout the world, of a miraculous birth for a great god or hero.

The story of a miraculous conception for Jesus is only related in the Gospels of Matthew and Luke, in rather different versions, and is in some tension with other Gospel accounts that speak of Mary's failure to understand Jesus' mission or of his cousin John the Baptist not being sure if he were the Messiah, even though a truly miraculous conception should have made that pretty clear. In Christian tradition, there later developed an added belief that Jesus' birth, too, was miraculous, leaving Mary fully a virgin, and the noncanonical Gospels record various miracles Jesus performed as a child. One, making a clay bird and then getting it to fly away, is mentioned in the Qur'an, but such stories seem frankly petty, and some of them (there is one about punishing an objectionable school teacher) are even unsavory when looked at objectively.

It seems clear that miracle stories tend to get more dramatic over time and that legends of amazing and wonderful events (that is what *miracle*, from the Latin *miraculum*, means) grow greater as the years go by. When we read of medieval accounts of miracles—St. George killing the dragon, virgins (St. Uncumber, one of my favorites) instantaneously growing beards to put off unwanted suitors, and the house in which Jesus was born flying through the clouds to Norwich and coming to rest at Walsingham, happily not too far from the bearded lady—we may well feel a twinge of skepticism.

As the centuries rolled by, the unspecified number of magi (probably the reference is to Zoroastrian priests) who visited Jesus in his house in Bethlehem some time after his birth turned into three kings, each named, who visited the manger, together with a crowd of shepherds, angels, cows, and sheep. The story gets more detailed as time goes by, and that is a good clue that human imagination is hard at work. Are all the miracle stories, then, products of human imagination, and if so, how does that affect religion?

As we examine the religions of the world, we find many undoubted instances of myths and legends and some common themes of miraculous births, superhuman deeds of valor, and visits to and returns from the world of the dead, surrounding the great heroes of faith. Nobody can think they are all true—they contradict one another about many things—and it seems a little arbitrary to say that everybody else's reported miracles are legends, whereas the miracles of our own tradition are all true. So it is reasonable to approach the subject of miracles with a skeptical mind.

Moreover, most miracle stories arose within a worldview in which angels and demons were fighting for dominance and for the souls of men and women and in which storms, earthquakes, and plagues were caused either by demonic influence or were some sort of divine punishment. Many of Jesus' miracles were, in fact, exorcisms of demons, who often recognized him as the Son of God and had to be commanded to keep quiet. He was fed in the wilderness by angels and tempted by the devil. In that world, there was not just a supreme cosmic consciousness, God. There were legions of spiritual powers—good and bad—causing things to happen in the world in accordance with their own plans and ambitions.

In that world, there were no laws of nature. Miracles, wonderful and awe-inspiring events, were to be expected, as the supernatural spirits fought and sought to demonstrate their power in the events of nature and history. Almost every event was caused by direct spiritual action, and miracles were just a particularly powerful and impressive expression of such action. Moses' miracles in Egypt were better than the miracles of the Egyptian magicians, because his God was more powerful than theirs. When God can do almost anything God wants, uninhibited by laws of nature, then it is only to be expected that the Divine Being will demonstrate his superior power when the occasion demands it. But when we have given up that general notion of the world and of God, can we still retain any meaningful concept of *miracle*?

The Discovery of the Laws of Nature

A divine miracle, for a believer in God, is an expression of the presence and power and purpose of God in an extraordinarily impressive event. Or, for non-theistic traditions like Buddhism, a miracle is an expression of the amazing power of a liberated soul that has transcended the physical limitations of ordinary human beings.

Miracles in this sense, extraordinary expressions of spiritual power, are a problem for science because events in the world are no longer thought to be directly caused by supernatural spirits. The birth of modern science in the sixteenth century occurred partly because of the exclusion of such spiritual causes from the natural world. Francis Bacon (1561–1626) aimed to separate "metaphysics" (the investigation of the ultimate nature of reality, aided by Aristotle's formal and final causes) sharply from "physics," which was to be concerned only with efficient and material causes. Final causes, he said, were like the vestal virgins of ancient Rome, dedicated to God but barren. Empirical science must have nothing to do with them. The alleged purposes of finite objects, or of angels and demons, were not parts of science proper, which must only study the physical antecedents that bring about their effects in accordance with general, measurable, repeatable, and predictable laws.

René Descartes, in 1637, at around the same time or soon after, characterized rational method in thought as that of seeking evidence for your beliefs, dividing each problem up into its constituent parts, beginning with the simple and ascending little by little to the complex, and seeking an exhaustive enumeration of the topic under review. This method, in fact, owed something to the work of Robert Grosseteste (1186–1253), chancellor of Oxford University, who stressed the importance of analysis and measurement in observation and who saw mathematics as the hidden language of nature. This thinking was to open up a fruitful way forward for the scientific method, which seeks to understand complex things in terms of the laws that govern the behavior of their simple parts, laws that are to be discovered by close, repeated, and publicly verifiable observation and that are to be formulated in precise mathematical terms.

The triumph of the laws of nature was completed in the work of Isaac Newton, who constructed a few simple laws of mechanics that seemed to apply to all phenomena when they were considered in relative abstraction from the very complex real-world situations in which they were perceived by common sense. Projectiles seem to common sense to fall to earth after a while, and so Aristotle had thought they need a positive force or impetus to keep them moving. Newton demonstrated that the common-sense view is mistaken, since it is factors like air resistance and gravity that cause projectiles to fall to earth. Abstractly considered, in isolation from such real-world factors, objects will continue moving in a straight line without any special impetus, unless something stops them.

By using mathematical abstraction and postulating a set of universal principles that govern the behavior of the simple parts of physical objects, Newton, who published his great work *Principia Mathematica* in 1687, completed the revolution in physics that had begun with the criticism of Aristotelian principles by Copernicus and Galileo. The natural world could no longer be seen as the playground of supernatural spirits. It was the outcome of the application of a few universal rules of action to simple physical particles. Spirits had been driven from the universe. Henceforth, the universe could be seen as a machine.

This was a huge revolution in human thinking, but it was not prompted by opposition to religion. It rather recast religion in a new mode. The writers I have mentioned all saw mathematics as the language of God and humans as able to understand the universe mathematically because they were made in the image of God and so could understand God's language. Angels and demons were relegated, with gnomes and fairies, to a lower level of religion, and attention was concentrated on just one supreme and perfectly rational Spirit, who had designed the universe as a perfect machine.

Isaac Newton had no trouble with miracles and wrote a number of extremely boring books about the biblical miracles, pointing out that God could break his own laws if he wanted to. But he did not realize that this made miracles much odder than they had previously been. Miracles had been extraordinary spiritual acts but still acts of the same general (spirit-caused) sort that occur throughout the universe anyway. Now, however, miracles have to be transgressions of universal laws of nature. That is how David Hume defined them, and Hume used the word *transgression* advisedly, to point up the absurdity, as he thought, of miraculous intervention. Why should God make a set of beautiful and elegant laws, only to break them when the Divine Being felt like it? Does this not make God some sort of mathematical criminal?

Are Miracles Transgressions of the Laws of Nature?

In his 1748 work, *An Inquiry Concerning Human Understanding*, David Hume's full definition of a miracle is "a transgression of a law of nature by a particular volition of the Deity, or by the interposition of some invisible agent" (1955, 123n1). This has become almost a standard definition given to all first-year philosophy students. But that definition could not have existed before the time of Newton, and the use of the words *transgression* and *invisible agent* subtly convey the impression (and are meant to do so) that miracles are criminal acts by beings rather like fairies. So Hume's definition already begins to make miracles seem absurd.

The philosopher Richard Swinburne, author of one of the best modern philosophical treatments of miracles, *The Concept of Miracle*, is reasonably happy with Hume's definition, even though he offers as an alternative the much better formulation that a miracle is "an event of an extraordinary kind, brought about by a god, and of religious significance" (1970, 1). But the problem with Hume's definition is that it may conjure up a picture of a universe as a machine, in which every event falls under one or more of a set of universal and unbreakable mechanical laws and in which those laws, taken together, give a complete and exhaustive explanation of the universe. In such a universe, any breaking of the laws seems like arbitrary interference by some person outside the machine.

This picture was indeed held by many after the time of Newton, and it led to the deistic view that a Perfect Designer would make such good laws that no interferences would be necessary. Some even thought that the very existence of science depends upon denying the possibility that the laws of nature could be violated. For every event must have a cause; a cause is a preceding physical state plus a universal law; and if any exceptions are allowed, science and the rationality of the universe are undermined.

Christian theologians were especially influenced by the deistic world-view, and this sometimes led to a denial of the occurrence of miracles. Friedrich Schleiermacher, writing at the beginning of the nineteenth century and sometimes called the "father of liberal Protestantism," held that the miracles recorded in the Bible were literalizations of purely spiritual truths. The Resurrection of Jesus, for example, may have consisted in the remarkable spiritual experiences and visions of the apostles and in the new understanding of human existence these brought about. But Jesus' tomb was not miraculously empty, and his body did not literally rise from the dead. The twentieth-century theologian Rudolf Bultmann also regarded literal miracles as wholly legendary. Christianity, he thought, is about the possibility of a new understanding of human existence and about inner spiritual renewal. It was not about the occurrence of very odd facts very long ago.

It is certainly possible to have religion without miracles. A Muslim may say that the Qur'an is a unique literary and spiritual work without saying that it breaks any laws of nature. A Jew may regard the biblical record of the Exodus from Egypt as a highly exaggerated and largely symbolic account of what may originally have been a series of unusual natural disasters. A Christian may regard the New Testament miracles as exaggerated accounts of the inspirational effect of the presence of Jesus or as physical symbols of his spiritual status and authority. And a Hindu or Buddhist may similarly regard miracles as legends expressing in literal form the important spiritual teaching of the way to liberation from desire and despair.

It is probably true that all major religious teachers would regard the physical occurrence of miracles as much less important than the spiritual teaching of how to overcome what Buddhists call the three "fires" of greed, hatred, and ignorance and of how to achieve union with a Spiritual Reality of greater consciousness, wisdom, and bliss. Jesus, for example, apparently resisted all requests to provide a sign from heaven that would prove his authority (cf. Luke 11:29).

This suggests that miracles are not properly regarded as visible proofs of the existence of God. If they were, we might reasonably ask, as David

Hume does, for more evidence and for a host of personal miracles that might leave none of us in any doubt.

Nevertheless, if miracles, even when taken in a purely symbolic sense, testify to the superior reality of Spirit and to the possibility of spiritual liberation for beings embodied in a physical world, it might seem surprising if there were no physical symptoms of spiritual presence and liberation. There may be no demonstrative proofs of the existence of God, but surely one might expect some indications of divine presence, at least for those who wish to know more of God, who "have eyes to see."

For deists, the elegance and rationality of the laws of nature, the handiwork of the Great Mathematician, is such an indication. But it is quite hard to see that such a spiritual reality could have any active, personal relation to human beings or that humans could be transformed by relation to it if all the thoughts and acts of humans are caused solely by the laws of the natural world. Most religions are founded on claims that Spirit has acted in the world in some specific way—in freeing the Israelites, dictating the Qur'an, or becoming incarnate in Jesus. In nontheistic traditions, humans can be freed from the constraints of physical desire and suffering and become aware of a nonphysical dimension of reality. Awareness of a nonphysical reality must be partly caused by that reality (if knowledge is genuine, the object partly causes awareness of it). So, there must be some causal connection between spiritual reality and the physical world.

Even for a view like that of Schleiermacher, the apostles had visions of Jesus after his death. If those visions were genuine, this posits a causal interaction between the dead Jesus and the living apostles. This might not break a law of nature since perhaps all those who have died continue to exist in some other form after death and some of them even appear in visions to the living. But it would be a causal influence of the spiritual (after-death) world upon the physical world in which the apostles still lived.

If, in addition, the tomb of Jesus were, in fact, empty, this implies that the physical body of Jesus was transfigured into a spiritual form, and this would be a miracle in the sense of an extraordinary manifestation of spiritual power over the physical. Yet, for Christians, this is not just breaking a law (that dead bodies gradually decompose). All the dead, they think, are going to be transfigured at the general resurrection. Seen in that light, Jesus' Transfiguration—the resurrection of his physical body to a new form of life—is unusual in its timing but not in its occurrence.

In fact, a Christian might say, there is a spiritual law that all the dead will be transfigured and will rise again. Normally, bodies decompose. But, in special circumstances, perhaps if humans are wholly filled with the divine Spirit, that tendency to decompose is checked. In some cases, transfiguration ("assumption into heaven," in traditional terms) may follow immediately.

Of course, the objection may be raised that the invention of such spiritual laws is a totally fruitless fantasy. We can always invent invisible and untestable spiritual laws to justify ridiculous opinions. But they are totally useless to science as they lead to no new predictions, and the evidence for their existence is wholly speculative, not based on public and repeatable observations.

This objection is fair. These spiritual laws are not laws established by experiment, leading to fruitful predictions. What the believer is doing is accepting the testimony to a miracle and then thinking of some way of making its occurrence seem reasonable in the light of the alleged purposes of a God. Accordingly, much will depend upon whether it is reasonable to accept testimony to the occurrence of a miracle.

Miracles as Extraordinary Manifestations of Spiritual Power

To that question, I will return. But I will first complete the discussion of how miracles are to be defined. If and only if we could credit what has been said about resurrection, the most natural way to describe matters would be to say that the normal operations of nature (the decomposition of bodies) have been modified or transcended by extraordinary events that reveal the operations of a higher spiritual, but still entirely rational, law (the transfiguration of bodies into spiritual form).

What is at stake, therefore, is whether Spirit has a specific causal influence on the physical. Such influence may be relatively normal, as when someone feels a sense of the presence of God. It may be quite unusual, as when someone has visions of a dead person or when inspired words are placed in the mind of a prophet. Or it may be totally awe-inspiring and extraordinary, as when a physical body is transfigured into spiritual form.

Seen in this light, the definition of a miracle as the transgression of a law of nature seems inadequate. The physical world is causally affected by Spirit. Virtually all religious believers accept this, and their differences about whether miracles occur are differences about the extent, character, and unusualness of such spiritual causality.

The inadequate picture is to think of nature as a perfect, self-sustaining machine, a closed causal realm of universal and unbreakable laws. If nature is as a whole the manifestation of Spirit, then the laws of its operation will be manifestations of the nature of Spirit. To put this in theistic terms, the predictable regularities of nature will manifest the faithfulness and reliability of God, who wills that we should be able to understand and use those regularities. But if God is a supreme personal reality, it is to be expected that there will also be unique and more distinctly personal forms of manifestation, by which God is truly known in many forms of beauty, moral insight, and historical guidance. The universe will, in short, not be a machine. It will be more like (though not exactly like) a body, expressing both reliable regularities and specific personal actions.

We do not transgress the laws of nature when we use our bodies to express personal feelings and intentions. Such expressions are not wholly explained by the laws of biology (which does not deal with them), but they do not violate laws of biology either. So maybe God should not be thought of as "transgressing" the regularities of the cosmos, which we have learned to describe in mathematical terms, when God expresses intentions that cannot be wholly explained in terms of such regularities.

Science works on the assumption that every event has a cause. This is a postulate of the rationality of the universe. There is a reason for everything that happens. It is a dogma, in that it cannot be strictly proved, and it goes well beyond the available evidence. Religious believers most often accept that dogma, too. But they typically claim that not all causes are physical causes, and that accounts of the universe that only mention physical laws and causes are incomplete.

Purely physical laws have exceptions when they are modified by spiritual purposes. That follows from the fact that not all causes are physical causes. Where a nonphysical cause operates, it will supplement and modify the influence of purely physical causes. But why should we say that the physical law is "broken"? We do not say that the law of gravity is broken in a case where a change in the momentum of a system modifies the operation of the law. The introduction of an additional causal factor will obviously modify laws that would otherwise operate in a simpler manner. What we should say is that physical laws apply, unless other causal factors modify them. Then, they continue to operate but they are modified by another law. In the case of religion, such a law may concern the implementation of the ultimate purpose of the physical system as a whole.

I can see why miracles have been defined as transgressions of law. But it would be less misleading, from a religious point of view, to define a miracle as an extraordinary manifestation of spiritual power. There are no otherwise unbreakable laws that have to be arbitrarily broken by an external interference, and we do not have to think of some invisible person suddenly deciding on a whim to break a law. The key questions we need to ask are whether there is any spiritual causal power and whether it may sometimes manifest in extraordinary ways. When put like that, it is easy to see that God (if there is a God), the Creator of the universe, is a supreme, spiritual causal power—though it would demean God to think of the Deity as "an invisible person." And it is quite possible that God might manifest the Divine Presence in extraordinary ways. We would just have to look and see.

Hume's Argument That Miracles Are Absolutely Impossible

David Hume sets things up so that we would never find a miracle, however hard we look. Commenting on alleged miracles that occurred around the tomb of Abbe Paris, he concedes that many of them "were immediately proved upon the spot, before judges of unquestioned integrity, attested by witnesses of credit and distinction, in a learned age, and on the most eminent theater that is now in the world" (1955, 132). That sounds pretty impressive. But Hume's response is this: "What have we to oppose to such a cloud of witnesses but the absolute impossibility or miraculous nature of the events which they relate?" (1955, 133).

All reasonable people, he says, will take that assertion as a sufficient refutation. But how does he know that miracles (by his definition, transgressions of laws of nature) are "absolutely impossible"? The irony is that, according to Hume's own general philosophical principles, we cannot lay down in advance that anything is impossible. Experience is our only guide. Experience can only tell us what has happened so far, in our very limited life-span, in a small region of the earth. It cannot tell us what the future will be like or even whether the future will be like the past. It cannot tell us whether things are very different in different parts of the world or for people other than ourselves. It cannot tell us that there is any necessity in the laws of nature that renders them impervious to change or alteration.

One of the major conclusions of Hume's philosophy is that necessity cannot be shown to be an objective property of nature. We might think that the laws of nature are necessary, that there is some inner necessity that connects the same causes invariably with the same effects. But this is, he argues, an illusion. All we have is a "customary connection" made in human thought or imagination between two states, which have been observed always to have followed one another in the past (*Inquiry*, section 7, part 2).

Just because two states have been observed always to follow one another in the past, it by no means follows that they will always do so in the future. It does not even follow that they have always done so in the past, since we have only seen a tiny part of the past. So it seems that our belief that there are laws of nature that events necessarily obey is only a habit of thought, founded on very limited experience. It may very easily be wrong.

What on earth, according to Hume's own principles, could justify him in saying that an event that does not fall under a law of nature (such a law being no more than an invariable constant conjunction of two events) is "absolutely impossible"? Nothing more than habit or, we might as readily say, prejudice. It is not "all reasonable people" who will reject the possibility of miracles. It is incorrigibly prejudiced people who cannot rid themselves of ingrained habits of thought.

Hume actually concedes that events breaking laws of nature may occur, after all, but not, he says, where religion is concerned. "Should this miracle be ascribed to any new system of religion, men in all ages have been so much imposed on by ridiculous stories of that kind that this very circumstance would be a full proof of a cheat" and would justify all men of sense in rejecting it "without further examination" (1955, 138). A careful initial skepticism about reports of miracles has been replaced by a full proof of deceit, a proof so complete that it needs no examination. Prejudice has rarely been quite so clearly expressed in the history of philosophy.

Is There a Firm and Unalterable Experience That Establishes Absolute Laws of Nature?

Hume says that no proof is needed in particular cases because "a firm and unalterable experience has established" the laws of nature: "As a uniform experience amounts to a proof, there is here a direct and full proof . . . against the existence of any miracle" (1955, 123). But is it the case that a firm, unalterable, and uniform experience established the laws of nature? Whose experiences are we talking about here?

For thousands of years, nobody realized that there were any laws of nature. There were, of course, many observed regularities, but there were also many odd events that did not seem to fit into regular patterns at all. Common sense seems to show that things mostly happen regularly and predictably—the sun rises each morning and sets each evening. But common sense suggests that not everything in life is regular and predictable—what my children are going to do next or whether a volcano will erupt; in terms of common sense, these events are anomalous and unpredictable. I am not suggesting these are miracles. I am just saying that the common experience of most people throughout human history is that there are both regularities and anomalous and unpredictable events.

The very idea of a law of nature is, at best, a late-medieval idea that came to fruition in the sixteenth century. To frame the idea required genius, not common sense. It required a leap of faith that mathematics is the language of nature and a determination to probe beneath sensory appearances to reduce phenomena to the operation of unwritten, mathematically specifiable laws upon unseen particles of which visible objects were said to be composed. This is a huge leap of imagination. So, whose firm, unalterable, and uniform experience establishes a law of nature? Only people who can solve differential equations, who are capable of postulating unseen "atoms" underlying the objects we perceive with our senses, and who can devise precise laws stating ideal relations between those atomic particles. The experiences in question are not experiences of common sense. They are the experiences of intellectual giants.

Since Newton's day, the laws of nature have become exponentially more difficult, mathematically, to the extent that hardly one person in a million can even state the laws of quantum field theory, let alone understand them. The firm atomic particles that were supposed to be the foundation of matter have disintegrated into the "particle zoo" of neutrons, gravitons, positrons, quarks, and goodness-knows-how-many other flickering and transient entities. Only highly trained people with graduate degrees in physics who work with particle accelerators are in any position even to identify such particles. And the deterministic laws of Newtonian mechanics have been subsumed into stochastic laws of quantum and chaos theory and models of multidimensional space/time that seem to most of us indistinguishable from the visions of science fiction.

It is, nevertheless, true that many laws of physics can be said to be well established and that the formulation of such laws constitutes the triumph of modern scientific method. It is still all a very long way from common sense. It is an equally long way from Hume's own empirical philosophy, whereby you just construct human knowledge by inference from immediate sensory impressions.

Observation is important in modern science. But it is not a matter of attending very closely to the sensory impressions that occur in everyday experience. A physical scientist has to build an apparatus in which such things as temperature and pressure, radiation background and electromagnetic fields can be precisely controlled. Then, a theory has to be constructed in accordance with which certain future observations in this closely controlled environment can be predicted. An experiment has to be set up, and the results recorded by the use of sophisticated instruments whose readings need to be interpreted by a highly trained observer. Finally, wherever possible, the whole thing is repeated, varying the boundary conditions and usually modifying calculations to fit the observed results more closely.

Good scientific work in physics is not something that just anybody can do. It requires great mathematical skill, a fertile imagination, the ability to think up fruitful experimental situations, a sort of intuitive feel for an elegant theory, and the courage to challenge established thinking and try out apparently wild ideas. Any physicist who talks about a firm, unalterable, and uniform experience as the backing for the formulation of a law of nature will be rightly laughed out of the laboratory.

Quantum Theory and the Laws of Nature

Of course, theories and experimental results do get established, and a moderately competent scientist can trust and use them once they have been published by a thinker of genius and accepted by a reputable peer group. But those thinkers of genius will always be looking for what has been missed, for counterexamples that current theories cannot explain, and for anomalies and discrepancies that point to the need for new and possibly revolutionary forms of theoretical explanation.

None of that means that there are no laws of nature. But it does mean that we should not be too sure that we really know what they are or that we are on the verge of explaining absolutely everything by means of them or that we may not get a huge surprise at any time that may disprove all previous theories.

This happened to Newton's laws with the advent of quantum theory in the early twentieth century. The principles of Newtonian mechanics were not shown to be totally incorrect. They had worked well for over two hundred years and were a pretty reliable guide to how middle-sized objects, moving slowly relative to the speed of light, behave. But Einstein's theory of relativity subsumed those laws under a wider set of more fundamental laws and showed them to offer only a limited and incomplete explanation of gravitational attraction. They do not work for very small or very fast particles. And they omit all mention of the basic nuclear and electromagnetic forces that play a large part in determining the behavior of all fundamental particles.

In the light of discoveries in physics since 1905, when Einstein published his paper on the photoelectric effect, it has become accepted by all competent physicists that Newton's laws of motion and gravitation do not provide a complete, closed, and deterministic account of the physical universe. They are not complete because they fail to account for many physical phenomena. They do not form a closed system, for there are many factors they do not even mention—like dark energy, dark matter, quantum fields, and nonlocality—that modify the operation of Newton's laws in major ways. And they do not offer a deterministic account because we now know that it is impossible in principle to predict the future completely.

This is because Heisenberg's principle of indeterminacy means that we can never determine both the position and the momentum of a subatomic particle. So, we can never have precise knowledge of all the properties of an initial physical state. Not only that. On the "Copenhagen interpretation" of quantum events, there is nothing—certainly nothing knowable by us—that precisely determines a change in quantum state of a subatomic particle. Exactly the same physical state of an atom can have a number of alternative future states. That is, the same cause can have different effects, and we can assign no physical cause for which effect is actualized.

This finding undermines a highly cherished dogma of classical physicists, the dogma that every cause (every initial state) can have one and only one effect; that is, that causes sufficiently determine their effects. This is the dogma of physical determinism. Given an initial state and the laws of physics, all effects follow by necessity from their causes. No alternatives are permitted.

This dogma cannot be proved in any way. The most we could say, before the rise of quantum physics, was that, as far as we have been able to determine, the same initial states always give rise to the same effects—as Hume might say, unalterably and uniformly. Some philosophers (Immanuel Kant, for example) have thought that this principle of sufficient causality is entailed by the rationality of the universe and is a precondition of scientific research, for, if we introduced uncaused causes into the universe, we would have introduced a principle of nonrational anarchy.

Copenhagen indeterminacy undermines this argument. It introduces vast numbers of particular events that are not determined by any law that we know about. The reason this does not bring anarchy into the universe is that there are stochastic or probabilistic laws that govern the behavior of large assemblies of subatomic particles and that make the observable universe seem deterministic, insofar as all "random" quantum fluctuations usually cancel each other out when large numbers are involved.

However, they do not always cancel out. Chaos theory (which uses fully deterministic equations) shows that very small fluctuations in initial conditions can produce very large and unpredictable changes in macromolecular states. A common illustration is a metal ball poised precariously on top of a semicircular metal ring. The smallest force applied to the ball will tip it one way or the other, but it will fall either onto a switch that will ignite a nuclear bomb or onto another switch that will dispense a million dollars. This is an example of a tiny change that will produce hugely different effects. For quantum theory, there are millions of such tiny changes, and some of them will produce unpredictable effects on a large scale.

So, now we know that extraordinary and highly improbable events are possible without breaking any laws of physics. They will, in fact, happen but only rarely. To say that an event is highly improbable is not to say that it cannot happen. It is to say that it will happen but not very often. Most of the time the quantum indeterminacy of the universe will be invisible, and we will not observe the slight distortions of time and space that they, in fact, constantly involve. Stochastic laws are still laws of physics, but they allow extraordinary things to happen.

These would, of course, not be miracles if there were no God. But, if the prevailing interpretation of quantum theory is accepted, two dogmas of determinism have been comprehensively undermined—that every cause has one and only one possible effect and that all causes can be exhaustively specified and their effects, at least in principle, predicted.

There are laws, and, without them, there could be no science. But quantum theory has rendered obsolete a widely held eighteenth-century view that the universe is wholly determined by inflexible and universal laws that exclude any other causal influence and that completely explain everything that will ever happen.

John Polkinghorne speaks of "the patchwork character of scientific understanding" (2005, 11). Modern physics does not offer "a single causal web of known and determinating character." There is, Polkinghorne says, a major gap between the quantum realm and the realm of classical physics that has not yet been bridged by a fully integrated account. And quantum theory and general relativity have never been perfectly reconciled to one another. So, he concludes, "science has not demonstrated the causal closure of the natural world" (2005, 37). There may be an "intrinsic fuzziness" or "ontological openness" in nature that allows the operation of further, largely unknown, causal principles.

It looks as though modern physics is mainly concerned with establishing a set of precisely measurable regular relationships between artificially isolated phenomena under strictly controlled conditions. That such relationships exist and can be mathematically described is an amazing fact about our world, which did not have to be true. Einstein remarked that "the eternal mystery of the world is its comprehensibility" (1970, 61).

But the supposition that these relationships (these "laws") govern absolutely all phenomena without exception, that they are wholly unbreakable and unchangeable, and that there are no other causal factors to be taken into account in the real world is not supported by modern physics. As Polkinghorne says, "We therefore have no compelling grounds

for regarding current theories as being more than a form of approximation to actual physical reality as it is encountered in the limit of effective
isolatability" (2005, 34).

There is probably no statement about the fit between modern physics
and the objective world that is not contentious. But we can confidently
say that a closed and deterministic view of nature is neither a presuppo-
sition of nor a deduction from the practice and established findings of
modern physics. Universal physical determinism was suggested to many
by the work of Newton, though he did not subscribe to it himself. Contemporary views tend to be much more agnostic about the universal
applicability and all-encompassing range of physical laws. There is, after
all, no firm and unalterable experience that establishes the existence of
unbreakable and deterministic laws of nature.

As far as physics is concerned, there could be forms of spiritual causality in nature, though the methodology of physics would preclude a
study of them within physics proper. The strongest arguments against
miracles will not come from a belief that there are closed, absolute, and
inflexible laws of nature. They will come from the difficulty of establishing that any spiritual causes have ever been reliably observed. And that
is where David Hume concentrates his attack.

Can We Ever Trust Testimony
to the Occurrence of a Miracle?

Hume says, "No testimony is sufficient to establish a miracle unless the
testimony be of such a kind that its falsehood would be more miraculous
than the fact which it endeavors to establish" (1955, 123). But is this really
a reasonable requirement? Suppose an event occurs that violates a law of
physics. For Hume, that should only mean that a normally regular succession of events would, on some occasion, fail to obtain. Such a thing
may certainly be improbable, but it could happen. It is hard to quantify
the improbability with any certainty.

Hume, of course, in his chapter on "Miracles" in *An Inquiry Concerning Human Understanding*, holds that the probability of such an event
is zero, so we could never get a greater improbability. It would follow
that no testimony, however strong, could ever establish the occurrence
of a miracle. But his chapter on "Necessary Connection," in the same
book, establishes that, in fact, it is possible for an unprecedented event
to occur. Its improbability is a function of the number of times it has
been observed to happen. Thus, an unprecedented event is truly very
improbable with regard to normal human expectations, but it could
still happen.

Now suppose that someone, John, sees such a miracle and reports it to me. Could the falsehood of his report be miraculous? I suppose Hume means that its falsehood must be more improbable than the event he reports. If John is sane, sees the event in good light, has no reason to think he has been tricked, is honest, and reports it sincerely, it is very improbable that what he says is false. How improbable? Again, that is difficult to quantify exactly. But we could certainly say it is very improbable.

So, the reported event is very improbable, and the falsehood of John's report is very improbable. To put it another way, it is very likely that John is telling the truth, and what he reports is very unlikely indeed. Hume proposes that I should not believe John unless it is more improbable that what John says is false than that the reported event occurred. That seems a very strong requirement, but it is not as impossible as Hume suggests.

What we seem to have is a roughly equal balance of improbabilities. For Hume, they cancel each other out, leaving me in a state of total indecision. But I suggest that the balance can be tipped quite strongly on the basis of other factors not yet mentioned and not simply on the basis of a balancing of probabilities. It is, as Richard Swinburne points out (1970, chapter 6), because Hume fails to mention these other factors that his analysis may seem plausible. In the discussion in the next two sections, I shall gradually spell these factors out.

Why Improbable Events Probably Occur

The strange thing is that situations in which there is a low probability of a person's being mistaken yet reporting something highly unlikely occur not infrequently within science. Galileo's observation that there are spots on the sun was very unlikely, given the body of scientific opinion at that time. Should his testimony, then, have been ignored? In fact, it was, and the Inquisition was entirely reasonable, according to Hume's view, to disbelieve Galileo!

But Galileo was right, and it would not have been unreasonable to believe him, given his expertise and the weaknesses of the Aristotelian worldview, which could have been apparent to others if they had thought them through carefully enough. He could have been deceived, though he probably was not. What he observed was very improbable, given current scientific opinion, but that opinion was possibly (and turned out, in fact, to be) mistaken. Even in science, it is not unreasonable to bet one's career, and perhaps even one's whole life, on a theory regarded as highly improbable by one's peers.

Einstein did just that for the last twenty years of his life, refusing to accept quantum indeterminacy. He is still generally thought to have probably been wrong, but no one doubts that he was a great physicist, and all admire his tenacity. Nobody thinks he was actually irrational.

This is not, of course, just a matter of observing and reporting an improbable event. But it is a case where Einstein's authority (the rather high probability that he was right, given his past record) was balanced against the high improbability (given current opinion) of the totally deterministic view he was defending. This situation might indeed lead most of us to be agnostic, letting this battle of probabilities end in a draw. Yet some practicing physicists just have to commit themselves one way or another. They have to bet on Einstein's authority or on quantum indeterminacy. Their decision will help to determine the research programs they pursue and perhaps the whole course of their working lives. The point is that it is perfectly reasonable, and a positively good thing, that different scientists should bet different ways. It is a good thing that their theories go well beyond the evidence because this is a matter of great practical importance.

This precise issue is not yet resolved. There are quantum physicists like David Bohm who have propounded a consistently deterministic account of quantum phenomena, by introducing a "pilot wave" that would signal changes throughout the universe at superluminal speeds. But the consensus is still that many basic subatomic events are non-deterministic and that "hidden variables" like pilot waves are explicitly excluded by quantum theory. Perhaps the issue will be resolved one day. The hope of science is that there will be a testable resolution of such problems. But, at present, the situation is rather like that in religious matters, where there is either a God or there is not, miracles either occur or they do not, but there is no currently available way of deciding the issue definitively.

Expert observations of events that conflict with currently accepted scientific laws are the very stuff of scientific discovery and progress. The Bell theorem—that there are nonlocal connections between subatomic particles that have once interacted but have become widely separated—is widely accepted among physicists, even though it requires either affirming faster-than-light connections or treating separated two-particle systems as one very strange single object and even though it is extremely difficult to replicate experimental proofs of the theorem. In this case, the expertise of the physicists in question, and the mathematical elegance of the theorem, outweigh the inconvenience that there is no completely convincing way of reconciling it with the theory of relativity.

The moral of these stories is that what we might call "the probability of an event" is not an absolute and unchanging quantity. It depends upon a whole background context against which events are taken to be more-or-less probable. If there is no God, an event breaking a law of nature would seem to be quite improbable to us, though possible. But it would have no point and so would be relatively unintelligible. It would just be an odd occurrence, and we might be well advised, as scientists, to ignore it. Nevertheless, there might, in fact, be huge numbers of such events, unknown to and unobserved by us, so it might not be very improbable at all. It is only improbable relative to our experience, which we admit to be extremely limited.

If there is a God, however, what we will consider to be probable changes considerably. We might not want to go as far as Newton did and say that God could do anything God wants and leave the realm of physical law intact. Then, we would have a severe problem (not a scientific one) about why God does not just improve the universe and eliminate all natural disasters. We might want to postulate a universe that runs according to general and, on the whole, predictable laws. But we might also want to deny that such laws account for everything that happens or that everything can be completely predicted or that there can be no nonphysical causal influences. Modern physics provides some justification for taking such a stance. So, if we believe there is a God, the probability that there are spiritual causes at work in the universe is considerably raised. And so is the probability that some of those causes may be extraordinary.

The Resurrection of Jesus as a Paradigmatic Miracle

If there were a God, there would be at least one case of nonphysical causality, for God creates the universe. There is no general law that, whenever there is a God, there follows a universe like this. Any explanation of God's action would have to be what Richard Swinburne has called a personal explanation (2004, 35–51), in terms of a unique, unrepeatable purpose. So, God could make things happen in ways that could not be brought under any general law of nature.

If God creates the universe for a purpose, it is rather likely that there will be causal influences of God's purpose upon parts of the creation. It is likely, therefore, that there will be states of affairs, or perhaps aspects of states of affairs, that could not be brought under purely physical and nonpurposeful laws of nature. They would not be miracles, unless they were extraordinary, awe-inspiring, and specifically revelatory of God's presence or power. They might occur unobserved and undetected. But they would be there.

In this case, the occurrence of a miracle would still be highly improbable, relative to the normal way in which things proceed. But it might be quite probable that a miracle should occur if there were good reason for God to cause an awe-inspiring event that reveals something of spiritual importance. The context makes all the difference. To put it briefly, we would reasonably be much more inclined to believe someone's testimony to a miracle (a very improbable event) if that miracle fitted into, while perhaps also expanding considerably, a more general understanding of God's purpose for the universe.

Take the case of the Resurrection of Jesus, which Hume really had in mind in his discussion. Here is a claim by a group of people to have seen Jesus after his death. It is unlikely they were lying since most of them were martyred for their belief. It is unlikely they were deceived, for the appearances of Jesus were spread out over a length of time in various locations and corroborated by many observers. Yet it remains possible they were deceived or that original reports of their visionary experiences later got exaggerated.

The Resurrection itself is highly unlikely since people have not otherwise been seen to rise from the dead. Yet this judgment may change if there is a God, if God revealed to the prophets of Israel that there would be a Messiah, if Jesus were a great spiritual teacher, and if the Resurrection could be plausibly seen as a confirmation of the true Messiahship of Jesus. Then, the Resurrection would become intelligible as a disclosure by the Creator in and through the person of Jesus, that the ultimate destiny of humanity is to be raised from death to eternal life. All these things, it need hardly be said, are disputable. But they are an important part of the context of Christian claims that a miracle occurred.

In addition, Christian teaching is that humans are trapped in self-centered arrogance and can be liberated by the inner presence of the risen Christ. The message that Jesus died and rose again to forgive sin and to bring eternal life with God is both a challenge to reassess our lives and commit ourselves to worship the God revealed in Christ and the offer of a dynamic power to help us to do so. It provides a vision of human life as oriented toward supreme value and promises to transform human life with a new vitality.

This may sound a bit like a sermon. I do not mean it to be that, but it is only fair to stress that miracles are events of religious significance. They are meant to disclose the reality of God and to transform the lives of those who are open to that disclosure. Hume fails to mention any of this—not surprisingly, since he does not think there is any religious significance or any God. But it is inaccurate to represent a miracle as though it were just a very odd event that we simply have to consider dispassionately and without any personal involvement.

So, Hume says that he would not believe any testimony that Queen Elizabeth I rose from the dead and governed England for three months. The fact is that, however astonishing such an event would be, it would have no religious significance. It would not confirm in her courtiers their belief that she was a messenger of God or their ultimate hope of eternal life with God, and it would not, I presume, transfigure their lives by a sudden inrush of the Holy Spirit.

There are two main factors lacking in the imagined resurrection of Queen Elizabeth that were present in the alleged Resurrection of Jesus. One is a historical context—a long tradition of prayer and spiritual experience in Israel, which included the hope of a Messiah or spiritual liberator, together with a historical estimate of the spiritual insight and authority of Jesus. The other is the existential factor of disclosure, challenge, and personal transformation, by which some people, but not all, feel encountered by a reality of supreme value, disclosed in the risen Jesus, that can transform their lives.

Since miracles occur in a religious tradition, are connected with the lives of those who claim spiritual authority, and are claimed to mediate the presence and power of a Supreme Spiritual Reality, any estimate of the probability of their occurrence will depend upon your attitude to that tradition, that alleged authority, and that alleged spiritual reality. For Christianity, the crucial question will be not, "Can a dispassionate survey of the evidence give proof beyond any reasonable doubt that Jesus rose from the dead?," but "Is the reality of God mediated in a liberating way through Jesus, whose life is recorded in the Gospels and whose presence is known in the church?"

At this point atheists have to answer "no." But it is not irrational to answer "yes." For those who choose the latter answer, the probability of the disciples' testimony that Jesus rose from death must rise considerably. It will still not become a theoretical certainty. "Faith" enters in, not as belief wholly without evidence but as commitment to a loyalty and discipleship that evaluates the evidence for the existence of God in the facts of nature, the historical evidence of Jesus' life and teaching, and the personal experience of millions of believers, including that of the evaluator, in a positive way.

Miracles in Different Religious Contexts

I have dealt with the miracle of the Resurrection because that is what really concerned Hume, even though he misrepresented the belief abysmally. Other religions have their own miracles, their own disclosures of spiritual reality and transformation. This, of course, is used by Hume to show that the evidence for miracles is weakened even further by the fact that the miracles of different religions contradict one another.

Jews and Muslims do not accept the miracle of the Resurrection of Jesus. That is not, I think, because of a difference in weighing its probability in the abstract. Jews do not think Jesus was the Messiah because he did not bring in an age of peace and justice. Since he was not the anointed messenger of God, it would not be appropriate for God to raise him from the dead. In addition, disclosures of God come to Jews not through Jesus, but through the Law and the prophets. So they dislike the Christian rejection of the Law and the Christian insistence on the necessity of redemption by a human person, instead of by obedience to the Torah. For these reasons, the miracle of the Resurrection seems spiritually (not physically) implausible. It does not fit with Jewish views of God, God's method of self-revelation, and their own spiritual experience.

Muslims, in a rather different way, accept Jesus as a messenger of God but are hostile to regarding any human, including Jesus, as divine and to the Christian doctrine of the Trinity. So, they do not accept that Jesus, a true prophet, was crucified as a criminal. He did not rise from death, they think. Nor did he die. He ascended directly to the presence of God, from whence he will return on Judgment Day. And because they believe Christians are in general deceived about the divinity of Jesus, Muslims have some reason to distrust the testimony of the apostles to the Resurrection.

Thus, it is background beliefs about the nature of God, the nature of divine revelation, and the most adequate forms of personal spiritual experience that account for Jewish and Muslim skepticism about the Resurrection. Jews and Muslims have their own normative miracles—the Exodus and the Qur'an, respectively. It is these events that, for them, disclose the nature of God and challenge them to commit their lives to the quest for the Good.

The upshot is that miracles are only spiritually plausible and, therefore, only accounted worthy of belief if they fit into a background of beliefs about spiritual reality and how it is authentically known in historical and personal experience. Miracles are not indubitable events that will convince unbelievers—though that is the sort of thing unbelievers often seem to think that they should be.

This shows something important about religious belief. Religious belief does not depend upon a dispassionate analysis of evidence that leads to conviction beyond a reasonable doubt. It is always a commitment made in response to an insight that is individual and unique. Your miracles do not contradict mine. What you accept as a miracle depends upon what you think the Supreme Spiritual Power is and upon why you think it should ever act in extraordinary ways.

So, a Christian can say, "The Resurrection of Jesus is an event that discloses the purpose of a suffering and life-giving God and founds a new community for implementing that purpose." A Buddhist can say, "I see no such God and no such purpose. So, this alleged event seems not only unlikely but spiritually misleading. Therefore, I do not accept that it happened. But I would expect an enlightened being to be omniscient in all matters relating to liberation, so, to me, stories of the Buddha's superhuman knowledge disclose the nature of enlightenment and the spiritual goal of human life." In reply, a Christian is almost bound to say, "I am much more skeptical about such stories because I do not accept that the Buddha was really omniscient—he did not, for instance, know about God."

Thus, it is reasonable to accept the occurrence of miracles but only if they fit into a pattern of beliefs about the nature of a Spiritual Reality (whether God or the spiritual capacities of liberated souls) that is likely to act occasionally in extraordinary ways or that is likely to give rise to extraordinary human powers. Hume is correct in thinking that miracles cannot be presented as "proofs" of God, since it is only reasonable to accept them if you already believe in God or in spiritual reality.

Nevertheless, if you think there is a God who has a purpose for the world and you think the purpose has become obscured because of human self-will, then you may be surprised if there are no extraordinary manifestations of the Divine Presence and purpose. In that case, the occurrence of some miracles will confirm your preexisting belief. And miracles may not only confirm but also modify that prior belief in important ways—just as the Resurrection of Jesus modified the disciples' expectations about what the Messiah would be and do. In that way, the occurrence of miracles may be important to religious belief, though miracles will never function as independent proofs of the truth of a religious view.

Conclusion: Miracles and Scientific Law

Miracles have been prevalent in the traditional form of most religions. They are extraordinary events that show spiritual power, that of either God or a spiritually liberated soul. Their primary importance is religious, showing something about the presence and nature of spiritual reality and communicating a transforming encounter with such a reality. Since religions are mostly founded on the axiom that Spirit exists and has causal power, it would not be surprising to find some extraordinary physical manifestations of such power, probably focused upon some person who is believed to have an especially intense and authentic experience of Spirit.

Legends readily multiply, and human imagination is strong. It is, therefore, reasonable to be very cautious in affirming that a miracle has occurred. On the other hand, miracles seem to be possible even in the law-governed universe of modern science. For science does not show the universe to be a closed and complete causal web. For all science knows, there may be real spiritual causes, though science excludes them from experimental consideration since they are unlikely to be law-like and predictable in their operation. Such causes would modify (rather than "break") purely physical laws, and there is nothing in science that would make this impossible.

Miracles, however, are not "proofs" of God. An assessment of whether miracles occur will depend upon your background beliefs and upon whether you think transforming encounters with a Spiritual Reality are possible. It will depend upon whether you think the testimony to a miracle is reliable, upon whether you think the event falls within a wider intelligible pattern of spiritual purpose, and upon whether you think that what the miracle discloses is spiritually profound and important enough to warrant the occurrence of such an extraordinary event.

Questions can be raised at every stage of this discussion. The whole idea of Spirit, as a nonmaterial causal power, may be rejected. The admitted amount of legend, delusion, and fraud in religion may be considered to outweigh any alleged evidence in favor of a miracle. Even though Hume's specific arguments are quite weak, the evidence for miracles is often from a long time ago, reported by only a few witnesses who have a strong interest in the occurrence of miracles, and relating to events very unlike anything seen in contemporary closely observed experience. It may be thought that the success of the scientific method strongly suggests that all real explanations must come in the form of experimentally established and predictable assertions and that all real knowledge must be based on public and tested observations. Alleged miracles may then be seen as throwbacks to a fairy-tale, prescientific view of the universe that has not yet recognized that events happen in accordance with law and not by the will of invisible entities.

Nevertheless, I think any dispassionate thinker would have to concede that David Hume's arguments against miracles are not at all convincing and that the theory that the universe is a closed and complete causal web is no better proved by science than is the theory that the universe is created by God. Both theories go well beyond the strictly scientific evidence. There is something to be said for both. But as far as the question of this chapter is concerned, I think it has to be said that the laws of nature, as modern science understands them, do not exclude the occurrence of miracles. That, of course, does not settle the question of whether miracles occur, a question that must be settled on other grounds.

5. What Is the Nature of Space and Time?

(IN WHAT SENSE CAN TEMPORAL ACTIONS BE FREE?)

Space and Time in Traditional Religious Thought

BETWEEN THE SIXTH and the twelfth centuries in Christian Europe, Jerusalem was taken to be the center of the world, indeed of the universe. Paradise was in the East across the sea, with four rivers flowing from it, including the Tigris and the Euphrates. Dante, however, in 1319, located purgatory as a mountain in the southern hemisphere, with hell under the ground below it, and the earthly paradise at its summit. The heavens formed a perfect sphere about the earth and were made of quintessence, a changeless and incorruptible "fifth element." Time was often divided into three more-or-less equal parts—the first from the Creation to the giving of the Ten Commandments, the second to the Incarnation, and the third to Judgment Day. There was no thought of progress or change. Time began not too long ago, and time would cease not too far in the future, to be followed by an "eternity" of heaven or hell (with the slight complication of some waiting time to be spent in purgatory for redeemed but not wholly sanctified souls).

These views were due to a literal reading of various passages in the Bible, but they illustrate how different medieval Christian views of space and time were from any informed modern view. Heaven, hell, and earth were geographically connected in a more-or-less common space, and time was a short and unrepeatable prelude to eternity. So, Jesus "descends" into hell (or *Sheol*, the place of the dead), and he "ascends" into heaven. We now know that, if he began ascending two thousand years ago, he would not yet have left the Milky Way (unless he attained warp speed).

Indian religious cosmology is equally distant from modern scientific views. The god Vishnu, for instance, was incarnated in the world as a fish; a tortoise, supporting a mountain on his back while the elixir of immortality was churned from an ocean of milk by the gods; a boar who rescued earth from the cosmic sea; a man-lion; a dwarf; a warrior; Rama, who ruled his kingdom for a thousand years; Krishna, who defeated many demons; and Gautama Buddha, who oddly enough spread false teachings to delude the unwise. Thus, the earth has existed in many forms over a period of more than four million years (a *mahayuga*), and the gods often take form within it and exhibit miraculous powers. There are many different realms of being, and time is without beginning or end, each *mahayuga* being preceded and succeeded, after an interval of "cosmic sleep," by an infinite number of others. Within this vast cycle of endless repetitions, human souls are reborn, according to Sankara, after ascending to the moon, descending in rain, attaching themselves to plants, and being ingested by animals or humans.

Indian cosmology is very different from and much more expansive than the Christian and Semitic cosmology. But both cosmologies mix the space of this earth with the "spiritual space" of the gods, so that it is relatively easy to move from one to the other, and the gods and demons live in remote parts of space, visiting us at intervals. Both see time as something ultimately to be liberated from (by ascending to heaven or by attaining release from rebirth).

There are, of course, many ancient religions that do not have such a negative view of time. They are simply concerned with relationship with spirits, good and bad, who can alleviate the worst dangers of human life and bring fertility or prosperity. They often have a rather gloomy view of the afterlife, with nothing much to look forward to. But, as the great Semitic and Indian traditions developed, they stressed much more positive views of what may lie beyond the imperfections of time and, correspondingly, became more aware of the limitations of temporal existence. This is partly because they developed a greater sense of how the conditions of earthly life make it difficult or impossible to have truly intense and fulfilling knowledge of God or of the Ultimate Reality.

The idea that our temporal existence is somehow alienated from the Divine is often expressed in stories of a golden age when the gods walked the earth. Sometimes they still live on earth, on mountains, or in inaccessible lands far away. But often the "rainbow bridge" between gods and humans was broken, and now the underworld realms of the departed and the heavenly worlds of bliss, like the Tushita heaven of Buddhism, can be visited only in spirit, not in body. Traces of these views can be found in the Bible, where humans tried to build a tower between earth and heaven (Gen. 11:1–9). In the New Testament, Paul writes of a man who ascended to the third heaven or paradise—whether in the body or not, he did not know (2 Cor. 12:2). And, in Islam, the feast of the Mi'raj is celebrated on the twenty-seventh day of the month Rajab each year. The Mi'raj is a tradition (based loosely on the first verse of chapter 17 of the Qur'an) that the Prophet was taken by a winged beast from Mecca to Jerusalem and thence ascended by a ladder to the seventh heaven.

Some commentators have supposed that such tales show that early religion was both literalist, locating heavens and hells within or above the earth, and mistaken about the facts of geography. But studies of how legends grow more definite and specific over time suggest that literalism may be a later development of what were originally visionary experiences. Stories of sacred mountains inhabited by the gods, of towers reaching to heaven, and of stairways to the underworld seem to be based on a natural symbolism, whereby an ascent to life and goodness is symbolized as a physical ascent, and a lowering of vitality is symbolized as physical descent. Sacred space is primarily a symbolic space, and it is possible that the literalization of such symbols already presages a loss of archaic religious sensibility. Ancient religious views may have been primarily symbolic, but the rise of interest in the natural world, which presaged modern science, sometimes led to a literalization of those symbols and a blurring of the distinction between symbolic and real space and time. Yet it also led to a more accurate account of the physical space/time in which humans live.

The Development of Philosophical Views of Space and Time

Despite the literalizing interpretations of ancient texts, there grew up at the same time a very different tradition of interpretation, originating in the writings of philosophers. Probably occurring some time before the invention of writing (three or four thousand years before the common era), a line came to be drawn between the rational investigation of nature, prompted by sensory observation, and the symbolic images and narratives by which visions and spiritual encounters were expressed. In the sixth century BCE, in Ionia, on the west coast of modern Turkey, Thales had the distinction of being the first scientist in history. He asked what the world was made of and decided, perhaps because there was quite a lot of it about or more likely because he knew the myth of the origin of all things in a cosmic sea, that it was water. The important point was, however, that he began looking for unity and simplicity of explanation without reference to supernatural agency.

After Thales, the Greeks virtually invented philosophy, the study of the natures of things and of the ideas by which we understand them. Alfred North Whitehead has said that the whole history of philosophy is a series of footnotes to Plato, and it is true that Plato (429–347 BCE) and Aristotle (384–322 BCE), founders of the Academy and the Lyceum, respectively, in Athens, have exercised a dominant influence over philosophical thought ever since.

It is noteworthy that neither Plato nor Aristotle cared to relate their philosophies closely to Athenian religion. Socrates, in whose name Plato's *Dialogues* were written, was condemned to death for corrupting the Athenian youth, especially in matters of morality and religion. Plato participated in some religious rituals but was not able to make any coherent sense of the often riotous behavior of the Olympian gods.

Yet Plato's philosophy is the foundation of much subsequent religious thought and was enormously influential, particularly on the theology of the Eastern Orthodox churches, on Sufism, and on strands of mystical Judaism. Plato's most basic distinction is between appearance and reality. In the systematic development of Platonism, space and time and all observed objects in them belong to the realm of appearance, of what appears to human beings in conditions of ignorance. Reality is a purely conceptual world (the world of "Forms," essences, or Ideas), which is timeless and changeless. Presided over by the Form of the Good, which is beyond being and yet is the ultimately real, the world of Forms is a logically elegant, systematic, and exhaustive array of all possible states. In it are the archetypes of all possible worlds, and finite things are imperfect participations in or images of that real world. Thus, time is, as the *Timaeus* (the only work of Plato known in Europe in early medieval times) puts it, "a moving image of eternity."

Human souls have fallen from the quintessential realm of the stars into the world of appearance. By meditation and argumentation, by cultivating the love of the Good and Beautiful, they are to seek release from this world and return to the stars, their proper sphere, freed from the limitations of physical space, living in the changeless light of the eternal sun.

This is a heady mixture of philosophical/scientific speculation about the ultimate nature of reality and a spiritual vision of the soul as a spark of eternity trapped in the illusions of time. It never connected coherently with Athenian religious myths, and its connection with the literalization of texts about heaven, hell, and the end of the world was always ambiguous. But for centuries it has inspired the religious opinions of what became neo-Platonism, a mystical philosophy concerned with the ascent of the soul from involvement in the material world to union with the Good or the One.

When suitably amended to avoid talk of reincarnation, the evil nature of matter, and the essential immateriality of the soul, Platonism has become the intellectual foundation of much orthodox Christianity.

Christ, the *Logos*, is the eternal archetype of all things, and the human Jesus is "the image of the invisible God." God is the perfect, changeless, timeless, "One beyond being," who is the pure Form of Goodness itself. And the ultimate aim of the Christian life is conscious participation in the divine nature, *theosis*, or the return of the soul to its divine Source.

Aristotle was more the practical observer than the abstract mathematical dreamer. He probably did not have a very strong interest in religion, though he does speak of God as the highest and most perfect of beings and a worthy object of contemplation. But the medieval Muslim philosophers Ibn Sind and Ibn Rushd (Avicenna and Averroes, in Latin) used his known works to construct accounts of the nature of an intelligible cosmos created by a rational God. And, in the thirteenth century, Thomas Aquinas asserted what became for centuries the standard Catholic philosophy, for which the universe is a rational and comprehensible unity, the handiwork of a rational God.

Thus, the Greek philosophers transformed religions of symbol, myth, and imagination into intellectual structures of rational principle and conceptual rigor. What we see today in the classical systems of Judaism, Christianity, and Islam are traditions of ancient mythical thought, transformed by the charismatic influence of outstanding religious teachers and then interpreted by some of the key concepts of Greek philosophy. Early science, at that stage not distinguished from philosophy, did not oppose religion but transformed it from traditions of visionary experience and imaginative myth to the presentation of an intelligible worldview unified under the concept of one supremely good and intelligent Creator.

Both elements remained in play. But under the influence of Greek thought (and a similar process took place in India with the philosophers Sankara and Ramanuja, and in Buddhism with Buddhaghosa) a more-or-less coherent worldview was put in place. At its apex was one Supreme Reality, changeless, perfect, and nonmaterial. Space was, generally speaking, a half-real realm of appearance, in which individuals could exist alongside one another. There were other "spaces," like paradise, purgatory, and hell, but they were not accessible from or parts of this physical space. Time was an imperfect image of changeless perfection, and, in a truly liberated existence, it would come to an end.

So, the way was prepared for the separation of physical space and time from the symbolic space of spiritual existence and for the autonomy of natural science. But the whole physical world is still thought to have less reality than the being of God. The timeless is superior to the temporal, and the spiritual is superior to the spatial. In the end, this life is a preparation for a greater eternal life, and this space is unable by its nature to contain a direct and full manifestation of the Divine Presence, which is now clearly seen to be beyond physical representation and beyond the fragmentation and diversity of all physical things.

The Classical View of God as Spaceless and Timeless

In accordance with these views, and in a paradigmatic statement of the classical tradition, Thomas Aquinas' view of God, outlined in *Summa Theologiae,* 1a, questions 2–11, is that God is wholly simple, perfect, good, limitless, omnipresent, changeless, and timeless. The crucial concept is that of divine simplicity. God is not composed of parts in any way. So, God's goodness is identical with God's power and identical with God's existence and identical "with whatever else is similarly said of him" (question 3, article 3). Properties that seem to us to be diverse are, in God, united in an indivisible way. God cannot even logically be broken into parts. So, God must be timeless since time has parts (before and after). God is, therefore, changeless since there can be no change without time.

There are great conceptual difficulties with this description of God. It has been argued that the idea of a being, all of whose properties are identical with each other, does not make sense. But philosophers like Aquinas are arguing that God is not a substance with many properties anyway. God is beyond all the categories of thought we have and so should not be thought of as a "thing" that may or may not have various attributes. God is, as Aquinas puts it, "*esse suum subsistens,*" the pure actuality of being, existent by its own power.

This makes God strictly incomprehensible, in that we cannot imagine what such a being is like. Yet we can form a vague idea of a being that is the source of all finite and separable beings, though in itself it is unitary and purely actual, without any division or potentiality, an "unlimited ocean of being."

We could only speak of such a God in remote analogies and symbols, and we must always confess that, as Aquinas says, "we cannot know what God is, but only what he is not" (1a, question 3, introduction).

It may seem that such a God is indistinguishable from nothing, and it is indeed important to recognize that the God of classical religion is not a thing or finite in any way. The Divine, in this worldview, is as far from being a "person without a body" as one could imagine. Eastern Orthodox theologians tend to distinguish the divine *ousia*, the essential nature of God as it is in itself, from the divine *energeia*, the ways in which God manifests the Divine in the finite world. Then we could say that God is an ineffable plenitude and perfection of being that can make itself known to finite persons, perhaps in many finite names and forms.

The manifestations or disclosures of the Divine would then point toward, though would never fully encapsulate, their underlying source. Such a God would blind our intellect by excess of light rather than dissipate into empty nothingness. As Dionysius put it, God negates anything we can think but in the direction of greater perfection, not of mere denial. God is good but greater than anything we can think of as good. God is wise but not in any sense we can conceive. It would be misleading just to say that God is not good or wise. Rather, God is not less than good (perfect) but is so much more that we cannot imagine what such goodness is like.

Whether or not this is all thought to make sense, the doctrine of divine ineffability is central to the great classical traditions. Without paying attention to it, classical religion cannot be understood. One reason for the anthropomorphism that is so pronounced a feature of some contemporary religion is that the classical tradition has been forgotten or rejected, so that people cannot see that the concepts and images of faith are symbols of the Divine, and not pictures of it, whether visual or verbal.

However, sometimes the classical tradition has been viewed, even by its knowledgable adherents, in what may be thought to be an unduly restrictive way. Because God is not changing or temporal in the way that we conceive such things, it has sometimes been concluded that God is not changing or temporal at all—even though we might have thought that God would be changing and temporal in a higher manner. I will return to the question of what this might mean. But, historically, it is the case that change and time have often been excluded altogether from the Divine Being.

One reason for this is the argument, from the ancient Greek philosophers, that, if anything changes, it must get either better or worse. But if God is perfect, God cannot get any better, and it is unthinkable that God could get any worse. Therefore, any perfect being must be completely changeless. And if there is no change, there is no point in having any time either.

In addition, time was thought to be of negative value, something it would be better to be without. In the first place, the past no longer exists. It has passed away and may well be forgotten. Indeed, if an infinite time has elapsed, there would be an infinite amount of information to remember, and maybe even a Divine Mind could not contain a literally infinite number of bits of information. In the second place, the future does not yet exist. So, anything might happen, and there may be some nasty surprises lying ahead. At any rate, there would seem to be a huge number of future events that could not be known even by an omniscient being since they do not exist. And that seems very unsatisfactory. In the third place, the present only exists for a fleeting moment, and then it is gone. That also seems very unsatisfactory since, if you are just beginning to enjoy the present moment, it disappears as soon as you try to concentrate on it.

All in all, the nonexistence of the past and the future and the transience of the present render time a most unsatisfactory form of conscious experience. How much more perfect it would be if the entirety of time—past, present and future—could be contemplated as a whole. It would all exist, as Boethius put it, in one "unending life existing as a complete whole all at once" (1969, 5, 6). And that is just how the classical view of God envisions the Divine.

Negative and Positive Views of Time

Surprisingly, perhaps, some Christian thought takes the supremacy of timelessness over temporality so far that even life after death is conceived as a sharing in timelessness. The thought of an experience somehow including the whole of time all at once recurs in more recent thought. Jurgen Moltmann has written that "in the eschatalogical moment all times will be simultaneous" (2002, 261). That is, at the end of linear time, the whole life of the universe will be wholly present, and so there will be "a future for what is past." The past will not be lost but will exist in the eternal life of God, in which there is no longer past or future but only one equal coexistence of all things.

The Dominican Simon Tugwell similarly thinks of eternal life as "the taking possession, all at once, of a whole lifetime, including all its details, in a final perfection which makes such a lifetime precisely a whole" (1990, 158). He goes even further and asserts that a continuation of linear time after death would be unbearable: "Where heaven, then, draws all time together into a wholeness in which even failures and disappointments become glorious, hell is the apotheosis of frustration, going on and on and on, without ever reaching any sort of consummation" (170). "The final fulfillment of man consists in perfect stillness or immobility" (149).

The philosopher Bernard Williams has written of the boredom of a life continuing without end forever. Perhaps for the first few billion years, there would still be new experiences to relish. But, in the end, would we not plead for the whole process simply to stop? As a friend on vacation with me in New Zealand said, as we passed a sign to a magnificent waterfall, "Oh, no, not another magnificent waterfall! Let's just go back to the hotel."

So, eternal life can be conceived of as a transcendence of time and a sharing in timeless eternity. I have to confess that I find such views incoherent, inasmuch as they imagine a "timeless life after death" as somehow a *result of* historical existence. Since it must, therefore, come *after* earthly time, it logically must be temporal after all, even if it does not consist of measurable durations.

In any case, it is not obvious that temporality is bound to be an imperfection. Two main questions arise here—does change imply imperfection, and is time inherently unsatisfactory, as it is experienced by us? Clearly, many people have thought so, but this may not seem obvious. Time is a condition of change. It allows things to change their state. Sometimes such changes are for the worse. As the hymn says, "Change and decay in all around I see." But sometimes changes are for the better—as organisms grow and develop, they can realize more of their potentialities. But does all change necessarily make things better or worse?

Suppose I change from being a football player to being a baseball player. That would be a major change, but would it make me better or worse? If I were about equally good at both, we would surely say that I had just decided to do something different, but I had not got either better or worse, as such. So, a God could do an infinite number of different things. All of them would be excellently done. But, in the process, God would not have become more or less perfect.

For some medieval philosophers, a potential thing is less perfect than an actual thing. Thus, if God changed, God would move in some respect from potentiality to actuality. In that sense, God would improve. Aquinas holds that there can be no potentiality in God because God has to be fully actualized. God has to be doing everything that God ever could be doing. God never leaves anything undone.

However, this leads to some odd consequences. If God is always doing everything that God could possibly do, then there is never anything God could do that God is not already doing. If asked, God would have to say, "I am already doing all I can. I cannot do any more." And that begins to sound like a limitation on omnipotence.

As I confessed in chapter one, I am not opposed to putting logical limitations on divine omnipotence, so I can hardly complain about this problem. But we might wonder whether it is really a perfection to be unable to do anything new. Might it not be better to be able to do an infinite number of new things? Perhaps not, if this were a matter of going on and on and on, without ever getting anywhere. But perhaps every moment is its own goal or an intrinsic part of the goal. It is not that we are always trying to get somewhere else and never arriving. Rather, each creative moment is eminently satisfying on its own, and the thought that there is an endless series of such moments increases that satisfaction infinitely. The activity of creating new things may be in itself a great positive value.

The idea that creating new artistic works is good is perhaps an idea that flowered in European Romanticism in the nineteenth century. Even the Renaissance had seen art as a re-creation of what existed in the previous golden age of classical Greece and Rome. Medieval thinkers, influenced by neo-Platonic thought, had often seen art as an imperfect tracing of Forms that exist eternally.

Augustine, one of the first great Christian Platonists, wrote, "When you hear of a good this and a good that . . . if then you can put them aside and perceive good itself, you will perceive God" (1991, 244).

According to this strain of Platonism, you should actually turn aside from all particular beautiful things in order to attend to unchangeable and eternal Beauty itself. The universal is more real than the particular. As Anselm put it, the ideas of things as conceived in the mind of God have greater reality than particular things that exist in space and time and are poised precariously between being and nothingness.

It was probably the advent of natural science that helped to reverse this judgment and hold—what most people ordinarily now think—that particular material things are more real than universal ideas and that, if things do not exist in space and time, then they probably do not exist at all.

This is a more Aristotelian thought: if ideas really exist, they do not exist in a world of their own, but only as embodied in particular things. So, careful attention to the particular is not to be set aside. It is the proper path by which to discern the universal in its many images.

With this reversal of judgment, time itself took on a new importance. Whereas it had been seen as a fragmented image of eternity, carrying decay and loss in its very nature, now it came to be seen as the arena in which new particular beauties, greater complexities, and richer possibilities could be creatively realized. Time is not only the realm of perpetual loss. It is more positively viewed as the realm of perpetual possibility. New and better things are possible. Only because there is time can there be change. And only because there is change can there be originality and genuine creativity.

This perspective took centuries to gestate, for the Aristotelian view, new to Christian Europe in the thirteenth century, had first to be shorn of the assumption that there was a fixed norm of essential natures that all material things strove to actualize. Then, the growth of evolutionary thought had to generate the idea that the new might be better, more complex, and more valuable than the old. Only then was the time ripe for a perspective for which the creative process itself was to be greatly valued, precisely because it generated the new and unique. There was a goal of things in time, but it was not eternally specified in advance, as it were. It was constructed in the process of creativity; thus, the goal could not even be said to exist without the temporal process. The goal did not have to be a static point of stillness and immobility, as Simon Tugwell put it, somehow existing at the end of the process and summing it all up. The goal might *be* the process, though to be seen as such the process would have to be seen in its total context, so that the true meaning and significance of its parts could be seen. And its creations, though never final, would have to be preserved and valued forever.

So, there is a very basic divide between different views of time. For one view, time is a tragic process of decay and loss, uncertainty and transitoriness. If there is a perfect form of existence, for gods or humans, it must be beyond time, in changeless and undivided eternity. But, for the other view, time is a positive process of creativity and novelty, freedom, and discovery. Any perfect form of existence would have to include time, as the expression of freedom, creativity, unique individuality, and the fully personal life.

God, the perfectly realized being, would not be simple, in the sense of being without any complexity at all and would not be without any potentiality. Divine simplicity can be construed in a different way, as the indissoluble and coinherent unity of all compatible perfections, which is not composed of smaller independent parts but is One by the total integration of all possibility, rather than by negation of complexity. Divine power can be construed not as pure actuality without any unrealized possibilities but as the unlimited potential for new forms of being, as the actual and unlimited ocean of creative possibility.

Flowing Time and Block Time

I have pointed to the influence of the natural sciences in prompting a more positive view of time, for science emphasizes the full reality of the particular and the temporal. It reveals the way in which the cosmos has grown from initial simplicity to integrated complexity. It points to the possibility of improvement and creative change and the importance of human responsibility in shaping the future, at least on this planet. And, not least, it demonstrates the importance of individual genius and new discovery, both in understanding nature and in artistic activity.

Yet science, too, is deeply divided in its views of time. Many physicists feel a natural affinity with the medieval view that time is an illusion or a subjective perception of what is in fact a nontemporal reality. This is because of developments in physics in the twentieth century. In classical physics, Newton had seen space and time as absolute receptacles into which material objects could be put. This was not, as is sometimes thought, a materialist or mechanist view. Newton regarded space and time as the "*sensoria*" of God, the means by which God was aware of finite material objects, and he believed that gravitational action at a distance was the result of the direct action of God—though he excluded this view from physics, remarking that he "framed no hypotheses" on the matter.

Space and time, for physics, remained very much what they were for common sense. There were three dimensions of space, at right angles to each other, and space was a transitive and symmetrical set of possible relations between solid and precisely locatable material objects. That means that if A is to the right of B, and B is to the right of C, then A is to the right of C, and you can travel backward and forward between A, B, and C. Time allowed just one transitive but asymmetrical relation— past, simultaneity, and futurity. You can only travel in one direction in time—forward—so the time relation is not symmetrical.

But there is a problem with time. It moves. Or, rather, things are always moving along it, passing inexorably from past to present to future. So, time seems to grow in extent, as the present keeps on moving into an open future. That is how common sense considers the matter. My past grows ever greater, and I seem to be poised on a point that is always moving into the unknown. But, for Newtonian mechanics, it is not like that.

Newtonian laws of nature are time-indifferent. They work equally well forward or backward in time. If you think of nature as made up of small particles of solid matter, Newtonian laws of motion allow you to predict their motion from any given initial state, either forward or backward. We could predict all states of the universe from the beginning or from the end of time equally well. So, it is not true that the past is fixed, whereas the future is open. Past and future are equally fixed, and the present moment is a rather arbitrary selection out of all the possible points in time that are, in some sense, already fully determined to be what they are.

So, the physicists' view of time began to diverge from the common-sense view. This divergence grew rapidly from the beginning of the twentieth century. Einstein's theory of special relativity connected space and time into one four-dimensional continuum and renounced the view that time is an absolute flowing quantity. For relativity, time and space are closely interconnected. For example, the speed of light is an absolute limit that cannot be exceeded by any physical particle. But, at speeds very near to light-speed, time slows down dramatically. A space traveler who wanted to travel to another star in our galaxy, supposing (impossibly) she managed to travel at close to the speed of light, could get there and back in a few years of her time. But, when she got back, she would find that her whole generation, and her children too, had died long ago. At the speed she was traveling, time passed very slowly. But, on the more slowly moving earth, time passed more quickly. So, she stayed young, while everyone she had left behind grew old and died.

It may seem from this that the secret of endless life may be to travel at the speed of light. Unfortunately, at that speed (at least according to standard understandings of relativity), one would also have infinite mass, so obesity would become a major problem. In addition, if you actually reached the speed of light, time would stop, and you would not have any experiences at all. It hardly seems worth it. Conversely, of course, if you traveled very slowly, time would move much faster, and, in a very slow physical system, you might have huge numbers of experiences in a very short time. John Barrow has suggested that this is another way to get endless life or at least subjectively endless experiences while still being in time. Such paradoxes have been explored by physicists, though the possibility of exploiting them seems rather remote.

The serious point is, however, that time and spatial motion are intimately related. There is no absolute rate at which time flows. In relativity physics, it is even impossible to say that two events, widely separated in space, happen at the same time. Simultaneity is relative. For some observers, the two events would seem to happen at the same time. But, for an observer moving at a different speed, they may happen one after another—and even the order of succession could appear to be different.

Thus, the common-sense view that events happen at specific points in an objectively flowing time is replaced by the view that temporal flow is an appearance to specific observers of a deeper reality in which time and space are coexistent. Physicists often speak of space/time as a four-dimensional continuum. A space/time grid can be constructed in which the three dimensions of time are usually laid out as one coordinate and time is taken to be another.

The lifetimes of objects and people can be mapped as "world lines" on the four-dimensional map of space/time. Whereas it seems to us that we are continually moving through time, on a space/time map our whole lives from beginning to end are laid out as a line through three dimensions of space and one of time. Modern physics has frozen us into an immobile space/time, and our experience of moving through absolute space with a series of locations in an absolute time has been reduced to the status of a mere appearance or illusion. The underlying reality is the world line in space/time that exists in timeless mathematical reality and never comes into being or passes away. It is truly "eternal," and Einstein found in this one of the consolations of physics. Our past is never lost; for, in space/time, it is timelessly and forever there, as part of our own unique world line. It shall be there eternally, so our immortality is assured.

Perhaps only a mathematical physicist could be consoled by that sort of eternal life. Most ordinary people want some further sort of experience that is better than this one. But, as we have seen, some theologians regard the afterlife as timeless, too, so perhaps Einstein's thinking was nearer to that of some orthodox religious views than he suspected.

The view that time exists "all at once," from beginning to end, is usually known as the "block time." It contrasts with the view that there is a fixed and continually growing past and a continuing movement into an open future, called "flowing or processive time." For most physicists, the flowing-time view has been given up because there is no objective rate at which time flows, no one leading edge of the past that creeps forward simultaneously throughout the whole universe. Relativity theory seems to have quashed that idea.

God and the Possibility of Multiple Space/Times

Is it really true, however, that a common-sense flowing-time view is committed to absolute simultaneity, to the opinion that time cannot be different for different observers? I doubt whether common sense has any such ambitious and wide-ranging theories. All common sense wants to assert is that my past grows larger and my future is open. Obviously, anyone closely related to me in spatial terms, anyone belonging to the same species whom I am liable to meet, must roughly share the same leading edge of time with me. In terms of physics, anyone within my light cone must be capable of being temporally related to me.

If pressed, I would probably say that any other conscious beings in the universe, wherever they are, must have a similar local sense of temporal process, and the ordering of events in their local time must be fixed. But there is no particular reason that these two processes, which will never encounter each other, should be locatable within some common, objective flow. There can be different processive times that are not locatable within one supertime.

Such a possibility is inherent in relativity physics, for which space and time are seen as relations between events, rather than as containers for events. If time is a relation, T, between two events, B and C, then it is quite possible that there should be no event—say, A or D, that is connected by T to either B or C. That is, B and C would form one, extremely short, temporal process. If you ask the question, "What happened before B?" the correct answer would be "Nothing." B has no relation T to anything other than C. There just is no A. Similarly, there is nothing that happens after C. So, our initial feeling that there must have been something before B is shown to be misleading, once we see that time is a relation between events.

But the fact that nothing happened *before* B or *after* C does not show that nothing exists *except* B and C. There can be other events (X–Z) connected by an internal relation T, even though they are not connected by T to B–C. Then, we have two processive times not temporally connected to each other. They will not exist before, after, or even at the same time as each other. But they may certainly exist, and they may both be quite proper times.

The same goes for space, obviously. There may be many space/times not spatially or temporally connected to one another. That means we could never get from one space/time to another by moving in any direction or by waiting a very long time. It would seem that there could be no causal connection between them, at least in any ordinary sense, since a causal connection, as we ordinarily understand it, involves a temporal connection between cause and effect.

Where would this leave God? Most people would not hesitate to say that God is not in space, yet God can know everything that happens in space. God can know everything that happens in every space there is, however many spaces there are. This is not a big problem for God.

It seems natural to say that God is not located in time either, since God is the creator of both space and time. There is a causal connection between God and time, but it is not an ordinary one. It must be a nontemporal connection, such that everything at every time depends upon God. God would be a nontemporal reality that generates time or many times. This means that God does not just generate the first moment of time and then leave it to go its own way. God must generate every time in the same creative act. Since God is not in time, it is easy for God to know everything that happens in every time, without being in any of them, just as God can know all that happens in every space, without being in space.

Such a view of God seems most consonant with the block-time thesis. Since God is nontemporal, there is no change in God. So, God does not first of all think what universes God might create and subsequently decide to create one or more of them. God's thinking and God's acting have to occur in one and the same nontemporal act. Moreover, God's making the last moment of some time exist has to occur in the same act as God's making the first moment of that time exist.

It immediately follows that God knows, in the same nontemporal way, every moment of time. If you ask the question, "Does God now know the future?" the answer is "No, God does not *now* know anything" because God is not in time. But God knows, completely and by direct vision, what lies in our future. And God knows what is our future in the very same act by which God knows the past and by which God creates both past and future.

In other words, there is no past and no future for God. And there is no difference for God between knowing past and future and creating them. God's knowledge, perhaps uniquely, creates its own objects, and God knows completely everything that ever has been and that ever will be. God can have complete knowledge of a possibly infinite number of space/times, but God does not see them as before, after, or at the same time as the others. God sees them nontemporally, as not temporally related to each other but as sets of temporal relations.

There could also be two space/times that have temporal but not spatial connections. That would be just to say that there are no relations of a spatial sort between them, but there could be some temporal connections—they could exist at the same time, for instance. This could be established if, for example, you went to sleep in one space/time and woke up in another, spatially unconnected one. The temporal connection would be established in your experience of one thing's happening after another. But there would be no physical means of getting from one to the other. It could be that the specific physical properties of these worlds were different. Thus, heavens and hells and many other worlds are conceivable in terms of modern physics without any sense of paradox. That, of course, does not at all establish that they are real—only that they are physically possible.

There is a qualification to be made here. You could only move from one space to another if you, the very same person, could be reembodied in a different space. If you think that literal sameness of body or brain is essential to being the same person, this would not be a possibility after all. Common sense has no problem with thinking that I could wake up in a different body, but that is a big question that is yet to be discussed (in the next chapter). Assuming it is possible, the symbolic spaces of ancient myths might represent (though probably in highly imaginative terms) real spaces other than this, to which journeys could indeed be made in dreams or visions or possibly after death, though not in the physical body.

Modern physics opens up, in an unexpected way, the possibility of different spaces, of different sorts of space, of different times, and of different space/time universes. It seems to confirm the possibility of a nontemporal underlying reality that is the real cause of what appears to us as the temporal flow of experience. It could be that the underlying reality is an impersonal and mathematical one, with elegance and intelligibility and mathematical purity but no awareness or intention. Nevertheless, it is worth noting that the classical idea of God is not a million miles away from the underlying intelligible world of modern physics. If you thought that the intelligible world was expressed in temporal form in order for finite consciousnesses to come to exist and understand it, you would be very near the classical idea of the purpose of God in creation.

Is Time an Illusion?

A problem remains about time. There is no problem, perhaps, about God's knowledge of the future (our future, that is). But there is a problem with freedom and with our sense that time passes or flows. Can it really be an illusion that we pass from one moment to the next and that we decide what we are going to do next, whereas, in fact, our whole lives are fixed in an eternal present?

The philosopher G. E. Moore once gave a British Academy lecture titled, "A Refutation of Idealism," in which he undertook, among other things, to refute the view that the sense of the flow of time was an illusion. A major part of the refutation, reminiscent of Samuel Johnson's response to George Berkeley two hundred years before, was that Moore knew he shaved before he had breakfast. And he was more sure of that than he was of any arguments to prove that time was unreal. It was, in other words, a defense of common sense against the fantasies of philosophy and mathematical physics.

What lies behind such a defense is the question of whether we are ultimately going to rely on common sense or on science for our view of what is real. There have been battles between common sense and science before, and science has usually won. The earth does go around the sun; physical objects are mostly empty space; and colors do not exist when we are not looking at them.

Still, we have observations that confirm earth's orbit of the sun, and we can see that the sun appears to move over the sky, though the sky actually moves around the sun. Physical objects feel solid, they repel one another, and no scientist pretends they do not. And colors are not nonexistent; it is just that they can be shown to depend upon the occurrence of electrochemical events in the brain in response to the stimulus of specific wavelengths of light.

These scientific facts, though surprising, do not show that our common-sense observations are incorrect or nonexistent. They show only that our observations may be misinterpreted or give rise to inferences that are false (that the feeling of solidity means that there are no gaps or that the perception of colors means that they exist on unperceived objects).

In the case of time, can it be that our observation that time passes is misleading and that, in fact, it does not? We would have to be able to distinguish between how it appears to us and how it really is and show why it appears as it does. The difficulty is that time is a fundamental form of all appearances. Without it, there would be no appearances at all.

What physicists typically do is regard time as a coordinate dimension with the three dimensions of space. But, actually, it is quite different in kind. It is not, for instance, at right angles to the spatial dimensions, as they are to each other. It is not reversible. It does not appear to be there all at once, its parts laid out alongside one another, as space does. It is phenomenologically different, which is to say that it appears to be not a "dimension" at all, in the same sense that they are.

Mathematically, of course, it can be represented as a "dimension"— that is, as a measurable coordinate along with others in a system of coordinates. But then mathematics can represent almost anything as a set of coordinates or abstract relationships. This fact in no way implies that, in the real world, the objects designated by the variables in the coordinate system are alike. It is just useful for some purposes to treat complex objects as abstract quantities, and the results can be very revealing about the behavior of real-world objects. But it would be a mistake to think either that the mathematical formalism has captured everything of interest about real-world objects or that, because two objects can be treated similarly in a mathematical model, they are similar in all respects in the real world.

Mathematical Models
and What Reality Is Like

This problem of mathematical formalism and what it represents becomes particularly acute with the general theory of relativity and with quantum physics and quantum cosmology. General relativity tells us that space/time is curved. Interpretations of quantum theory tell us that there may be ten or eleven dimensions, of which space/time is only a selection of four, most of them so small that we cannot see them. And quantum cosmology suggests that, below the Planck length (approximately 10^{-35} cm) space itself breaks up into a sort of topological foam, rather than being a continuum.

What we have is, as Bernard Carr puts it, "A sequence of mental models, each of which is progressively removed from common-sense reality" (2004, 54). Are these models telling us the truth about a reality that our senses disguise from us? Or are they mathematical abstractions that do not stand for anything objective but are pragmatically useful in helping us to understand common-sense reality better? Or is there some other way of understanding them?

In the formalism of quantum field theory, electrons are represented as probability waves in Hilbert space, and the square of their amplitude gives the probability of locating a particle at a specific point on a prepared surface. Now ask the question whether that is what electrons "really" are, and you will get a variety of diverse answers.

Many quantum physicists will simply say, "Don't ask." The mathematics works. It produces accurate predictions. It is a beautiful formalism. Yet it doesn't necessarily tell you what is really out there. Thus, leading quantum physicists like Niels Bohr thought that the mathematics is definitely a model, not a picture. It does not represent what is really out there. It is a useful abstraction that gives us predictions we can use (though only probabilistic ones). The real world is the world of observations. Mathematical physics tries to explain it and is very successful, but, as to what is really there, underlying the appearances, the mathematics does not tell us. This may be very frustrating for physicists, and debate continues to rage among those interested in such abstruse questions, which it is not necessary for physicists to resolve in order to get on with their work.

My point is simply this: modern physics need not be taken, and is very widely not taken, as a form of "direct realism," telling us what the world is objectively like. It can very well be taken, without any harm to physics—and possibly with some benefit to common sense—as a set of mathematical models that point to some hidden underlying structure of what appears to us but that do not undermine the reality of what we see. What we see is real. What underlies it and explains its ultimate origin and nature, we do not know. Mathematical models provide useful abstractions that help us to understand reality, but they do not help us to picture reality or delve into its ultimate nature.

We could take the mathematical models of space/time, or of a ten-dimensional space/time and of the many space/times that are used in some physical models, precisely as abstract models. They point, no doubt, to what Bernard d'Espagnat calls a "veiled reality" underlying this. But they do not undermine the reality of what we experience; they only provide an abstract schema of Ultimate Reality without introducing us to its final mystery.

We may not wish to allow physicists, or the classical theologians either, to tell us that time is an illusion, whereas the underlying reality is a timeless whole. We can say that the flow of time from fixed past to open future is an irreducibly real feature of both our experience and of the world as it is. We do not have to say that there is one absolutely simultaneous "now" with which all flowing times have to be correlated. There may be many flowing processes, not temporally correlatable with one another.

Where now will God stand? God will stand at every leading edge of every process, moving with it toward its own open future. God will not be confined to a particular time but will move forward with many non-temporally related times. It follows that the divine experience will not be linear in the way that human experience is. It will enter into all processive times and will, thus, not be reducible to one linear temporal series into which they are all put.

This is well beyond the possibility of human imagining, and some may think that the idea of an experience, even a divine one, that contains temporally unrelated segments of time is incoherent. There is no problem with the idea of such unrelated segments as such. The problem is with their being elements of one experience. However, if God can experience many unrelated space/times anyway, as the classical view seems to imply, it should be possible for God to experience them as processive, if that is what they really are. We might say they will be related in God's unitary experience, but they will not be spatially or temporally related to each other. In this way, God will be both supratemporal and temporal. The idea does not seem to be incoherent, though I can understand someone thinking it is inconceivable. No more so than some quantum physics, perhaps!

Temporal Flow and Freedom

What is the point of a processive view of time? It allows God to do new creative things, it allows finite agents to be free and creative in an open future, and it allows God to react to such free acts in a fully responsive way.

A wholly nontemporal God could not allow creatures autonomously to decide even part of the future, for then God would have to take account of their acts in constructing the next slices of time. And that would mean that God was temporal since God would first have to see what creatures did and then, at a subsequent time, respond. The non-temporal God must, therefore, will the creatures' free act and the divine response to it in the same act, and that act will be the one divine act of creation.

As a matter of fact, most philosophers and theologians have been entirely happy with that situation. When a person prays, they say, God causes the prayer and has eternally decreed the response to it. That, and everything else in time, is wholly determined ("predestined") by God. And such divine determination is entirely compatible with the exercise of free creativity and choice by creation because "free" action is taken to be action in accordance with your desires. You are free if you can do what you want. Your desires are set by nature. They are determined by previous causes and the laws of nature. Or, in the religious case, they are determined by God. You are not free if someone forces you to do something against your will. So, freedom is as "determined" as compulsion, but you are not compelled as long as you can do whatever you wish. Therefore, freedom and determinism are wholly compatible.

The determination of everything by God, which follows from divine nontemporality, is not the same as physical determinism or determinism by previous states and the laws of nature. God might determine everything without using general laws of nature at all, or without using them all the time.

But if God determines everything, then God determines people to do evil and to harm others and—in some views—determines them to suffer in hell because of it. John Calvin stated, "All are not created on equal terms, but some are preordained to eternal life, others to eternal damnation" (1989, 206). It is small consolation to be told that you acted freely in doing evil because it was what you wanted to do, when God put those desires into you and then punishes you for having them.

Many people feel that if you are going to be punished or rewarded for your acts, it must have been possible for you to do other than you did. It is not only that you did what you wanted. More is required—you could have chosen to act in accordance with a different desire. There were open alternatives, and it was up to you to choose between them. However, others feel that such an open choice would be no more than an arbitrary, uncaused event, and nobody deserves to be punished for an uncaused or undetermined event either. So indeterminacy, and a future of open alternatives, does not resolve this issue.

The Copenhagen interpretation of quantum physics does show that it is possible to have indeterminate events in nature—in fact, it claims that there are millions of them. An indeterminate event is not an event without any cause. It may have lots of causes, lots of factors inclining it to happen. But it is an event without a determining cause—without a cause that ensures that this precise event, and no other, will happen.

As David Hume pointed out, it is hard to see how a cause could ensure that a subsequent event would happen and that no other event could possibly happen. How can the present determine the future in this way? In quantum physics, the present does not determine one and only one future. It offers a limited range of alternative futures, and nothing that we know of actually determines which one happens.

Such indeterminacy does not seem to have any particular value. It seems like leaving things to chance rather than rational and responsible control. But that reference to rational control is significant. To have rational control of a process is to guide it to a goal that is taken to be of value. An intelligent agent can select one goal, out of many possible goals, and then select a process to achieve that goal.

Initial physical states and the general laws of nature lay down limiting conditions on what sorts of goals are possible and on how they may be achieved. But they do not consider goals or select means to them by conscious deliberation. Where, then, do goals exist, and what causes them to exist? They exist in minds, and what causes them is deliberation about possible futures and a comparative evaluation of those futures. This requires a capacity for knowledge, abstract thought, evaluation, and some control of the processes that can lead toward an envisioned goal.

Such a capacity can be exercised with various degrees of skill, attention, and application. To some extent, skills can be taught, attention can be focused, and application can be brought to bear. Intelligent agents can be held responsible for the goals they choose and for the effort they do or do not put into achieving those goals.

Among the goals that may be chosen are some that increase beauty, knowledge, and the happiness of others. There are others that disregard those things or that may even harm others in the pursuit of personal happiness. To make a responsible choice is to envision possible futures, evaluate them, decide on a personal goal, and begin to execute a process leading to it. This is not a matter of pure indeterminacy or randomness. It introduces considerations of thought, evaluation, decision, and execution. Those are the considerations upon which an attribution of personal responsibility is based. To the extent that agents are thought to be incapable of rational decision, of unbiased evaluation, and of intelligent choice or to be unable to influence their own actions by such rational activities, that those agents are exempted from responsibility. Thus, animals like dogs and cats are generally not held morally responsible for harmful acts, though some (mostly British) people think that dogs, at least, are borderline cases.

For views like this, attributions of responsibility presuppose the existence of rational agency, with capacities of thought, evaluation, and choice that are not within the province of the natural sciences, purely physical causal states, or the laws of physics. Nevertheless, if such views were true, physical processes could be modified by rational (or irrational) actions. In that case, there would be alternative possible futures, between which a responsible choice can be made—thereby undermining the notion of physical determinism. According to these views, then indeterminacy is a necessary condition of rational and responsible action.

Since physical determinism cannot be proved and since indeterminacy is affirmed by most quantum physicists anyway, it looks as if a consideration of human responsibility gives good reason for affirming a processive view of time, in which open futures are at least partly fixed by the choices of rational agents within the process.

According to this view, freedom of choice is not limited to the indeterminacies of subatomic particles. But the fact that science admits indeterminacy at a fundamental level suggests that it cannot consistently deny the possibility of indeterminacy in natural laws in general.

This is by no means the end of the argument, which has raged in philosophy since ancient Greece and seems to be theoretically unresolvable. For many philosophers, it is unrealistic to posit the sort of independence of rational agency from the physical causal network that these views seem to suggest. A compatibility view is the one, they would say, that is most consistent with the scientific view that we live in a world governed by physical laws, and there is no other "magical" or nonphysical stuff that we can draw on to solve our ethical problems. No matter how we manage to analyze thought, evaluation, and choice—and it is agreed that no one has yet satisfactorily done so—they must, in the end, be resolvable into the interactions of the physical entities that are the only real things that exist.

But at least we can plainly see that this is not an argument that science is in any position to resolve in the foreseeable future. If anything, indeterminacy seems to have the majority vote in quantum physics. Whether that sort of indeterminacy is the sort that a "responsible-agency" view of freedom requires is another matter.

Process Philosophy and the Creative Temporality of God

I have been speaking of physical determinism and finite rational agency. These points may seem not to implicate God, but they do. For if it is important to rational agency that agents should make their own choices between alternative futures and not be compelled, however willingly, to do so by prior determining causes, then determination by God is also ruled out. That means God must leave some alternatives to be decided by creatures. If that is so, then what God does next will have to be a response to a decision made in time by someone other than God. God will be temporal, in doing some things after, and in response to, others.

For the classical religious traditions, this idea was unthinkable. Would it not make God vulnerable to all the imperfections of time? It is only in comparatively recent times—since the end of the eighteenth century—that the classical idea of God has been revised so as to make temporality a perfection and not an imperfection. As I have suggested, this is partly due to the influence of science, which made the particular and the temporal of greater value than the purely universal and the eternal.

Today, a temporalist view of God is most often associated with the process philosophy of Alfred North Whitehead, who was himself a mathematician deeply interested in relativity. He developed a view of God as having a threefold nature. First, there is God's primordial nature—including "all eternal objects," which function as "relevant lures of feeling" for all realizable conditions. Then, there is God's consequential nature—"the physical prehension by God of the actualization of the evolving universe." Third, there is God's superjective nature—the divine nature as "qualifying the transcendent creativity in the various temporal instances" (1978, 87–88; see also part 5, chapter 2).

If I may translate, the primordial nature is like that of the classical God. It timelessly encompasses all possibilities as archetypes of possible worlds. But, unlike the classical God, in itself it is relatively abstract or incomplete. Real, as opposed to conceptual, content is given by the consequential nature, within which the whole universe is encompassed as in a perfect "divine memory" but in a way that is without discord or frustration—"the dynamic effort of the world passing into everlasting unity" (Whitehead 1978, 349). Finally, the superjective nature is the influence God, both primordial and consequential, has upon the further temporal development of the universe, luring or urging it toward the Good or at least the Better. In the work of many process philosophers, the superjective nature tends to get subsumed under the primordial and consequential natures as their joint influence on the actual entities of the universe. But Whitehead himself may have had a more active influencing action of God in mind.

Nevertheless, for Whitehead, God is not the all-determining source of the universe. On the contrary, the universe consists of an infinite number of "actual occasions" or point-instant events, each of which "prehends" or is causally affected by the events that precede it in time, and creatively projects a new possibility or set of possibilities into the future. Primary causality belongs to these events, and God is the abstract ground of their possibility, the "enjoyer" (or "sufferer") of their self-accomplished reality, and the ultimate final cause that enters, as just one influencing factor, into their creation of the open future.

This God, who seems to some critics to be reduced to being a spectator of and a weak influence upon the causal process, is rather a long way from the all-determining God of Aquinas. Whitehead says, "God does not create the world, he saves it: or, more accurately, he is the poet of the world, with tender patience leading it by his vision of truth, beauty and goodness" (1978, 346). God is not sovereign; like the world, God is "in the grip of the ultimate metaphysical ground, the creative advance into novelty" (349).

For this reason, process philosophy has rarely been perceived by theists as providing an adequate description of the God they worship. But the philosophy has, nevertheless, had great influence in making ideas of the suffering, changeability, and temporal creativity of God more acceptable. After all, it may be said, scriptural ideas, no matter how metaphorical or symbolic they are, do speak of God as passionately responding to human actions, as conversing with prophets, responding to prayers, and even, for Christians, becoming incarnate in history. Perhaps the classical theologians were a little too dismissive of the implications of such beliefs.

The process view of God can, with very small adjustments, be reconciled with something much more like the classical view. God's primordial nature does not have to be "actually deficient and unconscious" (Whitehead 1978, 345). It can be a fully conscious selection of timeless perfections, something that every consciousness would choose if it could. The events that form the universe could be created, brought into being by God, but given their own autonomy. God's "inclusion" of the universe could involve a fully personal response to and interaction with "other" truly personal agents, while sharing in the joys and sufferings of such agents. And God could direct the universe to a final and inexorable goal, without overruling human freedom and its consequences.

In this way, the concerns of the classical view that God is perfect in actuality, that God creates all things, that God is other than finite agents, and that God will ensure the realization of the divine purpose could be combined with the process concern that God acts in a new way and has new forms of experience in creating the universe, that God does not overrule or determine the wills of finite agents, that God is responsive to the acts of finite agents, and that God will take such acts into account in creatively realizing the divine purpose for the universe.

Creativity and relationship are values that presuppose some form of temporality and change. If they are genuine values, then God will realize them, though in a higher and more perfect manner. This means that the past will not be lost but will be perfectly preserved in the Divine Mind, its evils mitigated and transformed. The present will not be a relentless pressure to move on but will be a combination of rest and free creative movement. The future will not be either threateningly empty or boringly repetitive. It will be be an unbounded space and time for new creative acts and forms of relationship, in which good purposes will be assured of realization.

Or so it will be if God is indeed, as God is classically said to be, "that than which nothing greater [of greater value] can be conceived." Post-scientific views of perfection or value often posit creativity and time, relationship and particularity, otherness and cooperation as positive goods. Postscientific views of what is real argue that particular spatially and temporally locatable particulars are more real than abstract universals. Adherents of these views find it difficult, as medievals did not, to think of timeless self-contemplation as the greatest of goods (though there may remain a place for contemplation of timeless perfection in every life).

Reality and Appearance

Despite this, much modern physics, in its positing of block time, has restored vitality to a more eternalist form of thought, regarding our experience of space and time as subjective appearances or even illusions. There can be many space/times, sliced in many different ways, and perhaps, in the quantum soup from which the universe originates, many such space/times actually exist with equal ontological reality (see Isham 1993). In this way, both common sense and classical atomistic material-ism, with its idea of precisely locatable physical particles in one absolute space/time, have been put in question.

But even appearances have a form of reality—they are appearances to conscious agents, the way the universe really appears to them. And common sense may be right in supposing that the world of block time, of multiple space/times, and of quantum soup is, as Whitehead put it, "actually deficient and unconscious." This is a world of possibilities (as quantum physics supposes that it is), and actuality has to be carved out of it by actual conscious agency. The world of possibilities is there. It is, for a believer in God, part of the primordial nature of God. It is that world of which the physics of block time speaks, a world without cre-ativity, relationship, or consciousness.

Actuality is realized by conscious creative action. Thus, the appearance of three-dimensional space and flowing time is a reality for consciousness, a consciousness capable of creativity and relationship. Subtract consciousness, and any "creative advance into novelty," any cooperation and community, any sense of flowing time disappears.

If this is so, theists could say that block-time physics deals only with the conceptual world of possibilities in abstraction from the consciousness of God in which it actually exists, just as it attempts to deal only with the material aspects of things in abstraction from the question of consciousness.

Platonism may have returned to physics, but it is radically modifed by the knowledge that, in the end, conscious observation is the test of actuality. The observed universe is not just an illusion. It is the actualization in time of the eternal possibilities of being. It can only truly be understood in the light of those possibilities. But human experience, flowing and three-dimensional as it is, must remain the point at which we most authentically touch reality. Not even the most sophisticated mathematical physics has the authority to prove that space and time, as we experience them, do not really exist. But it may show that there are other possible forms of space and time. It may show that the nature of reality in itself cannot be imagined, though its structure can be mathematically modeled. And it may show that, though we exist in a world of appearance, this is how reality truly is in relation to us and that it cannot be negated, though it may be more profoundly interpreted, by even the most sophisticated theories of quantum cosmology.

All these topics are highly contentious, and there is little place for dogmatism or for the assertion of final and obvious truths in modern physics. In such a situation, religious believers may reasonably think that to speak of different forms of spatial and even nonspatial existence and of different senses and experiences of time, as many religions do, is well within the bounds of possibility as they are drawn by modern science.

Immanuel Kant said that space and time, as they appear to us, are "forms of our sensory awareness." They are no less real for that. But they cannot tell us the ultimate nature of reality, and they may be capable of transformations that can only be dimly imagined in dreams and visions. Part of the attraction of religions is that, at their best, they offer visions of time transfigured by eternity and of finite particulars becoming transparent to infinity. At this point, and for some people, fundamental physics and reflective religion may unexpectedly and fruitfully converge.

6. Is It Still Possible to Speak of the Soul?

(DOES SCIENCE ALLOW THE POSSIBILITY OF LIFE AFTER DEATH?)

Buddhism and the Human Person

ALMOST ALL RELIGIONS AFFIRM that there is more to human beings than material bodies and brains. This "more," the spiritual dimension, is often held to be of greater reality than the material body, to outlast it and sometimes even to precede it. The heart of personal life, its essential nature, lies in the spiritual dimension. That belief, found in some form in almost every human society, is at the core of religion.

There are different ways of interpreting the spiritual dimension of human lives. These differences spring from different ways in which the spiritual is thought to be related to the material. It is fairly easy to define a material object—it is a publicly observable, locatable, and extended body in three-dimensional space. It is made up of many smaller parts—cells, atoms, and subatomic particles—but all of them are, in principle, amenable to public scrutiny, measurement, and analysis.

The spiritual is harder to define. A negative definition is simply that it is not material—not publicly observable, not extended in space, and not physically measurable. More positively, it consists of consciousness (immediate awareness of some object), it has the character of feeling (pleasure in or aversion to the object of awareness), it involves thought (the ability to identify objects and consider possible states as well as actual ones), and it involves goals or purposes (envisioned possible states that would give pleasure).

A human person can imagine a tropical island, consider that it would be pleasant to go there, and decide to do so. No one else can visualize my imagined island as I do, and perhaps it does not exist in space at all, so it certainly could not be measured. It looks as though there is a clear distinction between the spiritual and the material, that they are different in kind. This, however, turns out to be a very controversial view. Yet it is initially a very obvious one, and it has seemed so to many religious views of reality.

In Buddhist thought, the human person is analyzed into five *khandhas*, "heaps" or groups (I am using the Pali terms). First, there is *rupa*, the material elements of the physical body. Then, there is *vedana*, sentience or feeling, the sense of pleasure and pain. After that comes *sannya*, perception, the apprehension and recognition of external objects but also perhaps of bodily sensations. Fourth is *sankhara*, mental formations, like mental habits, thoughts, ideas, and decisions. And fifth is *vinnyana*, discriminating consciousness, which some have defined as the connecting thread of personal continuity.

These groups can be described in a number of different ways, but the descriptions I have given provide a general idea of the strong Buddhist interest in internal conscious states of the human person. The analysis is achieved by observation and analysis of personal experience, by observing the flow of feelings, thoughts, sensations, and decisions that form the content of human experience. No one else can feel my pleasure or pain. No one else can have my bodily sensations. No one else can make my decisions. And no one else can have the sense I have of one cumulative series of experiences, integrated in a unique way into a whole that governs how my present and future experiences will be perceived and responded to.

Thus, all these elements of experience are accessible only to me, and they exist within a total pattern that seems to be at least partly under my control. For I must decide either to let myself be controlled by clinging and desire or by following the Eightfold Way of moral practice, meditation, and correct views, to free myself from attachment to desires and achieve mindfulness, compassion, and equanimity.

As I become enlightened, I may remember all my previous births and lives. I will see how, according to the laws of karma, I have reaped the consequences of my deeds and desires through many lifetimes. I will see how the series of feelings, thoughts, sensations, and decisions that constitutes my self has been the cause of my present experience. And I will see what I have to do to to achieve final release from the cycle of rebirth and achieve the experience of *nibbana*, of being without greed, hatred, and delusion.

There is a paradox in the way I have described the Buddhist view. It seems that great stress is placed on the uniqueness of access to "my" experiences and on "my" responsibility for gaining liberation. Yet a basic doctrine of Buddhism is the doctrine of *anatta*, of no-self. According to this doctrine, there is no permanent and enduring self that underlies all my experiences. There are just the five groups of experiences themselves, bound together in a particular series. They do not "belong to" anyone, so they are not really "mine." And liberation does not really consist in my self escaping from rebirth. It consists in the series, which has been bound together by attachment and desire, coming to an end, being "blown out," or being transformed into a wider consciousness, wisdom, and bliss, in which no sense of individual self, the alleged sole possessor and solitary enjoyer of experiences, remains.

Other Eastern Analyses of the Human Person

To understand the rejection of the doctrine of a permanent underlying self, we need to understand something about the Indian philosophy against which the Buddhists reacted. The Indian philosophical traditions analyze the human person in a different way from the main Western tradition. For many Hindu traditions, there is an individual soul (*jiva*) that passes from one embodied life to another. This consists, in one main analysis, of four basic elements. There is *manas*, the "lower mind," which governs the senses; *chitta*, containing stored memories, desires, aversions, and mental habits; *buddhi*, the higher mind, which knows, decides, judges, and discriminates; and *ahamkara*, the sense of selfhood or "I-ness." This sense of selfhood tends to identify itself, falsely, with the memories, aversions, and thought patterns of the mental elements. Liberation consists in overcoming this false identification and in achieving a state of pure consciousness, free from attachment and aversion. This analysis has strong affinities with a Buddhist analysis. Both divide the life of intelligent agency and feeling sharply from any particular physical body (for the agent successively lives in many bodies) and think of individual souls as sets of dispositions and capacities that are amenable to responsible discipline and development. Both seek to overcome the identification of the self with a particular personality or complex of desires and thoughts.

But for the Hindu tradition of Advaita Vedanta, beneath these sets of capacities there is *Atman,* the true self, which is identical with *Brahman*, the one Ultimate Reality. Liberation from rebirth is liberation from a false sense of self, as an individual and isolated being, to a true sense of self, as one undivided reality of supreme intelligence and bliss. Beneath the changing life of the soul, there is the unchanging life of the Absolute. If we can overcome the illusory sense of being a separate and lonely soul, we can find the one deathless eternal reality, the Self of all, at the center of our being, in "the cave of the heart."

A crucial point is that *Brahman* appears, for the sake of devotees, as

Ishvara, a personal Lord infinite in goodness, wisdom, and bliss. For most Hindus, the worship of the gods, usually all taken to be aspects of the Absolute personal Lord, is sanctioned. Even though the personal Lord may be part of the world of illusion, it is real for devotees and should not be negated. And with the worship of the gods goes the maintenance of Hindu sacrificial rituals and of the caste system, which places *Brahmins*, priests, at the peak of the social and religious hierarchy.

The Buddha rejected sacrifices, the priesthood, the caste system, and worship of a supreme God. He rejected the doctrine of *Brahman*, the supreme changeless Self, and the idea that we are all parts of such a Self. Yet Advaita and Buddhism are so alike that many scholars think that Advaita was propounded by Sankara as a way of absorbing Buddhist thought into the more overtly theistic Hindu traditions. If so, the absorption was so successful that Buddhism virtually disappeared from India until the twentieth century, when it once more emerged in critical opposition to the rigid caste hierarchies of popular Hinduism.

The similarity is that the idea of a reincarnating substantial soul is not part of either Buddhism or the Hindu tradition of Advaita. In both cases, what is reborn is the complex of dispositions and capacities that has been built up over many lives. And liberation is not the transfer of the soul to a better realm but the disappearance of that complex of dispositions, by being merged into a greater unitary and timeless reality that is beyond literal description. Whether it is called *Brahman* or *nibbana*, it is described as calm, passionless, cool, intelligent, and blissful and beyond all trace of individual personality.

The difference is that in Vedantic Hinduism the Absolute Self is the Creator, the source of all things by its self-manifestation. Such a Creator may conceivably help devotees by gracious action and is always a proper object of reverence and devotion. In Theravada Buddhism, there is no Creator—the world of suffering is not created by a good God—and liberation must be sought by rigorous self-discipline. There is no divine grace and no God to worship. There is only suffering and the path to the ending of suffering and the cool blissfulness of the Unconditioned.

Both these views, the one-self view and the no-self view, regard the human person as primarily a series of mental states and think that to identify oneself with any of these transitory states is a root error. The goal of spiritual life, to be found through moral practice and meditation, lies in overcoming attachment to a supposedly individual and distinct selfhood and in achieving a state that, though conscious, may be described as ultimately impersonal, without personality, desire, or the need for action and relationship.

This is not the only view of the human person that is held in Indian and East Asian forms of religion. There are many different views of the human person. Jains, for example, agree that attachment to desire is the cause of suffering and that liberation from rebirth is the primary spiritual goal. But for Jains, each human soul is a substantial and individual entity, which, in its liberated state, is solitary, omniscient, and blissful. In ancient Greek thought, Plato has a similar view that human souls are better off without their bodies but may have a blissful existence in a purely spiritual form.

Popular religion in most of these traditions, however, is content to aim at a rather less austere goal. What is hoped for is a better rebirth in a happier world. Some forms of Hinduism (like Bengali Vaishnavism) and even some forms of Buddhism (like the Pure Land school) locate the ultimate human goal in existence as a loving devotee of Krishna, the supreme personal Lord, or in a western paradise or Pure Land, ruled by Amitabha Buddha or by some compassionate boddhisattva. There are many hells and heavens, between which souls may cycle for millions of rebirths. Our best hope is to find an ultimate heaven with a pure form of embodiment where we can live happily forever.

Semitic Ideas of the Soul

The Semitic religions begin from a different place. According to the ancient Hebrew tradition from which they spring, individual personality, history, and relationship are of primary importance. If there is any goal for human life, it is not the overcoming of desire and individuality but achieving a transformed sort of altruistic desire and socialized individuality, in a society of loving-kindness and harmony.

At first, in that tradition, there was not a great concern with any sort of life beyond death. As such a concern formed, both out of a sense that the suffering of the innocent could not be the end of their lives and that it must be possible to know and love God more fully, the model for immortality came to be that of the resurrection of the body.

This was imagined in many ways, but it always involved the continuance of some sort of bodily and social life. For the Hebrews, *Nephesh* is the life-giving principle of all organic beings. Humans are said to be "dust," into which God breathes life. No great attention is paid to the contents of the mind and meditative self-observation. In the main Jewish tradition, humans are viewed as thinking, acting lumps of matter, and it would not be considered a good thing to abandon one's own personality or one's friends. The best thing would be for God to re-create the material universe in a more perfect form and put everyone into it.

There are two main variants of this general view—one that still distinguishes body and spirit quite sharply, though it holds that they are closely bound together, and one that can live with a wholly materialist interpretation of human personhood, though the materialism in question has to be of a rather special sort.

The Christian idea of the soul was classically formulated by Thomas Aquinas, following Aristotle's *Peri Psyche*, "On the Soul." The soul is defined as the "Form" of the body. Every physical object, in Aristotle's philosophy, has a Form or essential nature, that which makes it what it is. In organic beings, this Form is called a soul. So, plants and vegetables have souls. A potato, for instance, embodies the Form of "potatoness." The more like the Form of potatoness a potato is, the better it is as a potato. No material potato could ever be perfect, and all material potatoes embody their Forms to a greater or lesser extent. So, the Form is not a material thing. It is more like a conceptual entity, rather like a mathematical entity, that can be expressed more-or-less well in many material instances.

There are vegetable souls and animal souls. But the most important sort of soul is the intellectual soul, expressed in human beings. An Aristotelian has to discover the distinctive properties of a human animal. These will define the Form of human personhood. For Aristotle, and for Aquinas, who were both philosophers, the most distinctively human property is the ability to do philosophy or to think. The human soul is whatever it is that gives human animals the capacity to think abstractly and to make moral decisions.

Aristotle differed from Plato in insisting that Forms must be expressed in matter. They do not have a completely independent and superior reality. Form is real, and matter is real, but Form and matter have to go together to compose a truly existent thing. It follows that the human soul does not truly or properly or "by nature" exist without a body. It gives to a piece of matter a distinctive set of intellectual capacities. That is its function—the soul stands to the human body as potatoness stands to an individual potato.

Modern philosophers are not much impressed by references to potatoness. They tend to drop that idea and speak only of the distinctive capacities of a human animal. Then, to speak of human souls is to speak of the intellectual and the moral—and perhaps the emotional—capacities and dispositions of human beings.

This is, broadly speaking, a materialist interpretation of the soul, or at least it is compatible with some forms of materialism. To say that humans have souls is to say that they have distinctive capacities. Religion is particularly concerned with some of those capacities, especially those related to moral action, intellectual understanding, artistic sensitivity, and—the key religious concern—the capacity for conscious relationship to an Objective Reality, whether a being or a state, of supreme beauty and goodness. Religion is concerned with enhancing qualities of soul, of intellectual, imaginative, and moral practice. It is not, in this view, concerned with the existence of a separable spiritual bit of human beings. If there is life beyond this one, it will consist in the resurrection of the body, not in the continuance of a disembodied invisible object. This is the more materialist version of human personhood in the Semitic tradition.

However, such a materialist interpretation would not completely have satisfied Aquinas. It is part of his philosophy that Forms can have substantive existence (*Summa Theologiae*, I, question 76, article I). God, for example, is a pure disembodied Form. Despite Aristotle's arguments with Plato, Forms can have a separate reality in some cases. Even for Aristotle, God is spoken of as "pure thought" without a body, and it is disputed whether he thought part of the human soul could exist beyond bodily death.

Aquinas certainly thought it could and was committed to the existence of the soul (in purgatory, for instance) after death but before the resurrection of the body. He said that the soul can exist "unnaturally and improperly" without the body, even though its true function is to vivify the distinctive capacities of a human body. It follows that the agent of thought and morally free action, which is what the soul is for Aquinas, is not essentially (though it is properly and naturally) embodied. Souls could think and act without having a local and physical body, though to be properly and fully human they would think and act in an embodied way.

One way of putting this is to say that the very same thing that can think and act as a human animal can also, in principle, think and act in other aspects of embodiment (assuming that purgatory is another sort of embodiment), and it can also think and act without any physical embodiment at all. We can imagine having sensations and thoughts without having any physical body, and though that does not prove such a thing is possible, it is conceivable.

For Aquinas, a soul that exists without a body (like the souls in purgatory or heaven, for example) does so by a special act of God, and it does not really exist as a person in the full sense until it has a body in which to have experiences and act in an intersubjective world. Moreover, each soul is uniquely fitted to a specific body, and it cannot simply have a totally different body while remaining the soul of the same person. So, in the classical Christian view, it is important that, in some sense, it is the same body that gets resurrected, however different its properties might be.

This is not so far from a materialist view as is sometimes popularly thought. But it does require that a human life is not wholly dependent upon the continued existence of one specific material body and, thus, that human consciousness is more than a by-product of material events in a particular body, fated to perish with the disintegration of that body.

The Spectrum of Religious Views of the Human Person

Religious views of the human person are, thus, very diverse, and they might even be said to cover every possible form of relationship between conscious experience and material existence. There are five main views that various religious traditions have used. The one-self and the no-self views, of Vedantic Hinduism and Buddhism, respectively, agree that conscious experience and the capacity to control to some extent the content of that experience is distinctive of the human person. But the goal of spiritual life is to transcend individual human experience in some more universal form of consciousness, wisdom, and bliss.

The dualist view of one continuing and potentially disembodied substantial self is not widely held, though it can be found in Jainism. It shares with the first two views the belief that the ultimate goal of human life is the transcending of individual personal existence as we know it and the attainment of freedom from all material existence. That ultimate liberation is considered to be beyond community, relationship, and action. In the liberated state, there are countless individual souls, all omniscient and blissful, but having passed beyond desire and the need to act.

The fourth possibility is that human personhood esentially includes something like a material body, though it may be very different from our present body. Pure Land Buddhism, for instance, looks to a transformation of material existence in different forms of embodiment. The final goal in this view is some sort of individual and social existence, attained only by the sort of control of conscious content and disposition that the first three views emphasize.

Semitic views of the soul are broadly similar but reject the idea of many lives and rebirths, and so place much more emphasis on the vital importance of this earthly, material, embodied existence. They generally accept that resurrection may be in different forms of embodiment and that the ultimate goal of liberation or salvation is to be achieved by forms of moral and mental discipline (even if this discipline is construed as prayer instructed by divine grace).

Finally, the fifth view, also more common in the Semitic traditions, makes material existence in one specific body a necessary condition of human personhood. It holds that bodies can be resurrected in what must actually be a rather different form and agrees with all the other views in giving human life a goal, to be attained by disciplined control of consciousness, feeling, thought, and action.

Meditation may not feature largely in the Semitic religious traditions, but careful self-examination and firm resolution of the will do. There may be no attempt to transcend individual personality by merging with a Cosmic Self, but there is an attempt to overcome the selfish ego, possessiveness, and self-centeredness and to become a channel for a divine power and love that flows from beyond the individual ego. There may be no belief in many lives during which you can determine your own future fate, but there is a belief that you bear responsibility for the character of your future life.

There are differences among these views of the human person about whether the ultimate goal contains any form of material existence and about the extent to which the body is a necessary element of personal identity. But there is agreement that the practice of religion involves a knowledge of one's own personal life that is only possible by meditation or introspective self-examination, that the character of your life can be changed by discipline, meditation, or prayer, and that the goals of such practice are to achieve liberation from possessive and egoistic feelings and thoughts and attain consciousness of a higher state of wisdom, compassion, and joy.

Reductionism and the Reaction against Descartes

How does modern science affect such views? It may seem that science simply does not concern itself with them, any more than it concerns itself with music or literature. Science is not concerned with introspective analysis of personal thoughts, feelings, and purposes or with methods of prayer and meditation or with questions of the ultimate goal of human life. Most of the time scientists are careful specifically to exclude questions about subjective experiences, values, and purposes from their investigations.

When, at the beginning of the twentieth century, attempts were made to found a scientific psychology that would be based on reports of introspection, it was quickly abandoned as fruitless. It gave rise to no significant predictions, no general explanatory theories, and very little experimentally testable data. There were just subjective reports, of mild human interest but incapable of generating any new laws of nature. Introspective psychology was one of the great scientific failures of the twentieth century.

For some years afterwards, in an attempt to put psychology in the realm of science proper, behaviorism and reductive materialism became fashionable. B. F. Skinner saw humans as nothing more than complex stimulus-response mechanisms. B. A. Farrell wrote, "A human being is a modulator of pulse frequencies, and nothing more" (1970). Francis Crick, one of the discoverers of the structure of DNA, wrote in *The Astonishing Hypothesis* that "you, your joys and your sorrows, your memories and your ambitions, your sense of personal identity and free will, are in fact no more than the behavior of a vast assembly of nerve-cells and their associated molecules" (1994, 3).

These "nothing more" statements are rather perplexing, particularly because these authors do not agree with each other on exactly what it is that humans are nothing more than. They all seem keen, however, to assert that humans are nothing more than something, whatever it is. The point of agreement is that humans are certainly not spiritual beings in any sense, beings each with a rich and unique personal experience, a measure of responsible control over that experience, and a possibility of continuing to have experiences beyond the death and decay of a specific body and brain. Religious views of the human person, it seems, are all excluded in principle.

Gilbert Ryle, in *The Concept of Mind*, produced a very sophisticated defense of what is, in effect, a form of behaviorism (though he always denied being a behaviorist). He argued that "mind is what body does" (1949) and that mental operations like imagining, feeling, and thinking are public and socially learned activities of the person, observable, in principle, by others. They are not private states taking place in an invisible theater, inhabited by what he called "the ghost in the machine."

The machine is, of course, the Cartesian or Newtonian idea of the physical universe, as completely determined by mechanistic laws. The ghost is the Cartesian "thinking thing . . . which doubts, understands, affirms, denies, wills . . . and feels" (1960, Meditation 2). Descartes found its existence to be beyond the possibility of doubt. For Ryle, and for many other modern philosophers, the ghost cannot only be doubted, but it is almost certainly not there.

In modern psychology and philosophy, there is perhaps nothing that is hated more than what is called "Cartesian dualism." This is the view that there are two kinds of substances in the world. Material substance is extended in space and publicly observable. Mental substance is not in space at all and can only be observed by the "owner" of thoughts and feelings. The two quite different substances are mysteriously linked, perhaps, Descartes thought, through the pineal gland. At any rate, there is some sort of causal interaction between mind and matter, even though no laws of such causation have ever been formulated and no energy seems to be exerted in such interchanges.

The anti-Cartesians quickly descend into rhetoric, speaking of "a shadowy inner agent who is pulling the strings" or of a "ghostly controller." Mental events are described as "spooky events," which have "magical connections" with real physical events. Daniel Dennett asks, "Are there entities, either in our brains, or over and above our brains, that control our bodies, think our thoughts, make our decisions?" And responds that any such idea is "either empirical idiocy . . . or metaphysical claptrap" (1992, 413). Later, Dennett states that his own theory of consciousness (what explains consciousness) is that conscious experiences are to be identified with "information-bearing events in the brain—since that's all that's going on" (459).

The phrase *that's all that's going on* sounds familiar. This is another "nothing more" account. It may seem, both to empirical idiots and to metaphysical windbags, that there are sensations, thoughts, and feelings that can only be apprehended in introspection by one person and that it is very important, though also very difficult, to become aware of them. But all such idiots and windbags (and that includes all those Buddhists and Hindus who spend their lives meditating) are mistaken. There are nothing more than events in the brain. There are no introspectible events at all.

The "problem of consciousness," for such a view, is to say how the illusion of being an individual thinker, perceiver, and feeler ever arises. In what does it arise, and who or what is having the illusion? If an illusion exists, then there is, it would seem, something more than simply a brain event. There is also the illusion, and an illusion, though it involves false beliefs, is something: it is an apprehension of something that seems to be other than it is. But the "seeming" exists.

For hard-line materialists, however, the "seeming" only seems to exist. Daniel Dennett says, "Only a theory that explained conscious events in terms of unconscious events could explain consciousness" (1992, 454). This means that you can only explain consciousness by showing that it does not really exist. What actually exists is strands of narrative, sometimes artificially put together to form one invented central narrative of a "self," but mostly disconnected and plural sequences of beliefs and judgments, like the programmed sequences you get in a computer. Consciousness is a set of "physical effects of the brain's activities," just like the output of a computer program, with the peculiar property that "they give rise to illusions about their own powers" (16).

This, claims Dennett, or something very much like it, is the only way to give an account of consciousness "within the framework of contemporary physical science" (1992, 40). For a properly scientific account, "dualism is to be avoided at all costs" (37) because it is "fundamentally anti-scientific." These statements assert that only science can give an account of material and unconscious objects, that only science gives an account of what is real, and, therefore, that immaterial or properly conscious objects cannot exist.

The Double-Aspect Theory of Brain and Consciousness

However, we might think that science must be guided by the facts and that scientists cannot specify in advance what sorts of things can be facts. If, indeed, science can only deal with publicly observable and measurable objects, then if there are facts that are not publicly observable or measurable, science will not be able to deal with them or at least will not be able to incorporate them into a body of law-like descriptions of nature. That does not mean they do not exist.

There may or may not be facts, states of affairs, that are not publicly accessible or precisely measurable. If there were, how could we know? Only by experiencing them. But we do experience sensations, images, thoughts, and feelings that other people can know nothing about, unless we tell them. That is not an antiscientific statement. It leaves the practice of science wholly intact. So, Dennett's view seems to be founded on a dogmatic materialism rather than anything that science actually says.

Yet modern advances both in neuroscience and artificial intelligence tend to leave practitioners with a deep suspicion of dualism. Such work tends to show that there is a physical basis for conscious phenomena and that there are not two distinct worlds, one of conscious events and one of physical events. Somehow, in studying the brain, scientists are studying consciousness. Brain and consciousness seem to be two aspects of the same thing. According to this view, the phenomenal appearances of thoughts and feelings are not denied, but those appearances are only falsely taken to be distinct from brain events. In fact, they are the same events, apprehended from a different point of view, from the point of view of the person whose brain it is.

According to such a view, the existence of conscious states, of mental content known in personal apprehension, is not denied. But such states are said to be "identical with" physical brain states. Cognitive psychology since the 1980s rarely hesitates to affirm the existence of conscious states. "No longer do serious scientists and practitioners refuse to discuss consciousness," writes David Milner (2006, 138).

In two areas in particular, there have been major advances in the study of consciousness and the brain. Experimental studies, especially of monkey brains and of humans with various cognitive deficiencies, have shown a range of surprising links between brain function and reported conscious experiences. And the development of brain-imaging techniques, particularly nuclear magnetic resonance imaging (MRI), has made it possible to monitor brain activities while specific mental tasks are performed.

Experimental studies have overturned some simple pictures of experience—for example, that electrochemical messages from eye to brain stimulate conscious experiences of colored three-dimensional objects, and that we then respond to these experiences by adapting our behavior, for example, to reach out and grasp a perceived object in front of us. This seems an obvious picture, but it is seriously inadequate.

One of the best-known cases is that of "blindsight," which can occur when a person's geniculostriate pathway is damaged. Patients may have no visual experiences at all in one-half of their visual field, yet they are able to respond to objects there with a high degree of accuracy. In one case, a patient could throw darts at a dart board he could not perceive and achieve a creditable score.

This seems to show that visual perception, the occurrence of colored shapes in consciousness, is not necessary to intelligent and accurate response to stimuli. That is, we can respond to objects without seeing them. One patient was able to grasp a solid rectangular block, with her forefinger and thumb being positioned to do so, even when she could not visually distinguish that there was such a block present. It seems that there are two different quasivisual perceptual systems and that many different parts of the brain are involved, each contributing elements to a total experience. When one system is impeded, the other can still function (these cases are detailed in Milner [2006], cited above).

This extraordinary finding does not show that visual appearances do not exist. On the contrary, it only makes sense if they do. But it shows that conscious perceptions are not necessary to an organism's coordinated response to stimuli and that the brain can receive stimuli and initiate appropriate responses in the absence of perceptions. Visual perceptions heighten the accuracy of response, so it can be seen how, from an evolutionary point of view, they conferred a survival advantage. But this situation may give rise to the suspicion that visual phenomenology is laid on top of brain functioning as an addition to normal physical interactions but not as a wholly different sort of substance. Developments in the right hemisphere of the brain may have given rise to a capacity to construct visual imagery of the sort we know in our own experience.

The phenomenon of blindsight has led some theorists to think that it is physical processes in the brain that do all the real work in response to stimuli. Conscious perception is a by-product, a sort of luxury add-on, that contributes no real work to the behavior of humans. But it seems, on the contrary, to show that visual perception, though it is not necessary to responsd to stimuli, does increase the accuracy and effectiveness of response. So, it has a positive causal part to play. As the Nobel prize–winner and immunologist Gerald Edelman says, "The evolutionary assumption implies that consciousness is efficacious—that it is not an epiphenomenon" (1992, 113). If visual perception has survival value, that is precisely because it adds a new layer of causality to unconscious response. The strong implication is that consciousness is a real existent with some causal efficacy, and that it developed naturally as part of the brain's evolving complexity and integration.

A More Subtle Form of Duality in Neuropsychology

MRI scans, the more recent positron-emission tomography (PET) scans, and cerebral blood-flow studies have all established that many diverse areas of the brain are activated in what seem phenomenologically to be unified mental activities. This suggests that phenomenology (that is, what appears in consciousness) is different from observable physical brain processes. The observable processes are diverse and physically scattered. The phenomenological experience is of one unitary and integrated consciousness.

There is no question that specific sorts of mental activity can be located in specific parts of the brain. In one study (O'Craven and Kanwisher 2006), experimenters could tell, by seeing which part of the brain was active, what the subjects were thinking about. But these findings are sometimes reported in a misleading way.

It was reported in the press that scientists had now found the ability to "read minds." However, the facts are that the experimenters had found, by asking the subjects what they experienced, that one part of the brain was activated when subjects were thinking, for instance, about faces, and another part was activated when they were thinking about houses. Only then could they tell whether the subjects were thinking about faces or houses by seeing which part of the brain was active. This is impressive, but it is not quite mind-reading.

Correlations between thoughts and brain events could only be established by asking the subjects what they were thinking about—so the principle of sole access to your own thoughts had been retained. Experimenters could then tell what was being thought about, at least in a general way, by observing brain events and by assuming that the previously established correlations between location of activity in the brain and topic of thought still obtained.

Naturally, the experimenters cannot read any new thoughts. In fact, it is impossible to establish brain-thought correlations for every possible thought, since some thoughts and sequences of thought will presumably be original. In addition, the thought in question was artificially isolated and restricted. It was the image of a face or a house. No other thoughts were under consideration, and nothing in particular was to be thought about the face or house; it was just the occurrence of the image that was the object of study.

Human thought does not normally consist just in calling up isolated and definite images. Nevertheless, it is remarkable that any phenomenal features and brain states can be identified or correlated. It has been established beyond question that brain states of certain locatable sorts are correlatable with phenomenal experiences. It seems fair to assume that one does not occur without the other. And this ties them together more closely than a radical dualism may suggest. A natural proposal is to say that brain-state and phenomenal experiences are two complementary aspects of the same thing, one publicly accessible and measurable, the other private and not measurable in any exact way.

But this is a strange sense of identity, and it seems to come down to saying that, whenever a pattern of brain activity of a certain sort occurs, some phenomenal experience will occur, and vice versa. This is a strict correlation rather than an identity. Moreover, it seems to be a contingent correlation, since empirical investigations had to be carried out before the correlations in question could be established. The correlations could easily have been otherwise, and indeed most experimenters expected them to be otherwise, not quite so complex and involving so many diverse areas of the brain.

Is this, then, a sort of dualism, whether it is described as two different modes of access to one reality or as two closely correlated sorts of reality? The data of neuropsychology suggest, despite the protestations of some neuropsychologists and philosophers, that it is. For it is not just that there are two different ways of getting to a reality that is, in the end, described in the same way. Phenomenally accessed data (obtained by introspection) are described in a different way from publicly accessed observations of brain activity. Whereas brain activity is, broadly speaking, atomistic and made up of discrete parts, phenomenal perception is holistic and nondenumerable.

For instance, the phi phenomenon, so named by Max Wertheimer in 1912, is the process by which still pictures are shown to a person in rapid succession and that person sees one moving picture—the principle of the cinema. We may know that there is a rapid succession of still pictures, but what we see is one moving picture. The brain constructs a phenomenal impression of continuous movement out of discrete events in the physical world. The brain, it would seem, fools the mind. Is this an illusion? It suggests that what appears, phenomenally, is not identical with what exists in the physical world. It is how that world appears, as a result of processing by the brain.

Neuropsychological experiments make it clear that the occurrence of phenomenal experiences depends upon the proper functioning of the brain. Lesions to specific parts of the brain result in strange deviations in our phenomenal fields and in other respects as well. The importance of the brain is corroborated in the classic case of Phineas Gage, the American railroad worker in New England, part of whose brain was removed when a tamping iron passed through his cheek and out the top of his head. Before that incident, he was a conscientious and hardworking person. Afterwards, he became unreliable, shiftless, and a compulsive gambler. Antonio Damasio has recorded cases in which brain-damaged patients became psychopathic—disruptive, insensitive, and without remorse for their antisocial actions (Anderson et al. 1999, 1032–37).

It is hardly surprising that removal of parts of the brain will result in changes in perception or behavior. If I remove all your brain, I expect that you will stop thinking altogether. But it is initially more surprising to find that people's moral sense will be disturbed or may disappear when a specific area of the prefrontal cortex is damaged. This seems to strike at the very root of personality and imply that what we are and do, our very characters and personalities, are dependent upon, perhaps caused by, the functioning of our brains.

It does indeed suggest that the functioning of our intellectual and moral capacities depends upon the proper functioning of a specifically human brain. David Milner points out that human visual consciousness is able to create mental images at will and use them to plan or rehearse future activities. Damage to the parietotemporal region of the right hemisphere will impede this ability. And he suggests that monkeys lack this "cognitive prerequisite for the emotional experiences of remorse and foreboding, and ultimately, for the possibility of moral responsibility" (2006, 151).

If this is so, then the exercise of moral responsibility depends upon the possession of a functioning human prefrontal cortex. This conclusion is reinforced by the study of degenerative brain diseases, like Alzheimer's, which carry with them a progressive loss of memory and previously established personality traits. These facts have led writers like Antonio Damasio to say, "The distinction between diseases of 'brain' and 'mind,' between 'neurological' problems and 'psychological' or 'psychiatric' ones, is an unfortunate cultural inheritance. . . . [I]t reflects a basic ignorance of the relation between brain and mind" (1994, 40).

The object of attack here is the view that the mind is a distinct entity from the brain. It does not make sense to say that a mind can be responsible, free, and rational even when the brain is damaged, causing irresponsible, compulsive, and irrational behavior. It is not being denied that there is such a thing as morally responsible action or rational thought. What is denied is that such thoughts can take place in a purely nonphysical realm, whatever the state of the physical brain to which the thoughts are contingently connected.

Thought becomes rational and responsible when the brain permits it to do so. Thinking rationally depends upon the structure and functioning of a brain of a specific sort. In the absence of such brain functioning, thinking does not take place. If the brain is damaged, the thought process may well be impaired. This strongly implies that thoughts and feelings develop as the brain makes such development possible. They do not occur in a quite different nonphysical realm, in some sort of parallel world.

This further tightens the link between thought and brain. But it does not mean that thoughts are nothing but (there is that "nothing but" again!) physical brain activity. No matter how long you look at the sparking of synapses in the brain, you will not see a thought. You will not even know what a thought is if all you see are electrochemical discharges in the brain. It looks as though neuroscience has successfully shown the dependence of conscious experience upon the brain. But it has not reduced consciousness to observable states of the brain, and, in fact, it seems to presuppose that there needs to be an independent mode of access to conscious states that is not open to experimental science.

Computers and Artificial Intelligence

Some people who work in artificial intelligence argue that the case of the human brain is not really very different in principle from the case of very sophisticated computers. No matter how long you look at the physical hardware of a computer, you will never see sentences and thoughts. Yet computers regularly produce sentences and can answer questions we put to them. Those sentences are not nonphysical entities, in addition to the physical bits of which computers are constructed. Computers are made up of nothing but straightforward physical components. Yet they can solve problems, beat grand masters at chess, and answer complicated questions.

The fact that you cannot see the thoughts of computers by examining their hardware is, it may be said, analogous to the way in which you cannot see the thoughts of humans by examining their brains. In both cases, there is nothing present but physical components. Thoughts are the activities of complex physical systems. They are not additional "ghostly" or "spiritual" entities.

But do computers really think? There are two main reasons for concluding that they do not. First, no one believes computers are conscious. They do not represent the world to themselves or feel pleasure and pain. Second, computers simply follow programmed routines. They have no original insights and do not devise new proofs. They just do what they have been programmed to do, no more and no less.

The philosopher John Searle (1980) has invented the story of a "Chinese room," as an analogous case. In one version of the story, Chinese characters are sent into the room, forming questions, and out of a window come a set of answers. In fact, there are workers in the room who do not understand Chinese, but they have been issued a set of rules specifying things like, "If you receive character x, then you must send out characters y and z." They never understand what the questions or the answers are, though the answers are all correct.

A computer, says Searle, is like that. Characters go in and answers come out. But the computer does not understand what is going on. It just follows the rules programmed into it. Computers never give inventive or surprising answers (unless their wiring has gone awry). They make no leaps of imagination. They have no idea about what is going on. At the beginning and end of the process, someone understands the question and the answer. That act of intellectual understanding is something a computer can never have.

Such a conclusion is controversial. Daniel Dennett, for example, says that Searle's example is much too simplistic. Any Chinese room that could serve as an analogy for human consciousness would have to be able to pass the Turing test (that is, it would have to be indistinguishable in its answers from those a human person could give). But then the internal system would have to be so incredibly complex that it would no longer be like a simple digital computer program at all. "Understanding," Dennett says, "could be a property that emerges from lots of distributed quasi-understanding in a large system" (1992, 439). Complexity matters, and it could be that a really complex but purely physical system formed of lots of smaller subsystems, none of which was conscious, would understand what was going on.

There is no dispute that no actual computer or robot is conscious. The tasks at which computers outperform people are algorithmic processes that can be completed with extreme speed but whose routines are completely specifiable mathematically. There is no awareness or, what is closely connected to it, imaginative insight.

Proponents of "strong artificial intelligence" believe that some future, parallel-processing supercomputer could become conscious and creative. I see no reason to deny that. It amounts to saying that we could, in principle, construct a complex neural network that might generate consciousness, a sense of continuing self and of moral responsibility. Something like this is being imagined by those who envision the possibility of downloading memories and behavioral dispositions into non-human physical forms.

Freeman Dyson, for instance, defines life as "a material system that can acquire, store, process, and use information" (2002, 144). Then he envisages "a transhuman living in a silicon computer" and "a black cloud living in interstellar space" (after a novel by Fred Hoyle). And Martin Rees speaks of "thoughts and memories" being "downloaded into complicated circuits and magnetic fields in clouds of electrons and positrons" (2001, 117).

If we allow the future possibility of what at present are pleasing (or alarming) flights of fancy, this would not show that consciousness is "nothing but" electrons and positrons. It would show that consciousness is generated by complex arrays of electrons in the right configuration. Artificial minds will still be minds. It is a poor argument to say, "We are just like computers. Computers are not conscious. Therefore, we are not conscious." The argument should be: "We are conscious. We could, in principle, make computers just like us. Then computers would be conscious, too."

In fact, once we accept the notion that minds can be downloaded into other material forms, we are able to separate, at least in thought, the information content of minds and their specific physical embodiment. What computer analogies really show is not that we are just machines. They show that we—the very same conscious intelligent and responsible agents with a rich inner life of memories, hopes, and fears—could possibly be reembodied in very different forms. It would not be totally surprising, if and when this happened, to find ourselves coexisting with a number of artificially created intelligences—as well, perhaps, as dogs and cats and monkeys and who knows what else.

The Causal Efficacy of Conscious States

Those who oppose dualists (whom they tend to call empirical idiots or metaphysical windbags) have no patience with what they see as talk of a "ghost" or "hidden controller" or "little man inside the head watching events in the mental theater." Conscious states are not anywhere in space, and so, they say, it should simply be admitted that they are nowhere. In other words, there is none. To talk of conscious states is just to talk of states of the brain, and we know perfectly well where they are—inside the brain.

But sensible dualists, assuming there are some, do not want to speak of ghosts and little men in the brain. They just want to say that there are perceptions, thoughts, and feelings, in addition to electrochemical discharges in the brain. The Cartesian theater is the world itself, as it appears in our phenomenal fields. To whom does it appear? To the more-or-less unitary consciousness that *is* the functioning complex integrated brain, responding to stimuli from its physical environment. The materialist misrepresentation of the situation is that we think of the mental theater as a very small material object inside the head and the hidden observer as a very tiny body sitting in the theater. But we need to eject all such material elements from our picture. There is no physical theater inside the head. There is the brain, whose activity is registered to itself as a series of conscious events. And there is no tiny body in the head. There is the series of conscious events itself, a series of nonphysical properties of physical events in the prefrontal cortex.

At this point, a gap may seem to open up between what are called "substance dualists" and "property dualists." The property dualist will say that there are two different sorts of properties—physical and consciousness properties. But conscious states, though real, are properties of physical things (embodied brains). They could not exist without the physical things of which they are properties. The substance dualist, however, will say that there are two different sorts of things (substances),—physical things and conscious things (things that have conscious states). In this case, conscious substances (minds) could, in principle, exist without the physical substances with which they are, in human experience, strongly correlated.

I do not think this distinction is as clear-cut as it may seem. It depends upon making a sharp contrast between properties, which cannot exist alone, and substances, which can. However, there are well-known difficulties in saying just what a substance is, over and above the sum of its properties. For Buddhists and for logical positivists alike, a substance is just a collection of properties, and the question of what sets of properties can exist without other sets is largely a matter of contingent fact.

Once existent conscious states have been affirmed, it seems to be a matter of contingent fact whether they could exist without the physical states that are usually correlated with them. Perhaps the distinction between substance and property dualists is largely a verbal one—just another way of asserting, or denying, that some conscious states could exist without any physical states. And that does seem to be a question of fact that verbal definition alone cannot settle.

Both substance and property dualists agree that conscious events exist and are dependent upon the functioning of the brain. But there is something more to be said. In human experience, we do not seem to be just passive recipients of perceptions and thoughts. We seem to see, concentrate, attend, and think in an active way. This implies that conscious events—intentions and decisions—exercise a causal influence on physical events. Can events in consciousness exercise a causal influence upon the physical brain?

Much work in neuropsychology suggests that they can. I am not talking about highly disputed topics, such as telepathy or "psychic connections." I am thinking of the sort of evidence adduced by Malcolm Jeeves in his 2006 paper "Linking Mind and Brain." Research on Braille readers and other blind subjects revealed that habitual behavior has causal effects on the neural substrate of such activity (Sadato et al. 1996). The primary and secondary visual cortical areas of blind subjects were activated when the subjects performed tactile tasks. This is a case where it is not the physical events in the brain that cause experiences and activities, in a sort of one-way causal chain. It is a case where specific activities cause events in the brain that do not exist in normally sighted patients.

A brain-scan study of London taxi drivers (Maguire et al. 2000) revealed that the posterior hippocampi of taxi drivers were significantly larger than those of a non-taxi-driving control group. It seems that behavior and learning can cause local plastic changes in the structure of the adult human brain. That is, intelligent behavior can cause changes in brain structure.

It is not being claimed that there are some mystical or purely psychic causes of physical events. But it does seem that there is not simply a one-way causal path between brain and intelligent activity. Intelligent behavior can cause changes in brain structure and activity.

In the field of psychoneuroimmunology, there are many examples of changes in personal attitudes and in social situation giving rise to changes in cerebral and endocrine processes. The well-established placebo effect, by which a physically neutral drug improves health if the patient thinks it is going to do so, seems to show that beliefs can have physical effects. And it is fairly clear that resolving to adopt positive mental attitudes can have a marked positive influence on physical health. *The Handbook of Religion and Health* (Koenig et al. 2000) reviews two thousand published experiments designed to test the relation of religious beliefs to conditions such as heart disease, cancer, and depression. Most of these experiments suggest that there is a significant positive correlation between belief and longevity and health.

It may be, of course, that the brain causes both religious belief and good health. But the most natural view is that changes in social circumstances, in intelligent behavior, and in belief can produce effects on brain and body. Experimental work shows that conscious beliefs and practices supervene on behavior and responses to environment that do not need to possess a conscious element. But the available experiments also show that there is what is often called "top-down" causation, by which the brain is affected by a wider system of which it is a part. This includes not only the whole body in which the brain exists but also the field of social relationships and the environment within which bodies exist. Within these wider systems, thoughts, feelings, and intelligently directed behavior are not simply the effects of physical brain processes, working in a "bottom-up" way. They are conscious responses to the environment, and they can influence, to some degree, physical states of brain and body.

Nobel laureate Roger Sperry writes, "A mutual interaction between the neural and mental events is recognized: the brain physiology determines the mental effects, as generally agreed, but also the neuro-physiology, at the same time, is reciprocally governed by the higher subjective properties of the enveloping mental events" (cited in Gregory 1987, 164–65). For Sperry, consciousness is an irreducible working component in brain function—"the colorful and value rich world of inner experience, long excluded from the domain of science by behaviorist materialist doctrine, has been reinstated."

This whole area is highly controversial, and it is probably true to say that many neuroscientists tend toward a strictly materialist view, that minds are no more than brains. They would usually admit, however, that the "problem of consciousness" remains wholly unsolved, and it is not even very clear just what a solution would be, in purely physical terms. Very few have the confidence of Daniel Dennett, and that confidence has more the character of faith—commitment to a theory without overwhelming evidence because it seems to have practical benefits—than of verified theory.

Top-Down Causality

Those who hold views of the soul that originate in the Semitic traditions would not generally want to hold that the world of inner experience could exist entirely on its own, without any identifiable form of physical embodiment or context. But they would want to assert the possibility of different forms of embodiment and of a transfer of the inner experiences of a conscious being into differing environments (the "resurrection world").

So, it is important for them to believe that there really is an inner world of experience and that, in it, there originate morally significant causal intentions and acts that are not determined by physical states alone. The views of the neuropsychologists just outlined seem to support such a possibility. Such views, therefore, seem to rebut reductive physicalism—a physicalism that asserts that humans are "nothing but" physical organisms. There is a more subtle view, however, well propounded by Warren Brown (Brown, Murphy, and Malony 1998), what he calls "nonreductive physicalism." This, at first sight, seems to fit well with some Semitic beliefs about resurrection, but I doubt whether it is, in the end, helpful to call it a form of physicalism at all. According to this view, humans are purely physical beings, but thoughts, feelings, and perceptions are higher-level emergent properties of brains that have causal effects on the complex physical systems that are human beings. They are examples of what Warren Brown and Nancey Murphy, his coauthor, call "top-down causation."

Examples of top-down causation are extensive in biomedical and psychological literature. They include energy metabolism in mitochondria, by which a wider physical system governs or influences the processes that take place in intact cells; the production of three-dimensional information from two-dimensional images in visual perception; and the influence of working memory on the activity of neurons of the temporal lobe.

Warren Brown argues that there is no need to introduce any such entity as the soul, which he sees as an immaterial agent. Mental acts are causally influenced by neural systems to a very great extent. There is very little left, he says, for an allegedly immaterial "soul" to do. "The concept of a nonmaterial human 'soul' or 'spirit' as a causal force within the mental and behavioral life of a person is difficult to reconcile with what can be demonstrated scientifically about the impact of changes in brain systems on thought and behavior" (2004, 76). Nevertheless, he says, "conscious decisions and will are real phenomena that are effective in exerting a top-down (or whole–part) causal influence on the neurophysiological processes of the brain" (63). The patterns that emerge from complex physical systems have genuine causal powers. There are no new "entities" or physical forces involved, but there are new "levels of causal efficacy" (65).

The two beliefs—that there is not much causal work for a soul to do and that there are new causal powers in complex systems—are in some conflict with each other. It is incontestable that neural function is a necessary condition of mental activity in humans and that impairment of neural function leads to impairment of mental acitivity. But if there is any new causal efficacy in the brain, that is just what the soul is supposed to do. As long as there are consciously directed thoughts, deeply appreciated feelings, and attentive perceptions, there will be top-down causal activity. So, the objection that there is little for a soul to do seems very weak. The soul does precisely whatever higher mental functions do.

Still, it might be said, such functions make a soul superfluous. Why not just stick to top-down causality, and drop any talk of mental entities? But if you do that, what happens to "the colorful and value rich world of inner experience" of which Roger Sperry spoke? If it is not to disappear, and leave us with reductive materialism, we will have to say that there is more to physical entities than the publicly observable, colorless, value-free world of flickering subatomic particles of which physics speaks.

We might not want to call the colors, sounds, and smells we all subjectively experience "entities," as though they were objects in a shadow universe paralleling the physical universe. But they are appearances that are different from the world that is the causal object of their appearing. They are appearances of the world to consciousness, and consciousness itself is the way the world appears in immediate experience.

The problem with the whole–part model is that the whole must be composed of the same sort of stuff as the parts, however complex it gets. Sixty-five million colorless elementary particles, put together in a complex way, do not make up a single spot of color. They may, however, in a neocortex, cause the appearance of color and cause us to say that sixty-five million other particles that we are observing are colored in a certain way. The appearance of color is caused by complex causal processes, and it is the appearance of a complex causal process.

A tree looks green when observed by a human brain with functioning visual perceptual equipment. The green is not itself a complex brain system, which includes neurons as its smaller parts. So the whole–part model does not quite seem to fit. Rather, when one physical system causally interacts with another complex physical system, a green appearance of a tree comes into existence. The tree looks green; it is green when it interacts with a human brain and visual system.

We can identify the green with the physical tree, but only *as seen by* a human observer. In the same way, the brain looks gray, as seen by a human observer. When the brain undergoes neural activity, can we say that it thinks? Perhaps that is how its activity appears to the owner of the brain. But, again, this does not seem to be a case of a wider system influencing its smaller parts. If thoughts are appearances of neural events, it is rather that the thoughts are produced by neural events, and those thoughts sometimes cause the brain to be in some neural states rather than others.

The philosopher Jaegwon Kim (1994) has argued that once mental causality is admitted, physicalism has, in effect, been given up, and we have a dualist view of spirit and matter, no matter how much scientists dislike the thought. The question of causal efficacy is crucial. Are the only efficacious causal events physical, publicly observable, and measurable? If so, mental events are epiphenomena, with no real causal role. But if thinking can causally influence brain states, this is not a case of wider physical systems influencing smaller parts of themselves. It is a case of neural processes being influenced by states of consciousness. In other words, some sort of dualism seems inescapable. This is not really physicalism—the theory that nothing but physical entities exist—at all, even if it is called "nonreductive."

Religious and Scientific Views of the Person

Religions are not necessarily concerned with life after death—ancient Hebrew religion had very little concern with it. Most of the main religious traditions are concerned, however, with human liberation from egoism, hatred, greed, and ignorance, and access to a Supreme Reality of wisdom, compassion, and joy. This involves attention to and control of inner thoughts, feelings, and perceptions and, thus, a strong interest in states of consciousness—states the true nature of which may be hidden both from introspection and observation.

Most traditions have developed views of life after death in order to postulate a state in which egoism can be finally and fully overcome and access to the Supreme Good can be evident and immediate. The various models of Supreme Reality give rise to rather different models of an afterlife. They correspond to the five views of the human person outlined earlier in this chapter.

For the first three of these views (the no-self, the one-self, and the dualist view), consciousness and its contents have to be something that is capable of existence without the brain. Even for the fourth and fifth views (the spiritual-body and the replica-body views), it is doubtful

whether you should call a glorified brain that comes into existence perhaps thousands of years after the original brain has died exactly the same
brain. For the fifth view, it will be more like an improved replica of the
original brain. For the fourth view, it will not even be a replica since
it may take a wholly different form. So, all these major religious views
seem committed to the belief that human persons can continue to exist
in new and improved bodily forms (since the first three views usually
include belief in reincarnation). It is just a question of how new and how
improved they are.

These views assume that the thoughts and feelings of such persons
are not wholly causally dependent on brains, which are physical objects
governed by a specific set of space/time laws. There may be new brains,
but they and their laws must be rather different in an incorruptible
world. Thus, it becomes conceivable that thoughts and feelings could
exist without embodiment in this specific physical body. The connection
between a specific physical body and some consciousness has been loos-
ened. If the dependence of consciousness upon the brain is also thought
to be unnecessary, then it becomes conceivable that consciousness could
exist without any such physical dependence at all.

Perhaps thoughts and feelings could exist without being embodied
in any sort of physical world. Of course, if they did so exist, it is hard
to imagine how they would obtain new information, identify and communicate with one another, or perform actions. It looks as if they would
be stuck going over their old thoughts and feelings or doing boring stuff
(for most people) like pure mathematics. Interestingly, the Tibetan Book
of the Dead, which speaks of what happens immediately after death,
does precisely speak of a world of dream-like images, in which persons
work out the unresolved material left over by their embodied lives. But
this state does not continue forever, and it might eventually be unbear-
ably tedious if it did. Even then, however, the extreme dualist theory—
that ultimate liberation consists in an "isolated" state of omniscient and
unchanging bliss—might be a possibility.

But for religious adherents who think it important to preserve some
fairly strong sense of continuity with our present selves, extreme dualism
will not be wholly appealing. If there is to be any possibility of learning
new things or of communicating with others or of acting in new ways,
there will have to be something like a body to make the reception and
communication of information possible. It is for that reason that some
form of resurrection hypothesis is preferred by the Semitic faiths.

If some sort of double-aspect theory of the human person is accepted,
it becomes a question whether conscious states will exist in different
bodily forms or without any quasiphysical forms at all. Religious views

mostly affirm that understanding, feeling, thought, and sentience of some sort will exist without this body. But that is perfectly consistent with saying that such states and capacities in earthly life are completely correlated with states of the brains in which they are embedded.

For a believer in God, there is, in addition, one consideration that should exercise a major influence on the assessment of views of the human person. Believers in God seem to be committed to the possibility of at least one consciousness, that is, thought and intelligence, existing without a body. God has no body. And, however different and mysterious God is, it is at least more accurate to speak of God as knowing and acting than to say that God is unconscious and inert. So, theists seem bound to accept the idea that there can be conscious states without bodies. Buddhists also, who have no belief in God, believe that *nibbana* is a state of knowledge and compassion. For them, too, there is a desirable form of conscious existence that is not physical—though, like God, it far transcends anything that we can literally say about it.

Science cannot show that such views are false since science as we know it deals only with the physical—even neuropsychology deals only with reports of mental states or with neural or behavioral correlates of mental states and not with mental states themselves. Science can, I think, show that human consciousness, thought, and feeling develop with the development of the brain and can be impaired by brain damage. Human consciousness is brain-dependent, but there is a great deal of evidence to show that intelligent behavior and thought can exercise a causal influence on neural states.

Thus, it seems plausible to say that consciousness of some sort could exist without material embodiment, but it might be very unlike present human consciousness. Human consciousness is generated from and remains dependent upon a physical brain, though it can also influence neural states. The decay and death of the brain need not destroy consciousness, though it impairs the exercise of conscious abilities. Consciousness remains inert unless and until it finds a new form of embodiment that can reenable the exercise of its capacities. But such embodiments are possible—and if what religions say is right, some of them exist.

This implies a form of what Charles Taliaferro (1994) has called integrative dualism. Such dualism is not committed to the Cartesian thesis that nature is a machine or that mind is connected to body through the pineal gland. It is committed to the view that consciousness and its contents, though generated by the physical brain, are distinct kinds of existent entities and have causal influence upon some aspects of neural activity.

Because this whole topic is so highly disputed, it cannot be said that neuroscience or psychology, as such, dictates one particular view of the matter. But there is quite a lot of evidence that mental states and intelligent activity can causally affect the brain. Reductionist views can seem vastly counterintuitive, and nonreductionist physicalism does not really account for the apparently nonphysical nature of conscious content.

The soul is not a little (physical) man sitting inside the brain. But the human person seems to have a dual nature, having both a physically observable body and brain and a rich, colorful, value-laden inner world of experience and thought. These natures are tightly connected, and to separate them would be to leave this world in which we were born and in which we live. Most religious views think we can do this, precisely because the Ultimate Reality is a being or state of pure consciousness, and the goal of religious practice is to achieve union or perfected relationship with that Ultimate Reality.

Sophisticated religious views are wisely reticent about the exact form such union might take. The religiously important factors are that it should be in some intelligible causal relationship to the life lived on earth. It should enable persons to see their earthly life in the wider context of the divine knowledge and experience of all things. It should enable people to recognize and come to terms with the evil they have done and perhaps to find some way of making amends for it. And it should enable persons to grow further in knowledge and love of the Supreme Good, in ways impossible on earth. In these ways, religious belief is bound up with the possibility of achieving an ultimate goal beyond the death of the body.

I doubt whether science can have a definite view of such a possibility. Reductive physicalism would certainly rule it out. But a great deal of recent work in neuropsychology throws doubt on the truth of reductionism. My own view is that the most natural scientifically influenced position to take is that of integrative dualism. This would establish consciousness as an emergent reality that is logically but not (in this world) causally separable from a physical brain and body and that is capable of reembodiment. That would leave various religious claims about after-death existence as possibilities, to be assessed on other than scientific grounds—perhaps, ultimately, on experience of the objective reality of Supreme Goodness.

7. Is Science the Only Sure Path to Truth?

Religious Experience in the Semitic Traditions

IN MOST RELIGIONS, there is an important place for experience. In fact, if there were no distinctively religious experiences, it is doubtful if religions would exist.

Ninian Smart proposed a seven-dimensional analysis of religion (1997, 10–11). Most religions are distinctive in the experiences they favor and seek to sustain, in their myths or stories, in rituals, doctrines, ethical codes, social institutions, and material artifacts like temples or mosques. Different religions stress different dimensions, though most religions contain some elements in each dimension. Some religions do not place much emphasis on the occurrence of experiences and may even regard them with distrust if they lead to a questioning of orthodox beliefs. Yet it is rare to find the experiential dimension lacking entirely.

In Judaism, it is sometimes said that the most important dimension is that of keeping the Torah, or the moral and ritual tradition, and the cohesion of the community. Some Jews may be suspicious of undue introspection or of an exaggerated concern with one's own personal experiences. What matters is the community and the tradition.

Nevertheless, the community exists because it keeps the tradition and central to the tradition is belief that there is a creator God from whom the Torah derives and who, for the orthodox, gave the Torah to Moses. Moses is certainly said to have had distinctive visionary experiences. "The angel of the Lord appeared to him in a flame of fire out of a bush; he looked, and the bush was blazing, yet it was not consumed" (Ex. 3:2–3). God spoke to Moses out of the burning bush, and Moses hid his face, for he was afraid to look at God.

Many theophanies are recorded in the Hebrew Bible, and these are generally depicted as visions of a God who manifests and speaks. The content of revelation may consist of a set of laws (though it is not only that). But the laws are given through a prophet who sees and hears God. Whatever *seeing* and *hearing* amount to in these contexts, they seem to refer to direct apprehensions, analogous to or even mediated by means of sensory perceptions.

When personal experiences are distrusted in such traditions, it is because they may claim to contradict or supersede the original prophetic experience or because they may lead to an unhealthy concentration on some sort of emotionally powerful "peak experience" to the detriment of social and ethical commitments.

The prophet's vision of God and the prophet's mediation of God's message are taken to be absolutely normative, and nothing that threatens them can be encouraged. The stress in religion tends to be on authoritative experience, which mediates knowledge of God's being and will in a form with which all other alleged experiences must be consistent. The point is, perhaps, that adequate experience of God requires the fulfillment of specific conditions in the experient. The experient (in this case, the prophet) must be mentally well balanced, wise, morally pure, spiritually mature, and conversant with a set of concepts that are capable of conveying the nature of God with reasonable adequacy. It is because most people do not fulfill these conditions that the claims they might make about their experiences or the interpretation they may give to them are not necessarily to be trusted.

Christianity is quite reticent about Jesus' experience of the God whom he addressed as "Abba," Father. But Mark's Gospel recounts that, when Jesus was baptized, "He saw the heavens torn apart and the spirit descending like a dove on him. And a voice came from heaven, 'You are my Son, the Beloved; with you I am well pleased' (1:10–11). In John's Gospel, Jesus says, "I am in the Father and the Father is in me" (14:10). This is the strongest sense of personal union, and it is one in which the disciples can share: "I am in my Father, and you in me, and I in you" (14:20). But the disciples' experiences are always dependent upon and shaped by the primal union of Jesus and the Father, so again it depends upon a normative pattern established by one who was believed to be uniquely and consciously related to the Primal Reality.

The Prophet of Islam began his mission when he had a visionary experience in the cave, when he saw the archangel Gabriel and heard a voice calling him to recite the Qur'an. It seems that all the main Abrahamic faiths derive from the teachings of persons taken to have had a unique, intense, and direct visionary and auditory experience of God, an experience that gave them unique authority to proclaim the wisdom of God in their lives and teachings.

Even those Abrahamic traditions regarded as "heresies" by the orthodox, like Bah'ai, derive from the teachings of inspired prophets who claimed direct experience of God. It is misleading to separate "revelation" too sharply from "experience," as though revelation just consisted of words imparted to people who had no particular experience of God. The words may have authority. But that authority derives from the normative power of visionary experience of God and the unity with God such experience brings about, so that the prophet can become a living mouthpiece or even a human image of the eternal God.

It may seem like a problem that the authoritative experients—Moses, Jesus, and Muhammad—disagree with each other. They all claimed to apprehend one creator God of justice, mercy, and loving-kindness. But they provide differing accounts of what God wills and how to achieve it. This situation reinforces the point, which all traditions accept, that most religious experiences are fallible, and many are mistaken. That does not mean that they are not genuine experiences of God, but it does reflect the fallibility of most religious experiences and the great difficulty of deciding which, if any, are correctly described.

Religious Experience in Indian Traditions

The problem is considerably worse when Indian religious traditions are considered. There are a great many broadly theistic traditions in India, but all "orthodox" traditions accept the authority of the Vedas and Upanishads; in addition, different traditions look to teachers of wisdom who interpret those texts in various ways.

The Hindu scriptures are traditionally said to be learned from the gods by ancient sages. This is a form of verbal inspiration. As in the Abrahamic tradition, such inspiration is accompanied by an encounter with the gods by an enlightened sage. Such sages are often believed to be *avatara*, or personal embodiments, of a god. Thus, Sankara, founder of Advaita, the nondualist form of Hindu thought, is widely taken to be an embodiment of the god Siva. An avatar is omniscient and fully manifests the principle of divinity that is disguised or hidden in most humans. Followers of Advaita aim to realize the sense of union with the Divine themselves. In the modern form of Hinduism known as neo-Vedanta, the experience of nonduality becomes the main aim of religious practice, to which meditation leads.

Other forms of Hinduism, like Gaudiya Vaishnavism, are much more devotionally oriented. But Gaudiya Vaishnavism, too, aims at the experience of loving union with Krishna, an experience that the god fully realized with humans during his earthly embodiment. In these traditions, there is much disagreement about exactly how the object of religious experience is to be described, but there is an agreement that experience of a higher reality of intelligence and bliss is possible, that it has been achieved, even if rarely, and that it is achievable in principle by all, even if only in some future life.

Buddhist traditions reject any idea of union with an eternal Self or devotion to a Supreme God. But, if anything, they emphasize experience of higher states of human consciousness more than theistic traditions. When Siddartha Gautama achieved Enlightenment, it was after many years of ascetic practice, and it was an entrance into a higher state of consciousness. This experience is normative for disciples of the Buddha, but it is interpreted in very different ways by different Buddhist groups. In general, Theravada traditions concentrate on the practice of meditation, leading to nonattachment and a deep sense of inner peace that brings freedom from sorrow. Many Mahayana traditions, however, use texts like the Lotus Sutra that have been received in revelatory experiences from a living Buddha in a spiritual realm and have a more devotional approach to heavenly buddhas or boddhisattvas, those who are believed to have achieved Enlightenment.

There are many rules of practice for Buddhist monks, outlined in the *Vinaya*, or monastic discipline. But Buddhism is not primarily a system of social ethics. Its concern is with identifying and overcoming the causes of suffering by mental discipline. Rituals, systems of doctrine, and codes of ethics are primarily means to the achieving of a specific state of consciousness. In such schools of thought, experience becomes a primary goal of religious practice. But it might well be said that such experience is realistically pursued only by a rather small monastic elite. Most lay followers admire and encourage them but are themselves content with learning compassion and mindfulness in more mundane ways.

The Importance of Experience in Religion

Overall, it seems that distinctive forms of experience that may be termed *religious* are important to religion and that, without them, religions might not have come into existence. But there are many sorts and degrees of religious experience. At its most intense, a religious experience occurs only to a prophet or sage. Most religious believers may hope to have a vaguely similar sort of experience, to a lesser extent, or they may simply admire and trust the testimony of those who claim to have had it. Religious experiences in general are not inerrant, and adherents of each religious tradition are logically bound to think that most religious experiences (that is, experiences in the many traditions other than their own) will be described in ways that contain some errors of interpretation. All traditions are also painfully aware that the risk of deceit and deception, of mental imbalance and moral disorder, is always possible in human life. So, many religious experiences will be deluded, immoral, or unbalanced, and each tradition attempts to limit and counteract the influence of such experiences as much as possible.

In order to do this, most religious traditions contain revelations accepted as authoritative, and these can usually be traced back to some person believed to be in the best possible position to know the truth about Spiritual Reality. Being in that position involves possessing intellectual, moral, and positive mental qualities of a high order and being in an interpretative tradition that provides the possibility of a correct description of the experience. Only then will a claimed experience of such a person be accepted as a genuine insight into a higher divine reality.

Interpretative traditions differ quite widely, and religious experiences range from alleged encounters with a God or personal Spiritual Being to a sense of union with that which is Supremely Real or to entrance into a higher state of consciousness, free from suffering, greed, hatred, and delusion.

These types of experience are not quite as exclusive as may at first be thought. They share the sense of a higher reality of wisdom, compassion, and bliss. It is further descriptions of this reality as personal, as all-embracing, or as impersonal (we might say, though in an oversimple way, as God, *Brahman*, or *nibbana*) that produce divergences of interpretation. More differences arise when the descriptions get even more specific, detailing the precise "commands" of God or the characteristics of an enlightened being.

If this is the case, it suggests that religions may make a claim to access a higher spiritual reality in a number of different but not necessarily contradictory ways—by devotion, mystical union, or self-discipline, for example. The Ultimate Reality may be such that it has personal and impersonal, transcendent and immanent aspects. These can be taken as aspects of one rich reality, which can only be spoken of analogically in any case, rather than in complete and exclusive descriptions. However, religions then tend to congeal into competing traditions that claim sole possession of inerrant truth. At that point, either only one tradition can be correct, or they may all be correct in some points and incorrect in others (or, of course, they may all be incorrect on most important points).

Religious experience, the claim to apprehend a higher spiritual reality, thus seems to be essential to religion, though it is not an essential part of every believer's life. If all such claims are false or deluded, religion would seem to rest upon a mistake. In the world religions as a whole, the varieties of religious experience do not seem to present us with just a mass of total contradictions. Rather, the data look like a set of closely related and complementary claims at a general level, but that get complicated by doctrinal, ritual, and ethical differences that increase proportionally with increasingly detailed attempts to describe the precise character of the experienced reality and its relationship to ordinary human life and expectations.

Differing Interpretations of Experience

Do the sciences have anything to say about the possibility or genuineness of religious experiences? Religious experiences usually claim to be apprehensions of an Objective Reality. They are not just subjective feelings or purely mental phenomena. To that extent, they have the same basis as scientific claims, which are also founded on sensory experiences, apprehensions of an Objective Reality.

In science, however, there is a cumulative body of knowledge, agreed among all competent scientists, that can be experimentally confirmed. In religion, this is not the case. For that reason alone, some think that religious experience cannot provide reliable knowledge of any Objective Reality. So, we need to ask: can there be forms of experience the interpretation of which is not universally agreed upon and that are not experimentally confirmable and yet that give knowledge of Objective Reality?

I shall suggest that there are, that the scientific worldview is, in fact, largely an abstraction from ordinary lived experience, and that religious experiences form just one important subspecies of a large class of experiences that give rise to a body of nonscientific knowledge. In other words, science is not the only path to truth, though it is a necessary path to one sort of truth, truth about the publicly observable, mathematically measurable, law-like behavior of physical objects.

Many philosophers, from Thomas Aquinas to David Hume and Immanuel Kant, agree that all knowledge begins with experience. But they do not agree on just what "experience" is. And that is where we must begin.

Sensory experience presents us with visual, tactile, auditory, and olfactory data that are fused together into the apprehension of one experienced world in which we exist. But that world is experienced in many different ways. To some, it is a world of rich beauty and interest, while, to others, it is a boring and meaningless series of tedious impressions. Drugs like alcohol and cocaine are widely taken to alleviate the boredom of experience or to give an impression of greater significance and meaning to one's experience.

The world as we primarily experience it is not a value-neutral world of facts, to which we each have purely subjective reactions of pleasure and pain, liking and disliking. It is a world of beauty and ugliness, personal love and hate, promise and threat, security and danger. It is a world in which we are engaged as appreciative and creative or as indifferent and routinized, but always as involved, agents.

Existentialist writers, novelists, and poets, like Sartre, Camus, and Heidegger, have sought to capture the intricate texture of the lived world we inhabit, in which our personal integration of and response to experience gives a unique subjectivity to what Gerard Manley Hopkins called the "Inscape," the personal perspective from which we see and respond to our experienced world.

One of the things a scientific approach to the world does is to remove this rich texture of personal apprehension and response and construct a model of a depersonalized world of "pure objectivity," without purpose, passion, meaning, or value. This is not meant as a critical comment. It is simply an attempt to discern what science does to the richly interactive world of human experience in order to turn it into the value-neutral, publicly shared world of measurable, predictable processes with which the natural sciences deal.

The world of lived human experience is perhaps best expressed in literature, music, and art. In music, for example, an art without explicit cognitive content, we can enter a world of feeling that also speaks of different ways of being in the world. The sublime beauty of Mozart—the purity of line, the elegance of harmony, the freedom of spirit—speaks of a world other than our own, yet it shows that world in its most positive form, in a grace, formality, and decorum that mirror the limpid lucidity of the Newtonian modeling of nature as a beautiful machine and also the incisive rationality that was to be applied to human nature itself, dispelling the aristocratic traditions that had gone before. The darker side of the eighteenth century, the gross social inequality and the European colonization of the rest of the world, is hardly explicit here. That would come to some extent with Beethoven and the Romantics, whose music expressed the passions underlying the American and French revolutions and the rising concern with the "Rights of Man."

The point of this comment on the music of Mozart and Beethoven is to suggest that there are value- and feeling-filled apprehensions of reality that do give knowledge of what reality is like, but not in a dispassionately scientific way. My comment obviously expresses my own experience of and reflection upon their music. I can well imagine that someone else might regard this as a very superficial and perverse view, seeing significant connections where there is none, and interpreting the music in a very idiosyncratic way. But that is the nature of writing about music and about the arts in general. Disagreement is of the essence, and putting things in new and personal perspectives is what the appreciation of art is all about.

Are we to discount all this as just a matter of purely subjective taste? The music is, after all, just a sequence of vibrations or sound waves impacting the brain. Those, it may be said, are "the facts," and all the rest is reaction. The important thing to notice, I think, is that even this question can only be answered by a personal judgment, which we know will not be universally shared. If I say that the facts are "nothing but" sound waves and brain events and that all else is subjective reaction, I am going beyond experience itself and beginning to reflect upon how best to interpret it. Is the best interpretation to split experience up into bare facts and subjective reactions and to say that the facts belong to the objective world, whereas the reactions do not refer to anything in the objective world at all?

Must All Facts Be Publicly Observable?

This was the view of the logical positivists of the early twentieth century. The facts exist, and all values are purely matters of emotional response to them, of personal feelings of pleasure or pain, without objective significance. But logical positivism collapsed because it was such a very peculiar theory. For a start, what exactly were the facts for positivists? They were what David Hume had earlier called "sense impressions," and what the positivists called "sense data." But if these were the facts, did they exist when not being observed in an objective physical world? Apparently not. Colors, tastes, and smells, as they appear to us, do not even exist in the physical world. They are momentary phenomena. They appear, and then they are gone—though, luckily, we also have memory impressions, which are mostly very imperfect copies of what they were like.

So what is the physical world? Probably the best-known British positivist, A. J. Ayer, said that the physical world is a logical construct out of sensory data. We do not have direct access to the physical world. It is a sort of postulate, for correlating all our sensory data and those of other people, too, in ways we can understand. But what about those other people? Do they exist in the physical world? They can hardly exist in a purely logical construct. What we are left with is just sets of different sensory data. We have to postulate that other sets than our own actually exist, as well as postulating that a physical world exists. But we can never actually verify that either other minds or the physical world exists. We postulate them in order to make sense of our experience.

Perhaps we need not worry too much about the problems of positivism since it is extinct. But it is salutary to remember that, in the 1930s and for quite a few years, many people, including many professional philosophers, thought that it was the ultimate truth about what really exists. It is a salutary thought because, when we think we ourselves have found the ultimate truth about reality, we may do well to remember what happened to the positivists and ruefully confess that the same thing may well happen to us. We, and all our favorite ideas, may well become extinct—and sooner than we think.

There are two lessons to learn here. First, we must be duly cautious about making claims to ultimate truth—that is equally true for religious believers and for nonbelievers alike. Since almost everyone else has been wrong so far, we should not be too confident that we are right. Second, it is not possible to escape disagreement. People see the world very differently because they put different personal interpretations on it. Even when we agree that all knowledge begins with experience, we cannot agree on what exactly experience is. For the positivists, it was value-neutral sensory and memory impressions. For existentialist philosophers and phenomenologists, experience, before we get to work interpreting and analyzing it, is a much more complex, fuzzy, holistic, and value-laden affair. Splitting it up into objective facts and subjective reactions is already an interpretation. For are objects not really beautiful, or elegant, or threatening? Do our feelings not reveal to us something about the character of reality? Do they not have a cognitive dimension?

Of course, the reality we perceive does not exist, *as we perceive it*, when we are not perceiving it. But, then, the allegedly neutral fact—the redness of a rose, for example—does not exist as we perceive it, either, when we are not perceiving it. Its redness, we may say, is contributed by the mind in response to the impact of an objective physical aspect of reality upon us. Why should its beauty not also be contributed by the mind in response to the impact upon us of a nonphysical aspect of objective reality?

Well, it may be said, because there are no nonphysical facts. Beauty is not objective. Well, neither is color. At least color is caused by objective physical properties. Now we approach the heart of the problem. Are all objective properties physical? Might there not be properties of beauty, of elegance, of intelligibility, and of goodness? If the idea sounds strange, it may be because we have been indoctrinated by the dogma that all facts must be physical and value-neutral. But what is the status of that dogma? Can it be verified? It cannot. It seems to be what the philosopher Alvin Plantinga (1983) calls a "basic" belief, one that is not founded on evidence or more basic axioms. How could you justify or refute an assertion that "all facts are physical and value-neutral"? Perhaps you could refute it by coming up with some facts that are not physical—like God, for instance, or facts about mathematical truths or about beauty and goodness or about the nonphysical contents of other minds. But every time you try to do that, you will probably be met with the reply that they are not really facts. The phrase for that tactic is *winning by definition*. Well, it may be said, to be a fact something must be observable. But beauty and elegance are observable, mathematical truths are discerned to be the case, and God has been apprehended, at least by Moses, Jesus, and Muhammad.

Ah, yes, but real facts must be publicly observable and agreed on by everybody. The irony is that it is doubtful whether even natural scientists would reach a consensus on that statement any longer. Superstrings, for example, are not publicly observable, probability waves for electrons are not publicly observable, and superposed particle quantum states are not publicly observable. Nor are these theories agreed on even by all competent scientists. There are major disputes about the objective reality of probability waves, about superstrings, and about how to interpret quantum events. So, even modern science no longer insists upon public observability and universal agreement as conditions for attributing actuality to things.

With logical positivism, the situation was even worse. Not only did positivists not require that all events must be publicly observable, but they actually denied that any events were publicly observable or that we could possibly observe any other minds that might be publicly observing anything. The much-cited "verification principle" was not a principle of public verification at all. It was a principle by which I could observe some state of affairs by having one or more sensory data (See Ayer 1936). Since I cannot ever have sensory data of what is going on in other minds, I cannot ever verify that other minds exist, and so I certainly cannot appeal to them to verify some state of affairs. It looks as if the requirement that all factual claims must be publicly observable, testable, and agreed on by all is looking rather shaky.

The Worlds of Science and of Common Sense

The possibility of public verification is, of course, important to the natural sciences. However unobservable superstrings may be, the theory that applies to them is ultimately based on observations made in particle accelerators. The mathematical and theoretical element is pronounced in such theories, but it is generated from observations that have been carefully tested. Modern science really began when experiments were devised in order to observe what happens to objects in controlled conditions, hypotheses were proposed to account for such happenings, mathematical techniques were created to formalize the results, and repeated testing of those results established (or refuted) the hypotheses.

This methodology was extremely fruitful. It assumed that physical objects could be experimentally controlled, that their relevant properties (like mass, position, and velocity) could be isolated and measured, that they always acted in accordance with precisely stateable laws, and that they would always be observed, by any competent observer, to act in the same way under the same circumstances.

These assumptions were triumphantly vindicated. Science works. But they require a systematic abstraction from directly apprehended, common-sense experience. Instead of the holistic, *gestalt* character of everyday experience, phenomena were treated atomistically, as sets of isolatable particles. Instead of the temporal flow of experience, space and time were treated as abstract and, in Newtonian science, absolute person- and time-indifferent containers of events. Instead of the felt experiences of delight and revulsion, admiration and resentment, atoms in space obeyed impersonal laws of motion without consciousness or feeling.

In modern physics, the "objective world" has moved even further away from ordinary experience. Space/time is now curved and multi-dimensional. Elementary particles have become wave particle processes in Hilbert space. The basic laws of quantum physics have become extremely complex sets of equations that only postgraduate mathematicians can understand. And the real nature of whatever underlies Schrödinger equations and Heisenberg uncertainty relations has become completely unimaginable—less solid, atomistic, and predictable, more complex and entangled than Newtonian physics ever envisioned.

Few scientists question that there is an objectively real world and that scientific investigation reveals its nature with much success. But if the foundation of all knowledge is experience, there is a major problem about how very different the world of which science speaks is from the lived world of everyday experience. Some very tough-minded scientists (or theorists about science) assert that the real world is the world of science, even though that world, in quantum physics, has become extremely paradoxical and difficult to understand. The "experienced world" of flowing time, holistic experience, love and hate, freedom and resentment is an illusion of consciousness—which is itself an illusion of the brain.

But that is hardly a finding of science. There are no experiments to verify it and no way of gaining universal agreement about it. It is precisely an interpretation, a personal perspective, on the world. It is an interpretation that values science highly, that likes to deal in questions where agreement can, in principle, be obtained, that puts aside passion and political or religious intrigue, and that avoids like the plague what Freud called "the black tide of mud," by which he meant religion and superstition (quoted in Jung 1963, 173). Or, as Daniel Dennett said, "Dualism must be avoided at all costs" (1992, 37).

What is motivating this perspective is a deep hatred of the irrational and a strong commitment to "reason"—where reason is conceived as a proportioning of belief to evidence and where evidence is conceived as publicly available sensory data testable by experimental methods of controlled, measurable, and repeatable observations.

These may not, however, be very good definitions of either reason or evidence. Reason may involve a great deal more than letting all your beliefs be based on evidence, and evidence may include a great deal more than publicly checkable sensory data.

Is Science Value-Free?

Unfortunately, the tough-minded scientific perspective, like all perspectives, has a negative side that its proponents do not always see. In its concern to render all respectable knowledge value-free, it removes virtually all historical, political, ethical, aesthetic, personal, legal, and philosophical topics from the area of knowledge and deposits them in the dustbin of personal opinion or even of illusion.

For anyone concerned with human values, value-free science is something to fear. Science without values has the capacity, as religion by itself does not, of destroying the world, of building bigger and better bombs, of inflicting more inventive forms of cruelty on animals and humans in experimental technology, and even of rejecting the search for truth itself in favor of technical mastery and power.

If you say that science should not do that or that science at its best does not do that, you are importing values into science after all. You are saying that truth is a value that should be pursued, even if it is uncomfortable and unsatisfying. Compassion is a value, and modern science has usually been driven by a desire to improve the world and the lives of human beings within it. In recent years, we have come to see that science has a responsibility to save the world and to preserve its beauty and the diversity of life and landscape.

So, science should be driven by values: the values of truth, compassion, and responsibility. And it should also be committed to discovering values: the values of the intellectual beauty and rational intelligibility

of nature. But those statements, though they are of tremendous importance, are neither publicly verifiable by any scientific experiment nor
universally agreed on. They are not statements of science. They are statements of value that are embedded in the practice of "good" science (but
not, regrettably, of all science).

From the perspective of tough-minded science, such value statements are just matters of personal opinion or decision. They are not
true (though they are not false, either), and we cannot perceive their
truth by perceiving the world truly.

A different perspective would be that, if we see the intelligibility of
the laws of nature truly, if we see human and animal pain and happiness truly, if we see the fragile beauty of the earth truly, then those facts
will exercise a compelling attraction upon all those who are sensitive and
open to what their experience shows them. The facts themselves carry
intimations of transcendent and commanding value.

When such a sense is lost, science can become a mere means to exploi-
tation and greed, indifferent to the happiness of other creatures (since
happiness is, after all, a wholly subjective matter) and indifferent to the
fate of future generations. It has happened to many scientists, most notably in societies like Nazi Germany and communist Russia, and it can
easily happen again.

It is, thus, vitally important that scientists should have a disinterested
concern for truth, strong compassion for all sentient beings, and a sense
of responsibility for the welfare of the planet. Some scientists complain
that religion has no such concern, compassion, or responsibility. This is a
crude judgment, and we might just as easily complain that a purely tech-
nological and truly value-free science has no such concern either. What
should be said is that both religion and science need to be moderated by
morality, by the perception of value in experience.

What most major religions assert is that there is an absolute truth
(though we do not know with certainty what that is), that suffering is to
be overcome wherever possible, and that human, or even all, life should
flourish, for there is an Ultimate Reality that is the truth and that wills
the happiness and flourishing of all beings. Humans apprehend that reality in the sense of moral obligation, of being encountered by moral ideals
that demand our loyalty and commitment.

Those who are not religious would not put it like that. They may well
complain that the will of such an Ultimate Reality for the happiness
of all is not very evident or effective on this planet, so they may find
the hypothesis of a compassionate Ultimate Reality implausible. Nevertheless, they may still respond to the appeal of truth, compassion, and
stewardship, of beauty and intelligibility as supreme values, not rooted

in any transcendent personal Being but standing alone as worthy goals of human endeavor.

Such a response would not be religious, for it would not claim apprehension of any suprahuman and nonphysical realities or states. But it would be analogous to religious apprehension. For some, it is a form of experience of objective (not just invented) value, though what it would call for would be moral commitment, not prayer, worship, or meditation.

Value, Faith, and Science

What I am suggesting is that there are objective values—values that hold for everyone and that are more than matters of personal choice and opinion—that can be apprehended in and through ordinary experience. Their apprehension depends upon the development of an initial sensitivity, and the precise way in which they are seen and interpreted depends upon the deepest attitudes and beliefs of those who claim to apprehend them.

The tough-minded scientist will reject all such talk. There is nothing, such a scientist will say, to apprehend. There is only our own decision and the purpose we create for ourselves. Yet such a belief, too, is not verifiable or universally agreed. It is not a belief that forms part of any natural science. There is no demonstration of it that has been published in any peer-reviewed scientific journal. Yet it is a factual belief, a belief about what sorts of things are, or can be, facts, about what sorts of things there are.

At least one thing, then, has been established. Not all factual beliefs are scientific beliefs. Not all can be publicly verified or verified at all. Not all are universally agreed on. The statement, "There are no objective values, values that would exist independently of human beings" is a statement of (alleged) fact that is not subject to any scientific or public method of verification. Yet it is either true or false, and our decision about that may, in some cases, have very dramatic practical consequences.

You may reject the objectivity of the value of truth and yet commit your life to a search for truth. You may also theoretically accept the objectivity of the value of truth and never bother to do anything about it. Human beings are extremely irritating and irrational. But it would certainly be reasonable, if you thought there was an objective obligation to seek the truth about the universe, to do so with as little self-interest as possible.

Whatever their theoretical beliefs about the objectivity of values (and most practicing scientists perhaps have no explicit theoretical beliefs on the subject), the best scientists have been driven by a passion for truth at whatever cost. They have also been driven by a passion for beauty, for intellectual elegance, and for understanding. The equations of science may seem cool, purely rational, and without feeling. But great scientists are people driven by passion for truth, intelligibility, and understanding. It would not be too much to say that they are people of faith—faith, often despite the evidence and against all odds, that the world will yield up its secrets to patient investigation and that it will prove to be comprehensible as a fully intelligible reality, accessible to the human mind at its best.

What can justify the scientists' faith that there is no event without a cause or at least without a good explanation? What can justify the faith that the laws of nature will operate in the future as they have in the past? What can justify the belief that human reason is adequate to understand the structure of reality? As the Cambridge quantum physicist Paul Dirac said, "It was a sort of act of faith with us that any equations which describe fundamental laws of Nature must have great mathematical beauty in them" (quoted in Longair 1984, 7).

Not all scientists may have a strong faith in these propositions, but they must, nevertheless, act as though they were true. They must, that is, have practical faith, a commitment that often goes well beyond the evidence, a passion for truth and understanding that will not be undermined by repeated failure. Is this so very different from the passion of the religious believer that a different sort of truth can be found and understood, even though the way to it sometimes seems almost impossibly difficult and littered with the failures of past attempts?

"There is no different sort of truth," an atheistic scientist may say. "There is only our sort of truth, the sort that our discipline alone can discover." But that is precisely what is in question. The scientist is driven by passion—science is not, after all, value-free. And an assertion of the sole sovereignty of scientifically ascertainable truth is not itself a statement of science. The possibility exists that there may be a legitimate and admirable passion for a sort of truth that is not establishable by the methods of scientific inquiry.

Some Facts That Are Not Scientific— The Case of History

There are a great many factual claims that could not possibly be established by scientific methods. Some of them have been mentioned: most obviously, there is the claim that there are no facts that cannot be discovered by science. In order to test that claim, we first have to get some definition of science. This is subject to much debate, but the main characteristics of natural science are that its data are publicly observable, measurable, repeatable, and agreed on by all competent observers. The question, then, is: are there any data that are not publicly observable, measurable, repeatable, and agreed on by all competent observers?

What we need to do is to undertake a thought experiment (not a real, physical, scientific experiment) to see if we can think of any such data. This brings to light a function of reason that is not just an apportioning of belief to the evidence. For what we are asking is whether there is any evidence that does not count as scientific evidence. We think rationally about this question when we try to assemble all relevant information, classify and analyze it, discern patterns of similarity or difference within it, and possibly achieve an integrated, plausible, and coherent general interpretation of it.

This is an exercise not of experimentation but of rational inquiry. Reason addresses the data of experience, seeking comprehensiveness, consistency, coherence with other knowledge, elegance of classification, and awareness of all the implications of a proposed interpretation. It is more like pure mathematics than it is like experimental, natural science. One of the questions reason will ask is whether it is acceptable always to apportion belief to the empirically establishable evidence. Another is whether all forms of evidence have to be establishable by scientific, observational, and experimental, methods.

In pointing to the passion for truth and the faith in intelligibility that mark good science, we have seen that it can be reasonable and admirable to hold a passionate and morally grounded belief that goes well beyond the available evidence. And we have already discovered a question that cannot be answered by the methods of experimental science, no matter how long and complicated: "Are there any questions scientific methods cannot answer?"

But it might still be insisted that these points are about moral values and about matters of verbal definition. They are not really questions about facts. Are there any obviously factual matters that science cannot establish?

Consider some facts from past human history. Caesar crossed the Rubicon. That is either true or false; it is a historical fact (or a claim about one). Is it publicly measurable or repeatable? Obviously not. Is it agreed by all competent historians? It may be; but many historical claims are not agreed on, and there is no way in which universal agreement could be guaranteed. If we have read more than one history book, we should be aware that historians disagree continually. They are always providing new interpretations of past events and arguing about whether ancient historical records are legendary or strictly factual. Is it publicly observable? Obviously not; all we have are historical records; we can never gain access to the facts themselves.

This does not make us give up the attempt to understand history or deny that the past ever existed. It makes us aware that few historical judgments are absolutely certain or established beyond reasonable doubt. There is a truth to be known, but we will never have direct access to it and must be content with interpretations that will inevitably express our own preferences, beliefs, and inclinations. And we know that universal agreement will never be achieved.

To be a historical perspectivalist is to say that the facts of history will always be interpreted from a particular perspective and that such perspectives will probably always differ in ways that can never finally be resolved. But that does not make us doubt that historical truth exists. It might make us aware of the theoretical uncertainty of our perspective and of the usefulness of knowing about other perspectives that may be strong where ours is weak. But it will probably not make us give up our perspective or lapse into a complete agnosticism.

Sometimes, indeed, past facts are of immense practical importance—for instance, where a large sum of money belongs to someone only if it were bequeathed to him or her in the past. In a matter of great practical consequences, we might strive for one interpretation of history with all the passion at our disposal, with a passion that far exceeds a strictly neutral survey of the available evidence. It would be silly to say that we must always apportion our belief to the evidence. If we are lawyers, it may be our duty to argue a case strongly and to make the evidence conform to our committed view. This is not generally taken to be hypocrisy, much less irrationality. It is a practical commitment in the face of strictly objective uncertainty, in a case where we genuinely believe the facts are in our favor but where that is not beyond all reasonable doubt.

History suggests, then, that there are facts that are not publicly accessible or verifiable, measurable or testable, or susceptible to universal agreement. The evidence for such facts is often objectively less than certain, but it is often reasonable to believe more strongly than the available evidence strictly allows, if there is a great amount at stake, if we genuinely believe that the facts are as we judge them to be, and if there is no way of avoiding the issue.

These are the factors William James mentions in his famous essay, "The Will to Believe," first published 1896 (see Burkhardt, Bowers, and Skrupskelis 1978). If a belief is forced (you cannot avoid it), vital (of great practical import), and living (a realistic and plausible option), then, James suggests, it is rational to commit yourself to it even with less than overwhelming evidence. That seems to me to do no more than reflect the practice of good scientists when they believe that "there is no event without a cause," "there are universal laws of nature," or "the universe is comprehensible and mathematically intelligible." We admire the tenacity of Einstein who refused to give up belief in determinism in the face of Heisenberg's uncertainty principle. We may even admire Daniel Dennett's determination to avoid dualism at all costs or Richard Dawkins' refusal to read books of theology because he already knows they are rubbish. Much will depend upon our own perspective. What is certain is that there are few people who can live in the real world refraining from believing anything unless they have theoretically sufficient evidence for it. Human life is too short for that.

There are certainly facts of history. But they cannot be established scientifically, and they can rarely be established at all with theoretical certainty. There is much evidence for some historical facts, but, for many others, there is very little evidence, and narratives have to be filled in by what we think, on other grounds, is likely and by an imaginative patterning of the past shaped by our own experience of the present, adjusted as well as we can for cultural differences.

Facts about Human Motives and Goals

But at least, as positivists used to say, historical facts are observable in principle. They could have been observed publicly and checked if any scientists had been there to do so, even if they are beyond checking now. They might not be scientific facts, but at least they are the sort of facts that could have been observed.

However, history is rather more complicated than that. Many of the most interesting histories deal not just with observable events but with the motives, intentions, purposes, beliefs, feelings, and ideals of people. Are such things observable? In a way they are—we know what someone's motives or beliefs are by observing how he or she behaves. But there will almost always be disagreement about such matters, however much behavioral observation we undertake. We have to interpret observed behavior in terms of motives assumed to be in play. But can we be sure what those motives really are?

Behaviorists used to say that human agents are not in the best position to say what their own motives are. That is true. But neither are behavioral psychologists in a better position to say what an agent's motives are. The real driving forces and goals of human action may remain concealed to agent and observer alike. As Kant remarked, I can never be sure that I am really acting out of a sense of duty, that I am not deceiving myself. I simply have to do my best to try to act without self-deception and hope that I am succeeding. But if I ask the questions, "How far am I truly responsible for my actions? How far am I morally free to set my own goals, and how far are my actions due to dispositions I cannot really change?," neither introspection nor the most minute study of behavior will answer those questions definitively.

Kant concluded that I must assume that I am free, though I can never prove it—this is a practical commitment that must be total but that cannot be conclusively established on the basis of empirical evidence. For Kant, the assumption of freedom is a condition of the possibility of moral action, of acting on moral principles. But the assumption also rests on common-sense experience. I feel that I am free and am the cause of many of my bodily actions. But determinists will say that is an illusion, and how could I refute that? My evidence is just that this is how it seems to me—and that a whole set of beliefs about praise and blame, just rewards and punishments would collapse if how it seems were not the case.

Determined determinists can bring lots of evidence for the all-encompassing rule of physical causality. But they are nowhere near showing that all my seemingly free acts are actually caused by deterministic brain events. There is some evidence, but it is far from sufficient for such a conclusion, and it never amounts to a rigorous and exhaustive causal breakdown into purely physical components of specific, free, and responsible human acts.

These are cases in which there is a true view—either humans are sometimes free, fully responsible, and able to set their own goals (nonphysically determined), or they are not; either they have specific motives, or they do not. But it is impossible to establish a view with certainty. The claim is not that nobody knows my motives and goals but me: the claim is that nobody, not even I, can know all my motives and goals with certainty. These are facts of the matter. They are not establishable. But we often have to commit ourselves to one view or another on the basis of ambiguous and theoretically insufficient evidence.

Truth in Art

There are other cases, however, where I can normally be sure of facts that are not publicly accessible. An example would be the fact of what, precisely, I am now thinking (but not writing down) or of what I am now feeling. Such facts, mental facts, may or may not be known with certainty by me, and they may or may not be identical with some of my brain states; but I know what they are in a way that no one else can, unless I tell them. Thus, there are thousands of facts that are not physically observable, and the evidence for them is just my own experience, unverifiable by anyone else. They are even unverifiable by me because, once an experience has passed, I can never have any other experience that will verify that it actually occurred as I think it did. But that does not stop me from claiming that I have had many experiences.

Such facts often cannot easily be described. But in art, music, and literature, they can sometimes be not so much described as expressed. Music, for example, expresses attitudes and moods. It communicates emotional depth and feeling, a certain "felt apprehension" of the world. What it communicates are not publicly perceived facts in the physical world but what might be called "facts disclosed by feeling," ways in which the world is felt and responded to emotionally. Such personal apprehensions of the world do disclose aspects of what is seen. But the "seeing" is not a simple, universally shared perception. It involves creative imagination that is valued precisely for its personal uniqueness. It involves rare creative skill to express what is felt in a distinctive and original way. What is expressed is a unique feeling response to the world, and the expression requires a high degree of creative excellence. A distinctively personal and unique sensitivity and active creative power are required to produce a work of art that may express factors of perceived meaning and value in the experienced world with which the sciences do not deal.

The arts express not how the world is apart from all conscious apprehension but how it is when it is perceived and felt in a uniquely individual way. If I am a good creative artist, I may skillfully express what it is like to feel and be in the world as I am, with my mode of consciousness. Does this tell us anything about the world? It expresses how the world is for a particular consciousness. This can tell us something about the human condition, in its pain and happiness, its egoism and altruism, its melancholy and compassion.

One of the attractions of good literature is that it may convey to us ways of seeing the world, of living in it and experiencing it, that are quite new to us. No one disputes that we live in a shared world, but we see it so differently that the whole quality of our experience can be distinct. There is, thus, a sense in which we inhabit different worlds, carved out of differing aspects of our shared world, and those differences are in part a consequence of how we see the world, of what we ourselves are, and of how we actively interact with the world.

The arts can disclose aspects of reality, but those aspects are not publicly accessible, measurable, law-like, or predictable. Art expresses thoughts and feelings that disclose how reality is personally experienced. It, thus, expresses a rich inner world of meanings and values and also expresses aspects of the objective world that are only cognizable by means of such an intensely personal approach.

Is there a truthfulness in art? There may be truthfulness to the tragedy and hope, the ambiguity and significance, of the human situation. Art may show us how to respond deeply, though the facts of which it speaks are facts as they are revealed to humans who approach them sensitively and creatively. The moral lessons art may teach are not usually didactic. They present their distinctive viewpoints and leave us to respond. But some works of art may change our lives, as we feel that they present the possibility of more penetrating perceptions and more fulfilling ways of being. Such perceptions remain individual and always diverse. They are always a matter of personal discernment, judgment, and decision. This is the richness, diversity, and uniqueness of personal life, that life with which the humanities deal and which the natural sciences rigorously and in principle eschew.

Art at its best communicates—it expresses what it is like to be a unique personal and creative agent and what the world is like for such an agent. It can arouse in the observer an empathy for, a felt understanding of, that way of seeing and being in reality. We take observed sounds or marks or colors as expressions of ways of understanding other than our own and of aspects of reality that can only be apprehended by adopting such ways of understanding and feeling. Those expressions have the function of evoking in us, if we are attuned to discern them, a mode of consciousness and an apprehension of reality that can enlarge and deepen our own way of being in the world.

Though this is not religion, the parallel with the religious sensibility—the interpretation of phenomena as expressions of a Transcendent Reality that can only be apprehended through the adoption of a specific mode of feeling and consciousness—is clear. That is why, though art is certainly not all religious, there is, nevertheless, a deep affinity between the intensely personal apprehension of meaning and value in art and the personal apprehension of transcendent meaning and value that is characteristic of religion.

Science and the Humanities and Social Sciences

To all this, tough-minded scientists, if they are still there, will say that art is not about truth at all. It is an expression of personal taste, and it only confuses the issue to speak of such mystical-sounding things as expressions, evocations, perspectives, and feelings. Such things are for softies, aesthetes, and the scientifically illiterate. There is only one truth, one way in which things are. The human mind is weak and prone to delusion, so coming to know the truth is difficult. Science offers the only sure route to truth because it observes closely and repeatedly, tests out many possible explanations, and checks with others for agreement. It guards against hasty or ill-considered judgments. It is based on tested, carefully checked evidence. It has the best and only chance of saying how things are.

This is one idealized view of science. But there is another. Scientists may not be white-coated technicians dispassionately dealing with facts discerned by their laboratory equipment. They may be poets of the universe, "voyaging through strange seas of thought, alone" (as Wordsworth said of Newton), awestruck by the intellectual beauty of nature, passionate to understand its integrated complexity, creatively inventing new modes of explanation and new ways of investigating the natural world. Perhaps the creation of "the scientific world" is itself a work of art, of creative imagination. In that case, science is shot through with value and creativity. Truth and compassion, beauty and intelligibility, the patient struggle against prejudice and irrationality are its hallmarks. Its martyrs are those, like Marie Curie and Rosalind Franklin, who have given their lives in the search for truth. Its prophets are those, like Isaac Newton, Albert Einstein, and Charles Darwin, who have revolutionized human thought by the brilliance and originality of their insights.

It is, therefore, deeply misleading to separate science from the humanities and social sciences altogether, as if science were concerned only with dispassionate evidence and reason, whereas the humanities were concerned only with imaginative fantasy and subjective feeling. What is needed is a more integrated view of human knowledge in its total range, fascinated both by the regularities of the physical and by the uniqueness of the personal.

The humanities and social sciences take as their object of study the personal world of culture and history, of language and art, of political and economic activity. The natural sciences study the impersonal world of particles, atoms, elements, cells, brains, and universes. These are aspects of the same world, but one studies beliefs, purposes, feelings, and values, as expressed in languages, social institutions, and artifacts, while the other studies mathematical relations and the laws and structures of physical objects. In the human person, both aspects are integrated, the life of the body and the life of the mind being entangled and closely interwoven.

This difference in the aspects of reality that are studied brings with it a difference in methodology. Passionate curiosity, imaginative invention, and the search for understanding are common. But ideas have no physical structure; there is no way to measure them in quantitative terms; they follow no pattern of predictable regularity. The world of the humanities is the world of meanings, and meanings have to be understood by an effort of empathetic imagination, by learning to interpret experience as others do.

As the work of the philosopher Ludwig Wittgenstein helped to make clear, the world of meanings is not purely inward, individual, and private. Persons learn to think in a social context. Their inner lives are molded by their language, and we learn how others see things by coming to understand their language or by appreciating the nonlinguistic expressions of meaning in their art and social institutions. So, meanings are not completely hidden from view inside the minds of others. They are socially expressed and communicated.

Nevertheless, understanding a meaning is an intellectual skill different from the skill of a scientist who investigates the pattern of atoms in a molecule. Scientists need careful and technologically enhanced observation, experimental control of the object they study, and the capacity to repeat their observations. Humanists need to interpret visual or oral data as *communications*, as conveying imaginative visions and ideas. In this area, what you see is always a function of what you are. You have to learn to see things in a new way, even if you disagree with what is being expressed. Thus, you have to enter into a dialogue between how you see things and other ways of seeing. That dialogue may be fruitful or frustrating. It may enlarge your understanding or reinforce your prejudices.

There is no neutral, value-free access to the life of other minds and cultures. Social anthropologists try to be as dispassionate as possible, but they know there will always be a critical difference between one who naturally belongs to another cultural tradition and one who merely reports it, however accurately. They know that different anthropologists report the same data in very different ways, for interpretation and personal understanding are inevitably from a personal perspective. That perspective may be changed by interaction with another, but it will never simply be eliminated.

So, scholars in the humanities and social sciences expect diversity of interpretation. Indeed, they look for it as a way to counter their own limitations, and to offer new forms of insight. But that does not prevent them from developing commitment to their own personal view, and arguing for it as the most adequate view. For understandings of the world, like languages, are always fluid and changing and exhibit both a loyalty to their own history and tradition and a concern to embrace a more global perspective.

Perhaps the greatest lesson scholarship in the humanities and social sciences can teach is that historical change and human diversity are ineliminable aspects of the study of human beliefs. To place ideas in their cultural context and to be able to give the history of their development are to understand them better. Nevertheless, the question of rationality and truth is not lost in the admission of diversity and development. Rationality is expressed in the concern to place ideas in a perspicacious and intelligible pattern, systematically set out so that their logical relationships can be clearly seen. Truth is neither just what anybody thinks it is ("it's true for me") nor a matter of clear propositions picturing clear states of affairs in the world. Truth lies in a relation between concepts and reality, and the nature of that relation depends on the concepts available to a given culture and on the extent to which reality can be depicted accurately in such concepts.

It is possible that human language is inadequate to provide a comprehensive and fully adequate description of reality. Why should the world fit our concepts exactly? Concepts divide up the world, classify it, and systematize it in specific ways. One of the miracles of science is that the language of mathematics does seem to depict and illuminate the nature of the physical world—as Eugene Wigner put it, "The appropriateness of the language of mathematics for the formulation of the laws of physics is a wonderful gift which we neither understand nor deserve" (1960, 14). But the more beautiful and elegant the mathematics becomes—in quantum theory, for example—the less we are able to picture what the world it depicts is like or even whether it is depicting a real world at all.

Ordinary language more or less fits the trees and people and rocks we tend to bump into in everyday life. Mathematical language gives insight into the ultimate, but unpicturable, nature of the material world, the world of matter and beyond. But what other aspects of the world might there not be, and what different uses of language might we not need to depict them?

There is no reason that truth should consist only in the conclusive public verification of some precisely formulated statement in a human language. There are certainly some truths like that—the truth that there are forty-six chromosomes in the normal human genome is a good example. It is unambiguous and precise, and the statement corresponds to the facts. But truths about personal life are about a richly entangled, rarely fully explicit, constantly evolving, creatively interpreted set of thoughts and feelings. The language we have for expressing or describing such a life is limited and crude. We can hardly ever get a precise, unambiguous statement that corresponds to a mental fact, much less one that all of us could verify for ourselves. So, truth is much more a matter of degree, of metaphors that produce insight, if taken in the right way, of a more-or-less appropriateness.

There is, no doubt, only one way in which things are. But our language may not be able to state that precisely. Concepts may sketch it in a rough outline, with more-or-less adequacy and in rather different, even apparently conflicting, ways, if taken too literally. To gain a truly comprehensive and adequate view requires wisdom and sensitivity, and, given our human situation of vast ignorance and corruption of desire and will, hardly any one will manage to do it. Most of us will continue to live in a world of conceptual antagonisms, overemphasized inadequacies, and oversimple keys to understanding. The best we can do is to make of this situation a dialectic to enable wider understanding. The worst is to dismiss the views of others as ridiculous, being blind to the limitations of our own.

Religion between the Sciences and the Humanities and Social Sciences

This brings us back to the topic of religious experiences. In the life of religion, such experiences were seen to be fairly rare and to be associated with outstanding individuals of great wisdom and sensitivity. They were interpreted in different ways, depending on the concepts available to the cultures in which those individuals lived. But, at a general level, they seemed to have in common an apprehension of a Reality of Supreme Value, of beauty and wisdom, of bliss and compassion. This was interpreted as encounter with God or as union with a Reality of Supreme Value, either in a personal or an impersonal form.

Most religious traditions are at pains to say that the concepts in terms of which such experiences are described are metaphorical, not literal, for the reality is beyond precise description in any human language. It is also clear that conceptual interpretation enters into the description of experience, producing differences even at the highest level. But humans are, in general, so unbalanced and benighted that a great many so-called "religious experiences" will be pretty obviously harmful or irrational. For that reason, religions usually seek to make the normative experiences of their founding prophets or teachers authoritative for the tradition. They do not deny that believers in general may have religious experiences, but they do not grant them independent status or authority.

I introduced into the discussion an imaginary "tough-minded scientist" (but there are real-life cases of people who think like that), who argued that only scientifically established truths should count as truths and that religious experiences belong to the realm of subjective feelings and have no cognitive content. For such a person, religious experiences could certainly not be evidence for God: their interpretation is disputed, even at the most general level; there is no way of publicly verifying these claims; and many, perhaps most, religious experiences are irrational and occur to mentally unbalanced people. Evidence has to be available to everyone, publicly checkable, and carefully inspected to guard against trickery and delusion. Religious experiences fail these tests, so they are not evidence for anything, except the mental states of deluded maniacs.

Religious believers may be grateful that at least they are allowed to have mental states. But it is perhaps not so clear that their experiences are delusions. In this chapter, I have suggested that the claim that all evidence must be publicly testable, universally agreed on, and repeatable under controlled conditions, like much scientific evidence, is not really defensible.

In courts of law, there is rarely universal agreement—at the very least, the prosecution and the defense lawyers do not agree. The evidence cannot be repeated or controlled, and, if it lies in the past, it cannot be publicly tested. We have to make do with a lower standard of evidence and say that we rely on the majority judgment of people exposed to all available evidence, guided by expert opinion as to what the evidence suggests.

This is true of human history in general, where there is no question of control, repetition, universal laws, or universal agreement. There is evidence, and it should be made available to everyone. But there will always be differences of interpretation, and they will be partly due to differences in the personalities and experiences of the persons doing the interpreting. Some judges are better, more perceptive and discerning, than others. They are the leading historians, and most people will be wise to accept their guidance, even though experts often disagree.

When it comes to the thoughts, feelings, motives, and intentions of others, there is even more room for disagreement. Some are completely hidden from the observers' view. Many are ambiguous, and, even when the subject says what they are, many questions remain about how to interpret such statements and how much credence to give to them.

We know other people have thoughts and motives, but we have to rely for our knowledge of what they are on behavioral and linguistic clues that are more-or-less revealing and ambiguous. In such cases, the evidence is not always available to everyone or open to public observation, and it is almost always open to variant interpretations.

People often try to express how they see and feel about the world of their experience in art and literature. Literal description is eschewed, and metaphor and imagery are used to evoke in others something of what it feels like to live in the world as the artist does. But what is evoked depends even more upon the observer, who must engage in a personal interaction with the work of the artist in order to understand, in a uniquely personal way, what is being communicated.

We are now far removed from the alleged scientific world of impersonal control and analysis of publicly verifiable facts. The practice of science is not in any case, I have argued, as impersonal and value-free as this may suggest. But science does attempt to investigate a testable world of publicly verifiable facts. The humanities do not. They try to enter, though empathetic feeling, into semantic worlds that express perspectives on human experience, less literally describable or mathematically denumerable, more intensely felt and passionately committed.

These worlds are part of reality, too. They are worlds of thought and feeling, and sometimes they may change the interpretation we have of our own lives, as they present a perspective that makes sense of the complexity of experience in a way that nothing else has done.

Religion may no longer be the "queen of the sciences." But it may be a bridge between the humane world of empathetic feelings and the scientific world of objective facts. For there may be forms of objectivity that are only accessible through empathetic feeling and passionate commitment. Religious sensibility may be one, even the primary one, of such forms.

Basic Perspectives

Religions offer perspectives on human experience. What seems characteristic of a religious perspective is its placing all things *sub specie aeternitatis*, in the light of eternity, as related to a supreme actually existing Ideal or Value. Is there evidence for such a perspective? There can be no independent evidence for basic perspectives since they are what determines what sorts of evidence we will take seriously.

Statements expressing the basic perspective of science, like "every event has a cause" or "laws of physics are universal" are not based on evidence. Of course, we can say they have been confirmed so far, but their claims go far beyond what we have so far experienced. It is important that they are confirmed in experience. But they function as axioms of faith that make science possible.

Similarly, statements expressing the basic perspective of philosophical naturalism—like "there are no objective moral values," "all factual statements must be statements of science and can only refer to what is physical," "it is wrong to believe anything on insufficient evidence," or "all values are subjective"—are not based on evidence. They express fundamental axioms that determine the way in which we interpret all our experience. For a philosophical naturalist, they are confirmed by the fact that they make possible a no-nonsense, empirically fruitful approach to the world. Sir Francis Crick, for example, has said that his distaste for religion was a prime motive for the work that led to his discovery of the structure of DNA (reported in the *Daily Telegraph*, March 20, 2003). For him, religion supported theories about a mysterious "life-force" or spiritual basis for biology, and it was important to find a purely chemical basis for life. His view was confirmed by his discovery, but it was based not on evidence but on "distaste," or what I have called a basic perspective.

The basic perspective of religion is that there exists an Objective Reality of Supreme Value. One way to construe this is that the value is apprehended and enjoyed in a Supreme Consciousness, which also intends that Value to be realized to some extent in the finite world and especially in finite consciousnesses like those of human beings.

To believe in God is primarily to believe in the objectivity of value and purpose. That view is not based on evidence but is an axiom that makes a life of faith—of seeing all experience in the light of such objective value and purpose—possible. Such a belief is confirmed primarily by the sense it enables people to make of their lives (and will be disconfirmed if it does not do so). It is also confirmed by the greater vitality, happiness, and moral dynamism that it brings to those who accept it.

This is where experience assumes importance. The claim to experience a state or being of supreme wisdom, compassion, and bliss, when made by a person who is wise, compassionate, and blissful and who, with some plausibility, can be seen to be free from hatred, greed, and ignorance, gives experiential confirmation to the hypothesis of the objectivity of value.

Conceptual interpretations of such experiences vary, but that is because different cultures have developed different languages and concepts for expressing their experiences. An important area of convergence exists in claims to experience a reality of wisdom, compassion, and bliss. The divergences are like those found in any area where personal judgment is involved—history, the law, and descriptions of people's characters. It would be odd if such differences did not exist.

There is no possibility of public verification of religious experiences. But public verification is only possible where there is sensory experience of a common material environment. We cannot publicly verify any statements about feelings, thoughts, motives, and intentions or, in general, any data of personal consciousness. Tests for the authenticity of religious experience lie in consonance with other knowledge, internal coherence, and conformity with the occurrence of similar experiences by others.

The character and conduct of authoritative experients are important. But if they seem not only sane but extraordinarily well balanced, not only rational but extraordinarily perceptive, not only good but extraordinarily compassionate and unselfish, there is reason to give credence to their claims. Where religious beliefs seem to cause moral or psychological harm, we may find that the best explanation for that is to be found not in the religious beliefs but in the antecedent character of those who claim to have them. Of course, there are millions of damaged and unstable human beings, and one would expect many of them to be adherents of some religion. But if the question is about the character of those prophets and teachers who have authoritative and normative religious experiences, most unbiased observers would reckon them to be not evident deluded maniacs but among the wisest and best of humanity.

That is the case for taking religious experience seriously, as evidence for the existence of a Supreme Spiritual Reality. Those I have called "tough-minded scientists" will always be able to discount such evidence because it does not conform to their definition of evidence, as publicly observable and experimentally testable sensory experience. But perhaps we should make a clear distinction between that view—which is really a basic philosophical perspective—and natural science proper.

Natural science has little to say on the issue of the genuineness of religious experience because it is very difficult to devise any strictly controlled scientific tests for religious experiences. In the next chapter, I will return to this subject. In this chapter, I have focused on the question of whether there are limits to the methodology of science, on how the sciences relate to the humanities and social sciences, and on whether there are questions of fact and of reason with which science cannot deal. My argument has been that there are, and that the question of the truth-affirming character of religious experience is one of them. The arguments must be carefully assessed on their merits. My final barbed comment is that, if you do that, you will not be using the methods of any science when you do so.

8. Can Science Provide a Wholly Naturalistic Explanation for Moral and Religious Beliefs?

(HOW DOES MORALITY RELATE TO RELIGION?)

Religion and Morality in the Semitic Traditions

THE MORAL DIMENSION, both individual and social, is so important to religion that some scholars see religions primarily as ways of life rather than sets of doctrines or vehicles for certain sorts of experiences. Most religions contain all these elements—morality, doctrine, and experience—but they are weighted differently. The oldest Semitic faith, the Hebraic precursor of rabbinic Judaism, is often seen as primarily a religion of *Torah*. This can be translated as "law," but, in English, that word may convey a misleading impression of just a set of rules to be evaded wherever possible. For a Jew, the written Torah is the whole biblical narrative from Genesis to Deuteronomy, and the oral Torah is found in the Babylonian Talmud, the main object of study for Jewish religious scholars.

The biblical narrative is an account of history, especially that of the children of Abraham who are believed to be inheritors of a covenant with the God of Abraham, Isaac, and Jacob. It recounts that people were taken into slavery in Egypt, escaped by the help of God, and wandered forty years in the wilderness until they came to the borders of the promised land. The narrative defines the self-understanding of Jews as bound in a unique relationship to God, as saved from oppression by mighty acts of God, as wandering in the wilderness of the world, in a state of half-rebellion and half-obedience to God, and as heirs of a promise of justice and peace that seems to be indefinitely deferred.

The statutes and ordinances given to Moses by God—traditionally, but rather arbitrarily, numbered at 613—belong to this historical narrative. They define a way of life in relation to God, a way to true human fulfillment, in a society of justice, mercy, happiness, and well-being (*shalom*) in the worship and love of God, who is supreme goodness.

Torah is not a universal morality for the whole world. It sets Jews apart as a covenant people, and its ritual and food laws are quite distinctive. Even what may seem to be purely moral rules are seen as imitations of divine goodness or as recollections of a history of slavery, liberation, and hope. "Remember that you were slaves in Egypt" becomes a motivation for treating others with compassion, in recognition that God wills liberation for all creatures.

Because the rules belong to a historical narrative and define a way of relationship to God who wills human fulfillment, they cannot be lifted out of context and applied in a literalistic way, with no thought of the consequences of such application in very different circumstances. They need to be interpreted and applied by a judicial and scholarly process. This is living law, and its underlying principles must be sought and applied in historically appropriate ways.

There will always be a tension between conservative attitudes, which regard the preservation of a distinctive culture as important, and liberal attitudes, which are more inclined to revise ancient rules in the light of new scientific or moral insights. But for neither view is Torah just a set of unchangeable commands issued by an omnipotent tyrant who will ruthlessly punish all who disobey.

The law was given by God to a particular group of displaced and nomadic people in what we now call the late Bronze Age. The conditions of Jewish life have changed radically since then. With the destruction of the second Temple in 135 CE, all the sacrificial and ritual laws were rendered obsolete. Joshua ben Hananiah, around 100 CE, formally declared that the "seven nations" of Canaan are no longer identifiable, thus rendering all laws concerning the conquest of Canaan obsolete. Most of the punitive laws and some of the marital laws (concerning levirate marriage or the possession of concubines, for example) are also regarded as obsolete.

One reason for this is the eighth- to sixth-century BCE teaching of the major prophets, who insisted that justice, mercy, and loving-kindness are the heart of the law. Jesus was stating widespread rabbinic opinion when he said that the two most important commands of the law were to love God (absolute beauty and goodness) and to love one's neighbor as oneself. Rabbis must seek to interpret the law in the light of these commands and after thinking out their implications.

This revision does not reduce the ancient laws to irrelevance, but it calls for discernment of underlying principles and for new ways of applying those principles in contemporary situations. The law exists as a way of binding a particular people to God in a deeply personal relationship and as a way to human fulfillment in relation to God. The specific biblical rules are like normative precedents that must be creatively interpreted in many situations by judicial and scholarly argument and discussion. People sometimes miss the important role of argument and judicial disagreement in Judaism, though it is quite clear in the Talmud. The point about this being the law of God is not that its specific rules are unchangeable but that its principles preserve ways of life that encourage reverence and love for Supreme Objective Goodness (for God), an attitude of respect and care for all God has made, and a faith and hope that God's purpose for the flourishing of goodness on the earth will be realized.

Jewish religion gives morality a transcendent dimension, rooting it in love of a Supreme Objective Good and in a desire to make goodness known and effective in history. Like all human societies, Jewish society is in practice an ambiguous mixture of success and failure in this task and of insight and obtuseness about exactly what Supreme Goodness requires. But, in the Jewish prophetic tradition, religion is raised from being a commerce with spirits aimed at achieving greater personal success to being a submission of the heart to one supreme living and active moral Ideal.

Islam also sees God as setting out, through the Prophet, a way of justice and peace that will relate all human life to Supreme Goodness. It universalizes the idea of law (*Shari'a*), but bequeaths to its followers the same problems of interpretation and authority that make Judaism in practice a diverse set of communities united by the central thought of self-abandonment to God.

Christianity abandons the idea of a revealed written law, replacing it with the personal life of Jesus as the revelation of Divine Goodness—a revelation of the supremacy of suffering, selflessness, healing, and reconciling love. In all the Semitic traditions, then, morality is central to religious belief and entails respect and compassion for all personal life. But what gives morality its driving force is a vision of a God of supreme Goodness, whose nature is meant to be reflected in human society and whose final goal is the transfiguration of the cosmos by a fully realized personal unity with God.

Religion and Morality in Eastern Traditions

Buddhism and the renouncing traditions that largely originated in India do not have any belief in a supreme Creator who issues moral commands or who can establish a perfected community of love. Seeing that all life involves impermanence and unease or suffering (*dukkha*), the Buddha located the cause of suffering in attachment and inordinate desire. The path of release that he taught, the Eightfold Way, is a path of meditation, wisdom, and moral practice. Morality is an important part of the way to liberation. It is not a matter of authoritative commands but a means to liberation from sorrow.

It is not, however, a purely egoistic matter of finding release for oneself. Since a central doctrine of Buddhism is that of *anatta*, no-self, this is not a path of release just for oneself. It is the path all sentient beings must take to escape the wheel of rebirth. Some forms of Buddhist meditation concentrate the mind on the four noble qualities of compassion for all sentient beings, equanimity, happiness in the joy of others, and universal loving-kindness.

Coming to realize that there is no self, that nothing belongs to us, that we do not truly own anything, we are released from egoism and possessiveness, and we can eventually pass beyond desire to a state in which there is only compassion, wisdom and bliss—nirvana.

The Buddhist way is much more explicitly centered on meditation and disciplined training of the mind than are the Semitic faiths. The focus of such training is to achieve mindfulness and compassion. It is an inner path of purification rather than a code of social ethics. And it does not expect a truly just society ever to exist since this world is essentially a place where all sorts of destructive desires are worked out and final release entails leaving this world behind altogether. Things are getting worse, and, for traditional Buddhist schools, only in monastic communities is there a real chance of finding Enlightenment.

Nevertheless, there are many forms of Buddhism, and not all of them are world-renouncing. Especially in China and Japan, and quite recently in India, forms of "socially concerned" Buddhism exist, which emphasize the role of lay Buddhists and the possibility of enlightened living in ordinary society. Lay Buddhists have always been advised to follow the Five Precepts. They are: Do not take life. Do not steal. Do not misuse sex. Do not lie. And do not take intoxicants. These are moral rules, reminiscent of some of the Ten Commandments. But they are not given by a God. Rather, they are rules that increase compassion, altruism, and mindfulness and so may lead to a happier, more liberated life.

Buddhist ethics is rooted in a particular vision of human life and of the nature of the human self. Humans are fettered by hatred, greed, and ignorance, all of which inevitably lead to suffering. The way to end suffering and to see things as they truly are is to renounce possessiveness and clinging. Moral precepts outine the path toward release from sorrow. They are not absolute commands from some Supreme Authority but sound advice for achieving true insight into what it is to flourish as a human being.

Hinduism, unlike Buddhism, is explicitly theistic or even multitheistic.

What is characteristic of orthodox Hinduism is the key axiom that every-thing in the cosmos is part of *Brahman*, the absolute Spiritual Reality. *Brahman*, even for the most nondualist traditions, takes the form of a supreme personal Lord and can manifest in many different divine forms (the gods). The Supreme Lord is not a self-contained being, existing apart from the cosmos. For most traditions, it unfolds into the cosmos, and finite souls are conditioned parts of its unconditioned reality.

The key perception of this main form of Hinduism is that all things are parts of one Spiritual Reality, and that all human souls are, in some sense, identical with *Brahman*. As in Buddhism, meditation is a main path to spiritual discernment. But what is discerned is not that there is no permanent self but that all things are identical with, or in union with, the one Self of all.

This is clearly a different interpretation than the one given by Bud-dhists, but it may seem more like a matter of emphasis than of sheer contradiction. In both cases, the ordinary everyday personality is not a permanent self. It is something to be transcended. In both cases, there is a deeper reality of wisdom, compassion, and bliss, whether it is called a Supreme Self or a state beyond personal description. And in both cases, the spiritual path is one of passing beyond the everyday self to an aware-ness of that deeper reality—in the case of Hinduism, of seeing that "You also are that [Self]."

The supreme spiritual perception for Hinduism is the unity of all things in the Self. It is from this perception that moral conduct arises. When you see that all things are one, you no longer separate yourself as an isolated possessor of objects or ruler of other people. You will love others as you love yourself because, in fact, you are all parts of the same Self. As in Buddhism, there is transcendence of ego, and acts of compas-sion follow from discerning the spiritual unity of all things.

It may seem that rules of caste and custom dominate religious life in India and that they dictate very hierarchical and traditional attitudes toward society. But that is more a mark of preliterate rural culture than of religious faith. There is a link between conservative and nationalist attitudes and some forms of Hinduism, but, in such cases, it seems that the nationalist and exclusive attitudes manipulate elements of the reli-gion for their own ends. For belief that all things are parts of one Self of wisdom and bliss and that different people have different roles to play in relation to the Self (the basis of caste distinctions) does not license social exclusion and discrimination. It ought to generate attitudes of social sol-idarity and compassion since it is only by compassionate action that one can achieve release from the slavery of egoism. In the best spiritual teach-ers—like Gandhi and Ramakrishna, in recent times—it does.

Religion, like morality itself, can be used to bolster sets of values that are oppressive to many—the systematic subjugation of women throughout recorded history is often justified by appeal to "moral" values of family and sexual modesty. What is needed is not more morality but more of a sort of morality that takes the flourishing of all beings seriously and that opposes violence and oppression. Similarly, we do not need more religion but more of a sort of religion that reinforces compassion for all beings and nonviolence.

One would think that a religion that teaches the unity of all beings in one supremely wise and blissful Self and that teaches *ahimsa*, —respect for all sentient beings—as a key virtue is just the sort of religion we need. The sad fact is, however, that no moral, political, or religious system is beyond the possibility of corruption. Yet, in all the ambiguities and tragedies of our world, it is important to hold onto some vision of human nature that might give force and vivacity to moral action for universal human flourishing. When it functions authentically, religion does this, but not by issuing authoritative moral rules or appealing to ancient human customs. True religion seeks to move the heart to love virtue and to encourage the sensitive personal perception of goodness. It does not, and it certainly should not, encourage unquestioning and supine obedience to authority.

To a large extent, Confucian and Taoist attitudes toward morality, though not overtly theistic, share this outlook. To live in accordance with the Way of Heaven (*Tian*) or with the Way of Nature (*Tao*) is to have insight into what it is to be a full human being. Just as a good knife is a knife that cuts well, so a good human being is one who lives well, who realizes distinctively human excellences. To live a good life is to live in accordance with the Way of Heaven, a balanced and harmonious life that fulfills the distinctive potentialities of human nature and reflects a just perception of human possibilities.

The contrast between these attitudes and the Semitic emphasis on morality as a matter of divine commands should not be overstressed. For God, as the Supreme Good and the Creator of human nature, might be expected to desire the fulfillment of the distinctive potentialities God has placed in human lives. And, indeed, the main Christian tradition in ethics, influenced by Aristotle, has based morality on "natural law," which is precisely the fulfillment of natural human inclinations because they are created by God. Humanism, a concern for the flourishing of distinctively human excellences, is a shared moral perception between the major religions. But religiously based humanism sees human flourishing as involving conscious orientation to a more-than-human Spiritual Reality, whether that is conceived as God, nirvana, or the Way of Heaven.

There is an objective standard of goodness, perhaps realized in some personal or suprapersonal form. Morality, according to such views, is concerned not only with conduct but with the perception of objective goodness, so moral practice is not so much a decision of the autonomous will as a response to the discernment of an objective, more than humanly invented, value. It is such discernment that lies at the heart of religious faith, and it is that to which religious practice at its best points.

Morality and Sociobiology

Morality in general, it may seem, lies outside the province of the natural sciences. The sciences are concerned with how things are, and morality is concerned with how things ought to be. "There is no *ought* from an *is*" was at one time almost an axiom of moral philosophers. So no moral conclusions can be deduced from scientifically established facts. They must have some other source.

In recent years, however, a new science, originally called sociobiology but now more often called evolutionary psychology, has appeared on the scene. In 1975, the distinguished biologist E. O. Wilson published an influential book, *Sociobiology: The New Synthesis*, and he followed this up with *Consilience* in 1998.

Just as the structure of physical bodies can be explained by telling the story of their long evolutionary development, so, the theory goes, mental dispositions and capacities can be explained in the same way. The evolutionary story is one of how genetic mutations cause modifications in, for instance, the eyes, limbs, and brains of offspring. In the long struggle for survival over many generations, some of these prove adaptive and are passed on, while others are eliminated. We can now explain why our bodies, sense organs, and brains are the way they are by showing how each small modification that led to them was adaptive to the environment of its day and helped preferential selection over competing organisms.

The proposal is that our inclinations and preferences, our beliefs and thoughts, can be explained in a similar way. If humans have an inborn tendency to form specific moral or religious beliefs, this can be explained by showing that such beliefs had an advantage in the struggle for survival, perhaps hundreds of thousands of years ago. Beliefs, or tendencies to believe, got selected and inbred because of that advantage—or, in some cases, simply because they never got wiped out but carried on as by-products of the struggle for survival. Though they were never positively advantageous, they resulted from mutations that were not unfavorable enough to kill them.

E. O. Wilson says, "Ought is the product of a material process." It is "just shorthand for one kind of factual statement" (1998, 280). Not only can an *ought* be derived from an *is*. An *ought* is an *is*, of a specific type. What he means is that certain behavioral tendencies—for example, the tendency to protect your offspring, even at personal cost—were genetically determined by some mutation in your DNA. This tendency proved conducive to the survival of your offspring, who carry your DNA, even though it was not terribly conducive to your personal survival. But there are more of your offspring than there are of you, so your personal sacrifice propagates more of your DNA—including the tendency to sacrifice yourself for your offspring—than if you survived but all your offspring got eaten. Therefore, self-sacrifice has good survival value for your DNA. Even if, as Richard Dawkins once held, your genes are selfish, you, the organism that carries them, might be compelled to be self-sacrificing.

Altruistic behavior is the price some animals pay for being transporters of selfish genes. Such behavior, having had high survival value, gets codified into social rules, and then individuals say that they "ought" to obey the rules. The sense of obligation is the felt behavioral tendency to be altruistic, which was genetically inbred many generations ago. That is how the *ought* is an *is*. It is a tendency we cannot help and that can be explained by its past survival value in the evolutionary struggle for life.

This is an attractive theory in many ways, but I can hardly help feeling that something has gone wrong somewhere. When you ask what you ought to do, you review the alternatives and decide on a course of action for a reason. That reason is unlikely to be because the action was conducive to survival thousands of generations ago. There might be any number of reasons, but one frequently mentioned reason for doing what you ought to do is that the action will increase the greatest happiness of the greatest number or at least a reasonable amount of happiness for a reasonable number of people. A reason that is hardly ever mentioned is that the action will increase the number of DNA sequences that match some of those in your own body cells.

It is not just that we did not know about this until fairly recently. It is that, even when we do know, we probably do not care very much. Some people do care that their family line carries on, and they get great pleasure from the thought. But there are many more important aims in life than having lots of children. And once the children have grown up and left home, it would be unreasonable to say that you no longer have any reason for making moral decisions because nothing you do is going to propagate your DNA more efficiently.

What reason do you have for aiming at the happiness of others? Well, it might be said, it is just a reasonable thing to do since other people want to be happy, what people want (other things being equal) is good, and it is more reasonable to do good than to do evil. But it seems, at least at first sight, that Wilson is saying that what you ought to do is what you feel you must do because it has been genetically implanted thousands of years ago. That is your inclination, and if it is your strongest inclination, that is what you will do. If it is not, you will not do it. And that is that.

But, you protest, you have a choice. You do not have to do what you are naturally inclined to do. At that point, the sociobiologist might regard you sympathetically, and say, "Well, you would think that; that is one of your genetically implanted thoughts." And now we have identified a critical question: are all your thoughts and beliefs genetically determined, or are you sometimes free to choose? It may be true that you are caused to do some things by your genes. But can you also, at least sometimes, do something for a reason? And are these two compatible?

We have come back to the completely unresolved question of determinism and freedom. The fact that the question is unresolved and that there does not seem to be any way of resolving it does not stop people from having very strong opinions about it. Not only do people have strong opinions; they often say that those who disagree with them are just stupid.

I have already suggested that science has no answer to the question. How could any scientific experiment show not only that what you did was caused by some preceding physical event but that no other action could possibly have happened? Nevertheless, Wilson seems to be a determinist. "Rational choice," he says, "is the casting about among alternative mental scenarios to hit upon the ones which, in a given context, satisfy the strongest epigenetic rules" (1998, 199). Epigenetic rules are "the neural pathways and regularities in cognitive development by which the individual mind assembles itself" (139). So the strongest epigenetic rules are the most firmly established neural pathways, set up by a combination of genetic endowment and repeated behavior.

The upshot is that rational choice is something that happens to us. Various neural pathways compete with each other for dominance, and eventually the strongest, best established one wins. Our consciousness thinks that we are reviewing possibilities and choosing among them. But, in fact, choice is just a by-product of the brain processes that are all proceeding according to predetermined physical laws. We are condemned to live in a state of permanent self-deception. The physical brain is doing all the work, and there is no "choosing self" that has a causal influence on the future.

This is a fairly widely held view at present, but if the question is whether it is established by science, the answer has to be "no." In chapter six, I showed that many neuropsychologists think that conscious states, while closely correlated with brain states, are emergent realities, existing as aspects of very complex and integrated neural substrates. Most realities have some causal influence on their environment, so it seems highly likely that conscious states have some causal influence on the physical world surrounding them. Or, to put it another way, the conscious aspects of brain behavior have causal influence in virtue of their conscious content, not solely in virtue of their physical aspects.

Personal Explanation

Thoughts, attitudes, and moods make a difference to what happens in the world, even though such thoughts cannot be separated off as quite distinct entities from brain states. We ordinarily recognize this fact in speaking of what philosophers like Richard Taylor (1966) and Richard Swinburne (2004, chap. 2) call personal explanation.

Normal scientific explanation is nomological, or law-like. It cites a physical initial state in terms of properties like position, momentum, mass, and electric charge. It then cites a general law of the form, "Whenever X, then Y"—whenever a particle is moving with a certain velocity in a certain direction, it will end up at a specific location relative to where it is now, if nothing else interferes. And so, nomological explanation predicts a future state, the effect of an initial state plus the general law.

In personal explanation, we also begin with an initial state, but it is a state that has semantic content. It is a desire or wish that something should happen or an intention that it should happen. Being essentially an envisioning of a future state, mention of a future possibility is part of the description of the state. That makes it more than a purely physical state. It is a conscious state, with reference to a future possibility as part of its full description. No such reference is part of the description of any purely physical state.

Then, in personal explanation, we explain an occurrence by saying that someone intended to bring it about or brought it about for the sake of obtaining a state believed to be of value. That notion of "for the sake of" is what distinguishes personal explanation from nomological explanation, which is not for the sake of anything and which contains no reference to value.

We ordinarily explain human actions by saying that a person did something *in order to* obtain something else. This seems to be a form of explanation in terms of value and purpose, which is not reducible to a nomological explanation. The only way it could be reducible would be if the intended value were identical with some brain state that then caused a succession of further brain states in accordance with laws of physics. Each of these brain states would have to be identical with a conscious state, construed by the agent as thinking, planning, amending decisions, and pursuing a goal in a more-or-less rational way.

It would be wholly extraordinary if each brain state corresponded to a rational progression of thoughts, in a virtually miraculous parallelism of logically ordered thoughts and physically ordered neural states. For physical order has nothing intrinsically to do with logical order.

In a computer, a succession of physical states does correspond to a succession of logical inferences, but that is because the physical states have been intelligently set up by a program that determines their order, a program that was consciously designed. The program determines the physical states of the computer, but it needs some stimulus (an external goal) to trigger the program. Purpose and value enter at two stages of the physical process—in triggering it to arrive at an externally intended goal and in interacting with the program (by means of a keyboard, for instance) to set it on course to the goal.

Further, in a third stage, the result of a computer operation has to be interpreted by someone who can read the symbols it produces as having meaning. It cannot be said that a computer is an example of purely physical causation that happens to have a meaning and goal. The physical process has been designed, guided, and interpreted by a conscious person.

In brain processes, there is no "external person." It is the brain itself that has a conscious and intelligent aspect of its activity. That aspect triggers intelligent brain processes, guides them, and interprets them. We do not have to say that there is some purely spiritual ghost interacting with the brain. We can say that the sort of causality involved in rational thought and intentional action is teleological causality, a conscious aspect of neural states that brings about further neural states for the sake of an envisaged and valued goal—which is also a conscious aspect of some neural state.

The human brain, thus, exhibits two sorts of causality. There is nomological causality that operates when brain activity proceeds in accordance with purely physical laws. And there is teleological causality that has a directive or informational function in influencing neural states. Personal explanation involves teleological causality. It deals with activities of the brain but activities that are not brought about solely by physical or nomological (blind and undirected) causation. The brain, in its conscious aspect, envisages goals, values them, and seeks to bring them about.

Those who wish to reduce personal explanation to nomological explanation have to deny any real sort of purposeful action or human freedom and responsibility. They have to deny that conscious events, or aspects of brain events, play any causal role. They may think that teleological causality, bringing about something for the sake of an end, is very mysterious. But it is not any more mysterious than efficient causality, bringing about something in accordance with a hypothetical (if–then) law. Causality just is mysterious; you have to get over it. For common-sense thought, teleological causality is a basic sort of causality that can be seen in human actions.

Since this is the common-sense view and since no one has ever succeeded in showing that purely physical laws are the only causal factors in human behavior, reasonable people are entitled to accept teleological causality, even though there is no independent and conclusive proof that it is true.

This would mean rejecting the proposal that moral "oughts" are just the strongest forms of behavior that have been genetically programmed into us by their past survival value. We do sometimes have a real choice between different actions, and some choices are morally important. Of course, Wilson agrees with this, despite what he says about epigenetic rules. "We should be able to fashion a wider and more enduring ethical consensus than has gone before" (1998, 267), he says, if we see the biological roots of moral behavior. So, conscious knowledge can change our behavior, and we can devise and follow a wider moral code if we see how morality is rooted in human nature. Richard Dawkins says much the same thing: "We alone, on earth, can rebel against the tyranny of the selfish replicators" (1978, 215) Humans are free and responsible, and that means we can change our conduct for reasons, and we do not just have to do what the laws of physics make us do.

Explaining Altruism Genetically

But even if we can escape from the trap of genetic determinism, another trap lies in wait. Can evolutionary psychology really help us to see what a reasonable morality will be? The biologist Robert Trivers said, "Models that attempt to explain altruistic behavior in terms of natural selection are models designed to take the altruism out of altruism" (1971, 35). They are designed to show how altruism has been adopted because the offspring of species that are altruistic tend to reproduce and survive better than the offspring of species that are egoistic. Animals millions of years ago did not sit down and wonder whether they ought to be altruistic or not. Patterns of behavior and deep natural inclinations formed in them, and the altruistic patterns survived better than egoistic ones.

This is true only within limits, of course, and the best survival rules, as game theory shows, are those that favor limited, kin-preferential altruism and a good deal of lust and aggression, too (to keep the procreation rate up and the competition for food down).

Such evolutionary explanations are illuminating and seem to explain how humans show such paradoxical combinations of altruism and aggression. They help to show how we have come to have the inclinations and passions that we have. But so what? Does it follow that we ought to go on having them now?

Suppose we are free and that we can choose how to act for reasons. Is it a reason for being altruistic that limited altruism was a good survival ploy millions of years ago? It is not, any more than it is a reason for swimming now that our first ancestors were probably rather like tadpoles. It is always interesting to know how we evolved, what our imprinted behavior patterns are, and why they are the way they are. But if we can choose which inclinations to follow, we need some other reason for our choices.

Evolution has bred limited altruism into us, or into most of us anyway. But once we come to see this, we might come to see morality as "a collective illusion of the genes," as Michael Ruse (1995, 250) once memorably—though not entirely seriously?—described it. We see that we have a sense of obligation because such acts had high survival value millennia ago. But if we can get rid of that sense now, or at least weaken it, why should we not do so?

In *The Origins of Virtue*, Matt Ridley begins with a claim about biology that quickly, almost seamlessly, turns into a claim about morality. "Always, without exception," he says, "living things are designed to do things that enhance the chances of . . . their genes surviving and replicating" (1996, 18). Even as a statement in biology, this seems something of an exaggeration. Genetically based behavior that enhances the preferential selection of the animal's genes will obviously tend to get replicated. But so will behavior that has no such enhancement effect, that may even counteract it, as long as it does not actually kill off the organism, which gets preferentially replicated for other reasons. Nevertheless, genetically determined behavior will often favor the selection of the organism's genes and will not seriously impede such selection.

The move toward morality follows quickly: "A modern biologist seeing an animal doing something to benefit another assumes either that it is being manipulated by the other individual or that it is being subtly selfish" (Ridley 1996, 18, quoted from G. C. Williams). Thus, says Ridley, "altruism was just genetic selfishness" after all (19).

Ridley is at pains to say that this does not eliminate altruism; indeed, it explains it, as firmly rooted in our evolutionary past. But if humans are animals, then the claim is being made that a "modern biologist" will see human altruism as subtle selfishness—not the selfishness of the individual but of the genes carried by the individual. An altruistic action—like saving someone from drowning—is a piece of genetically determined behavior that has been biologically instilled into us because such behavior helped our remote ancestors to outbreed their competitors.

But the fact is that showing how we have come to have such natural inclinations does not even begin to address the question of whether we should change them or leave them alone now. If altruism is to survive as a rational policy, we must have a better reason for it than that it enabled animals to have lots of offspring in the far past.

When Richard Dawkins discusses morality, he says, "We can no more help ourselves feeling pity when we see a weeping unfortunate . . . than we can help ourselves feeling lust" (2006, 221). His circle of friends must be a very small group of kind and sensitive people in north Oxford. The pitilessness of humanity would be more apparent in Darfur or the favelas of Brazil. Such feelings of pity, Dawkins says, are "misfirings, Darwinian mistakes: blessed, precious mistakes." But if they are mistakes, caused by copying errors in DNA replication, why should they be called "blessed" or "precious"? Presumably because Dawkins cannot help liking them. But the terrible truth is that bolder and less conformist spirits can and do help it.

Pity can be bred out of people. Ironically, it was a perversion of Darwinism that set out most ruthlessly to eliminate pity, which Nietzsche regarded as a human weakness. The "social Darwinism" of writers like Ernst Haeckel, the notoriously anti-Semitic German racist who deduced from Darwinism the moral policy of exterminating the unfit and letting only the strong survive, is one of the factors that helped national socialism come to power in Nazi Germany.

One lesson to be learned is that the assumed facts of evolution, seen as "red in tooth and claw," are not always a safe guide to moral conduct. There may be some altruism in our past; but there is a great deal more violence, distrust, aggression, and hatred. This led the eminent biologist and Darwinian T. H. Huxley (1947) to say that the human duty is not to further the evolutionary trend but to oppose it as much as possible.

Nevertheless, Dawkins offers "four good Darwinian reasons" for altruism (2006, 219): a natural liking for kin; the expectation that if you do good to others, they may do good to you; gaining a reputation for generosity; and establishing social dominance. These might explain, as Machiavelli would say, why it is good to appear altruistic and why a certain amount of painless altruism might be advantageous. But these reasons are appeals to natural sentiments, which vary enormously between people and are very limited in their range, and to desires for personal pleasure and social status. A more stern-minded moralist would say that they are not genuinely altruistic at all, for altruism is action for the sake of good alone.

In the end, sociobiology does not seem to help us to make moral decisions. For we need to have reasons, not just causes, for our responsible actions, and we just have to decide what are going to count as good reasons for acting. There seem to be three main alternatives: a good reason for acting is that it will be for our own good; another is that it will be for the good of people we like; and a third is that it will be for the good of all. It seems equally rational to aim at any of these. It is reasonable to be a rational egoist in a world in which my pains are the only pains I am going to feel. It is reasonable to help my family and friends because I like them and am inclined to do so. And it is reasonable to aim at the general good because that is what a completely impartial agent (and reason is surely impartial) would do. All these reasons often conflict; in that case, we just have to decide what to do. Sociobiology will not help, and neither will reason alone.

The Difference Religious Belief Makes to Morality

But will religion help us to decide what to do? Some people think religion would actually make things worse. When we think of all the intolerance, hatred, and violence that religions have caused, we might think we would be better off without religion. However, intolerance, hatred, and violence are not confined to religion. Most regrettably, they seem to be deeply rooted in human nature, and they charactize societies that have no religious foundation at all, like the communist Soviet Union, Maoist China, Nazi Germany, or innumerable fascist dictatorships, nationalist political groups, and radical anarchist movements.

If we look at the claims of religion, as opposed to its sometimes harmful effects, the account given at the beginning of this chapter shows that most religions believe there exists a Supreme Value of wisdom, compassion, and bliss and that there is a fulfilling way of living as a human being, the aim of which is to achieve union, friendship, or harmony with that Supreme Value. A religious morality will not simply be a matter of human decision. It will be a way of responding appropriately to an Objective Supreme value or authentic possibility of existing (that is, a value that exists or a possibility that is authentic, whether or not humans know about it or agree with it).

Critics of religion often depict this as heteronomy, as supine fear of and obedience to a Supreme Power, whose commands all must obey on pain of death, or even of eternal hell. But that is not a religious understanding. If God, as the supreme value is termed in theistic religions, is supremely desirable—as a supreme value is—then the appropriate response to God is to desire to know God more fully, to delight in the being of God, and to aim at union with God as the most fulfilling possible way of life. The rules of morality are the means by which such union can be achieved, and they are rooted in an objective reality, not in autonomous decisions of the human will. Morality becomes a reasoned response to Supreme Value and neither a wholly autonomous decision about how to live nor blind obedience to a set of arbitrary divine commands.

Nontheistic religions also usually accept a spiritual dimension of reality. Even if it is not personal in nature, it embodies an ideal of harmony, wisdom, and excellence to which humans respond by imitating it or incorporating it into their lives. The "right" way to live is to live in conscious relationship to this Spiritual Ideal, and from that the rules of common morality follow.

Serious religious believers have a reason for altruistic conduct that is not available to nonbelievers, and that reason has overwhelming force. It is not that, if you disobey God you will go to hell—though it may be true that, if you finally and decisively turn away from the Supreme Moral Ideal, you will be lost in the despair and destructiveness of egoism. It is that loving God and enjoying the Divine Presence is the most reasonable and appropriate aim of human life. Loving God fulfills the highest human potentialities and brings the greatest happiness. And it entails following the commands God gives for attaining such ultimate human well-being.

As the book of Deuteronomy puts it, "Now, O Israel, what does the Lord your God require of you? Only to fear the Lord your God, to walk in all his ways, to love him . . . and to keep the commandments of the Lord your God and his decrees . . . or your own well-being" (Deut. 10:12). Love of that which is supremely good for its own sake and universal human well-being as the aim of the moral life are the central and distinctive themes of religious morality. Placed alongside those goals, the desire to gain social approbation and to look after the welfare of your own family seem pretty weak and unconvincing.

None of this will have much force for those who believe there is no God or spiritual reality. For them, God will be a human invention, and the so-called perfections of God will just be a projection of the ideals of a human society—probably, given the conservative nature of religion, an archaic and obsolete set of ideals at that. If you are skeptical about the objectivity of morals, you will almost certainly be skeptical about the objectivity of God, so appeal to God will be of no help to your morality.

In that situation, it may be better to rely simply on basic human sentiments of benevolence and affection and on devising rules for a reasonable degree of social security and harmony. If we see ourselves as evolved animals that have to cooperate to survive, we will not get a morality of absolute moral rules. But we will be able to construct a set of principles for living in society that may make life more satisfying for most people. And we might be more tolerant of those whose moral decisions quite reasonably disagree with ours.

Such a fluid, changing, constructed moral system may be preferred to the alleged divine commands of religion, which tend to be seen as absolute, inflexible, repressive of the opinions of dissidents, and supportive of the absolute authority of priests and supposedly divinely appointed rulers. A truly liberal, invented morality is preferable, it may be said, to an authoritatively imposed set of divine commands that reduces us to the status of moral infancy. And, put like that, it is hard to disagree.

There are forms of religion that insist on authoritarian, absolute, and inflexible moral rules. There are also forms of secular morality that are equally authoritarian, absolute, and inflexible. Liberal morality is not the sole preserve of the nonreligious. There can be liberal religious morality, too. And the argument for a religious view is that it provides an overwhelmingly strong additional motivation for altruism. For a liberal religious view, altruism is reasonable, and not only because it is what a purely hypothetical impartial agent would will. It is reasonable because it is what an actual impartial agent, concerned for the welfare of all (God), actually does will. Furthermore, the highest human happiness and fulfillment comes from conscious union with God, which can only be achieved as a result of genuinely altruistic action, of loving your neighbor (in the end, all sentient beings) as yourself.

The sciences cannot decide on this argument between secular and religious morality, in which each side tends to portray the other in the worst possible terms. To the extent that evolutionary psychology assumes a secular viewpoint, it may tend to take a negative view of religious morality, assuming religion to be a psychological reinforcement for social cohesion that had survival value in the past but may now be counterproductive. Yet, even then, the social functions of religion may, as the "father of sociology" Emile Durkheim (1963) argued, be a positive and beneficial element in the functioning of a healthy society. Sociology and psychology do not speak with one voice on this issue, though the weight of the evidence seems to support a positive view of the social benefits of religion (see Ward 2007). Neither discipline, however, is able to decide on whether or not any set of religious beliefs is true.

Psychology and Religious Experience

If religious morality is ultimately based on an alleged insight into a Spiritual Reality that defines or embodies supreme value, then it is based on a sort of experience that is closely linked to religious experience. But, as the last chapter showed, it is hotly disputed whether religious experiences can give any information about objective reality.

If it turns out that there really are no reasons for religious experiences, then we may look for an explanation in terms of causes. For instance, if I see pink elephants where there are none, the best explanation is that I am drunk and that alcohol is causing my brain to malfunction to produce hallucinations. Religious or moral beliefs could simply be caused by brain malfunctions, especially if they lead me to believe in things that do not exist.

Pink elephants clearly do not exist objectively, as they fail to have the causal effects that ordinary elephants have—they do not trample on cars, eat trees, or stand on people. Nor can they be seen by anyone else. We know they are hallucinations because they lack many of the properties of real elephants. I myself realize that, even when I see them in my drunken states. And, of course, when I am drunk, I am verifiably drunk—in a state known to be liable to cause people to see imaginary elephants.

The sort of moral and religious experiences that seem to be of a supremely valuable objective reality are not like that. They do not lack many properties of real objective values, for there are no such publicly observable properties. They are not felt by those who experience them to be imaginary, and they are not caused by unusual mental states that are known to cause false beliefs. Some of them may arise from unusual mental states, but such states may put us in touch with spiritual realities. It is almost impossible to tell whether or not they do when the realities in question are not publicly observable. But people who claim to have such experiences are rarely identifiably mad or unable to cope with ordinary life or otherwise irrational—the usual tests of mental instability.

One of the best-known treatments of experiences of spiritual reality is given by the psychologist William James, who studied unusual mental states in the belief that they might cast a sharper light on the nature of religious experience. In his classic book *The Varieties of Religious Experi-*

ence, originally published in 1902, James lists and classifies various types of religious experience. In suggesting general conclusions from his studies, he isolates a sense of communion with "higher powers" that is both satisfying in itself and leads to moral and personal improvement. As a psychologist, he writes that "the 'more' with which in religious experience we feel ourselves connected is on its higher side the subconscious continuation of our conscious life" (1968, 487). His personal opinion is that there may be many higher selves with which we establish relationship through the subconscious, but he admits that many different theological interpretations may be made of the basic experience of communion with higher spiritual powers. Being a pragmatist, he thinks that the mental and moral health that religious experience produces validates, or even constitutes, its truth. The effects "prove" the reality of the religious objects but do not entail any one specific religious interpretation of them.

Religious experiences have been the object of psychological studies since Edwin Diller Starbuck and James Henry Leuba initiated empirical investigations around the beginning of the twentieth century. In *The Psychology of Religion* (1899), Starbuck studied conversion experiences in Protestants. He found that about a third of the males he questioned and half the females had such experiences, that they were associated with puberty, and that, overall, they made for mental stability and commitment to social service, after a period of "storm and stress." He attempted to come up with neurophysiological explanations for conversion experiences and concluded that they eased the transition to maturity, and so had a positive psychological function.

James Henry Leuba (1925) adopted a much more naturalistic approach. He too studied conversion experiences and analyzed the writings of historical "mystics" like Catherine of Genoa. He apparently saw mystical experience as leading to the physical and spiritual realization of humanity, but he regarded it as a purely natural phenomenon, due to excited activity of the brain, rather than contact with any Objective Reality.

This conflict of transcendent and naturalistic interpretations has continued ever since, with naturalism being expressed in the work of Abraham Maslow and transcendentalism being evident in the writings of T. R. Miles, Michael Argyle, and David Hay. Maslow (1964) distinguishes between experiences of "self-actualization" and organized religion, which he criticizes as being a major enemy of religious experiences, imprisoning them in legalistic and bureaucratic institutions. There are "peak experiences" that were present at the origin of religions, but those experiences were entirely naturalistic, higher states of human feeling and awareness, though they increase a sense of personal wholeness and purposefulness.

Though such states are natural, they involve what Maslow calls B-knowledge or illumination knowledge. Such knowledge views the world without regard for human profit, in a nonegoistic way, and is focused on ideals in art, mathematics, science, morality, or religion. It can issue in a "plateau experience," which is a general satisfaction in all experience, taking into account peak experiences, but worked into an integrated view of life.

Maslow is an interesting example of someone who separates "transcendental experience" from religion and seems to embrace a nonreductive humanism. He does not find it necessary to appeal to any supernatural element in religious experience. But the fact remains that most people who have religious experiences do think they apprehend some sort of transcendent reality, and some account needs to be given of that belief.

Empirical Surveys of Religious Experience

Empirical research, mostly by questionnaire and social survey, generally shows that religious or transcendental experiences occur to somewhere between 35 to 55 percent of most populations. A. M. Greeley (1974) reported a 35 percent positive response in a national survey in the United States to the question, "Have you ever felt as though you were close to a very powerful spiritual force that seemed to lift you out of yourself?"

The Alister Hardy Religious Experience Research Centre in Great Britain asks the question, "Have you been aware of or influenced by a presence or power, whether you call it God or not, which is different from your everyday self?" In a British National Opinion Poll in 1976, 36 percent of the population replied that they had, and this proportion increased to 56 percent among those who had received education beyond the age of twenty. Interestingly, Charles Glock and Rodney Stark (1965) found that, in the United States, 45 percent of Protestants and 44 percent of Catholics said they had experienced a feeling that they were somehow "in the Presence of God." Transcendental experiences, apparently, occur to less than half of the religiously committed, and to about the same proportion of people in the population in general.

In the first surveys published by the Alister Hardy Research Centre, responses had to be sent in voluntarily, so it is a rather self-selecting group. Over four thousand responses were received to an advertisement in the national press. The vast majority of reports were of increased sense of purpose and meaning in life, though there was a small incidence of fearful or frightening experiences of evil. Experiences of Transcendent Reality, if these reports are to be trusted, are overwhelmingly beneficent, giving rise to an increased sense of well-being or joy. The vague sense of

"Something Other" is often, but not always, personalized into a deity. David Hay (1990) conducted surveys in the U.K., based on the Greeley and Hardy questions and claimed a 36 percent positive response. At present, the Hardy Research Centre is undertaking global surveys, using suitably adapted forms of the Hardy question. So far, a survey in China (an officially nonreligious country) has suggested results very similar to those in the West. The interviewees were all Han Chinese. Only 8.7 percent described themselves as religious, but 56.7 percent said they had experienced a spiritual being or power. It seems that, regardless of race or official religion, about half the human race sometimes feel themselves aware of a spiritual force, power, or presence beyond themselves.

There are many problems with such surveys from a strictly scientific point of view. They are often very culture-specific, being largely addressed to English speakers in the Western world and sometimes selecting those who are already religiously committed or at least interested. More recent attempts to broaden the range to non-Western countries are helpful here, and if the Chinese results are confirmed, there is a greater chance of seeing this sort of experience as universal.

The other major problem is in deciding just what sort of question to ask. The Hardy question could gain a positive response from those who believe in the exalted spiritual force of flying saucers or in the presence among us of alien presences from the stars. The questions are very vague and susceptible to many interpretations, and they do not clearly distinguish between irrational fantasy and the sort of mystical union claimed by major saints. But at least they represent an attempt to gain information about what humans feel and think, and they indicate that "transcendental experiences" are recognized by about half the human race. It seems that, in an intense and distinguishable form, they occur fairly rarely and that they are vague enough to be interpretable in quite a number of ways.

Suppose we left the existence of a Spiritual Reality as an open question: what would the results of these surveys show? That claimed experience of Spiritual Reality is not common to all and is not an everyday occurrence. Yet a significant proportion of people have such experiences, which can be interpreted in various ways. William James characterizes "mystical" experiences as ineffable but having some intellectual content, as transient, and passive. R. C. Zaehner identifies three types of religious experience—nature mysticism, monism (a feeling of unity with all things), and loving relation to God. Ninian Smart prefers a twofold division into mystical (unitive) and numinous (encounter with an "Other"). The conversion experiences studied by Starbuck seem very different from numinous or mystical experiences. And there may be something odd about isolating a particular sort of experience as "religious" when experiencing Transcendent Reality may often be a matter of how a person reacts to all experience, not something special and intense.

The collected data suggest that there is no single identifiable experience shared by all, but there is basic agreement in feeling a sense of unity with or close relation to a Spiritual Reality, a union that takes various forms. The experiences may involve sensory perceptions—of nature or music, for example—but they seem to be direct, nonsensory apprehensions of a nonphysical reality.

If the experiences are illusory, then a large proportion of humans are deluded about some of the most important experiences of their lives. If they are genuine, then a roughly similar proportion of humans lack any significant apprehension of Supreme Spiritual Reality. It is as if they were "Spirit-blind." A naturalist account, on the one hand, can be given in terms of "peak experiences" or unusual mental states, so a naturalist can explain why they occur. On the other hand, a believer can explain spiritual blindness as a result of the alienation of humanity from Spirit, which has made both religious and moral truths difficult to discern and even more difficult to live by.

What most surveys show is that those who have such experiences seem to be, or at least to feel themselves, happier, more balanced, and more altruistic as a result of their experiences. Surveys by the Oxford psychologist Michael Argyle (1958) analyzed data both from social surveys and from clinical psychiatric reports from Great Britain and the United States between 1900 and 1957 and concluded that religious belief cannot be correlated with any personality type or identifiable psychiatric illness.

Religious beliefs and experiences are not caused by, or strongly correlated with, any form of psychiatric illness. On the contrary, there is a positive correlation between religious belief and mental health and well-being, which is well-documented by Harold Koenig's *Handbook of Religion and Health* (2000). That does not prove that religious beliefs are true, but it confirms the hypothesis of evolutionary psychology that such beliefs have positive psychological and social benefits. The fact remains, however, that such benefits would not accrue unless the beliefs were independently believed to be true. Such a sense of truth is partly but importantly given by the intensity of religious experience, which carries a sense of objective truth with it. Yet, since there cannot be public verification of such truth, a naturalistic explanation in terms of strong psychological inclinations to form untestable beliefs can always be given.

Moral and Religious Experience

The result seems to be a draw. The evidence from personal experience for an objective Spiritual Reality is significant but not overwhelming. But perhaps it is misleading to concentrate on special "religious" experiences, whether of conversion, mystical union, or numinous feeling. If we do that, the crucial question seems to be whether the experiences can guarantee the reality of their objects. It is then hard to see what sort of guarantee could possibly be provided.

If we look back at religious morality, while there are intense experiences that convert some people to an altruistic outlook, the normal moral experience among religious believers does not seem to lie in the occurrence of intense, identifiable, and transient experiences. It is more a matter of interpreting many of life's situations than a matter of having a remarkable and discrete feeling state.

We do not normally speak of having "other-person experiences," of trying to describe what such experiences feel like, and then asking whether they show that other persons exist. We interpret the bodily behavior of others as the behavior of persons with thoughts, intentions, feelings, and desires. Our attention is focused on the persons, not on the nature of our feelings. And we are not trying to prove they really think and feel; we assume that they do, in order to have personal relations with them.

So, in regard to morality, we might interpret various events as demanding a moral response of compassion or as leading us to set aside personal prejudice in order to get at the truth. We do not infer the demand from our feelings; we accept that the demand is there. This may not seem religious, as we may feel we encounter a moral demand without believing in any God. But this is one important root of belief in God. For a Confucian, to feel the rightness of living in accord with the will of heaven is to respond to an element of reality. The physical elements of certain situations mediate the objective demand, the inmost moral structure of being. But because there is little or no talk of God, some may regard Confucianism as humanistic rather than religious.

Perhaps we could trace a spectrum of personalization in "transcendental" interpretations of morality. Confucian reticence about the reality of a transcendent being would lie at one end. Buddhism, being a "Middle Way," would appropriately speak of an objective state of compassion and wisdom. The Abrahamic faiths would lie at the other end, seeing compassion and wisdom as embodied in a personal creator God.

There may be no specifiable "feeling" to our interpretation of our sensory data as mediating moral claims upon us. What is significant is that some views of morality find it natural to speak of transcendent claims or ideals of beauty and goodness mediated through the objects we see, hear, and feel. Others find such talk unhelpful and think of morality as a matter of decision and the will.

We rarely speak of "moral experience," but we could (or some of us could) speak of apprehension of a moral dimension of reality. Religious morality ties such apprehension closely to apprehension of a Spiritual Reality. Indeed, it partly defines Spiritual Reality in terms of such moral apprehensions. Specific "religious experiences" would then be occasional and particularly intense feelings of such an apprehension. But the disposition to interpret all experience in terms of mediation of a Spiritual Reality, with a strong moral dimension, would be a more permanent, less intense, and often unnoticed cognitive orientation that might seem entirely natural.

Perhaps specific "religious experiences" could not establish the reality of their alleged objects. But maybe that is the wrong way to approach religious and moral cognition. It may not be a matter of inferring from inner states to unverifiable outer realities. It may rather be a question of whether we wish to divide "inner" and "outer" in this way at all. We might think of general interpretations of human experience and ask whether it is more reasonable to say that we experience a purely physical reality, to which we have purely subjective value responses, or to say that we experience a many-leveled, multifaceted reality that is mediated by means of our senses and involves our whole cognitive equipment, including our feelings.

If we do choose the latter option, surveys of "religious experience" may show that about half the population has occasional intense and memorable transcendental experiences, experiences of reality as more than purely physical. Such "peak experiences" may be given a naturalistic interpretation, but they do seem to be apprehensions of a spiritual dimension of reality, however they are more precisely interpreted.

We do not ordinarily speak of "moral experiences," but common sense assumes that there is an objectivity about morality; truth, happiness, justice, and beauty seem to exercise an influence upon us that is not causal but the influence of an ideal that calls us to realize it. As the philosopher J. L. Mackie (1977) said, believing in moral objectivity is just too "queer" if there is nowhere moral objects could be. There may just be "queer moral facts," facts of what G. E. Moore called "ought-to-be-ness." But a very natural place to put ideals of beauty, truth, and justice is in the mind of a God who is perfect beauty, truth, and goodness.

Morality can lead to religion, when the transcendental sense of goodness is linked to religious experiences of a spiritual sense of presence and power. If such a link is not made, morality can lose its binding and captivating force—as it is almost bound to do on a purely sociobiological account. As Michael Ruse once said, "A better understanding of biology might incline us to go against morality" (1995, 283). But equally importantly, religion can lose its moral basis and degenerate into a prudential bargaining with an authoritarian God, rather than being a free submission of the heart to a supremely beautiful and good Creator.

In conclusion, a purely naturalistic account of moral and religious beliefs can be given, but it is not the role of evolutionary biology to do so. Evolutionary biology can give us a better understanding of the development of our basic moral and religious inclinations and account for some of their peculiarities. But it cannot answer the question of what we ought to do or the question of whether, in our moral and religious lives, we are encountering a transcendental aspect of reality. The more we know about human nature from a scientific point of view, the better we will be able to reflect on what we should do. But science itself cannot tell us what to do, and our fundamental choice still lies where it always has: between seeing morality primarily as a matter for decision and seeing it primarily as a matter for discernment and response. Evolutionary psychology might help us to see that choice more starkly and to be better informed about the nature and limits of our choice. But whether morality puts us in touch with a Transcendental Reality remains, for science, an open question.

9. Has Science Made Belief in God Obsolete?

(ARE THERE ANY GOOD SCIENCE-BASED ARGUMENTS FOR GOD?)

The "Three-Age" View of Human Intellectual History

THERE IS A PICTURE of human intellectual progress made popular by Auguste Comte (it originated with Robert Turgot and Henri de Saint-Simon) that sees humanity as moving from the earliest stage of religion through a stage of metaphysics to the final maturity of science. Each stage supplants and renders obsolete the stage before it. The age of religion is the infancy of the human race, when humans formed animistic ideas of spirits in trees and storms, which could be influenced by magical techniques. In *The Golden Bough*, Sir James Fraser subdivides this first stage into one of magic, when the earliest humans tried to influence natural forces by magical rituals, followed by religion, when it was realized that magic did not work, and instead humans submitted in fear and imprecation to the mysterious gods who caused thunderstorms and earthquakes.

But prayer did not work either, so the more sophisticated humans began to do metaphysics, to think rationally about the nature of the universe. They were, however, armchair thinkers, like Plato, who never actually did experiments but just thought what things ought to be like (the planets, for instance, must move in circular orbits because circles are the most perfect Forms).

Only later, in sixteenth-century Europe, did experimental science get going, and at last humans came to know the real causal factors that made things happen, finally exorcising the ghosts of magic and religion from reality. Science shows us that supernatural spirits are both unnecessary and misleading fantasies. So, at last, we can face a vast impersonal universe with heroic stoicism, refusing to be deluded by fantasies of ghosts above the sky, seeing things as they are—blind, compassionless, unconscious, and indifferent to all things human.

That is part of a popular modern myth of human progress. Science will deliver us from superstition and infantile fear of the gods. By the cold clear light of reason, we will be able to devise a more humane, less authoritarian morality and plan the human future calmly and wisely, without bowing before unseen forces that demand human sacrifice—of the intellect, if not of actual flesh.

That myth was devised in the eighteenth century, when the cultured elite celebrated its emancipation from the brute passions of the working classes and more primitive races of the world—that is, from virtually everyone who did not own a country estate, run by those same inferior brutish lower orders.

The myth was destroyed in the twentieth century, the century in which scientific technology, applied to constructing weapons of war, led to more violent deaths than in the whole of previous human history. Science, the great liberator, had made it possible to kill more human beings in more terrible ways than had ever been imagined. The pitiless indifference of nature had taken root in the hearts of humans, and, from the most cultured civilizations in the world, the brightest and fittest members of a whole generation slaughtered one another in the greatest ritual of human sacrifice ever known on earth.

The evils of religious intolerance and warfare pale into insignificance by comparison with the record of emancipated twentieth-century Europe. That may lead us to think again about the alleged primitiveness of early humanity, as opposed to the rational thought of modern humans. Yet, from an evolutionary point of view, the intellectual capacities of prehominids, millions of years ago, must have been less developed than those of modern humans. There is no doubt that human knowledge has grown with the development of writing and mathematics, and it has grown more rapidly in the last few decades than ever before. We know that before the sixteenth century many human beliefs about the natural world were incorrect. And we can see in the recorded history of religion a development from belief in many gods and spirits of mixed moral character to belief in one God of supreme goodness.

That there has been a development in intellectual understanding is not in doubt. It is hard to exaggerate the revolution in moral and scientific thinking that has occurred in recent years. A universal charter of human rights has been drawn up, slavery has been officially abolished by most nations, equality of the sexes has come to be thought generally desirable, and care for animals has come onto the moral agenda. In science, the cosmos is seen as an intelligible realm of universal laws, evolution is established, and genetics and quantum physics have given us a dramatically new understanding of and control over human and physical nature.

All that is true. It would be odd if, in religion, there had not been a concomitant development in understanding. And there has been. The rise of biblical criticism, an increased awareness of the global diversity of faiths, the acceptance of new scientific understandings of the cosmos, the acceptance of freedom of religion and belief, and a clearer vision of the importance of universal human welfare as a religious goal have been hallmarks of a new understanding of religious faith as essentially concerned with universal human welfare and worship of a God who encourages personal creativity and compassion for all sentient beings.

The twenty-first-century world is one in which there have been enormous developments of understanding in science, morality, and religion. But these have been accompanied by relapses into the crudest barbarism. Human rights are routinely violated, slavery still exists in new and hidden forms, women are oppressed in much of the world, and animals are treated with extreme cruelty. New scientific understanding is widely used to create ever more terrifying means of destruction, including nuclear and biological weapons. The spread of global technology, despite its many benefits, threatens to render the world uninhabitable. New biological experimentation could release destructive organisms that could wipe out human life. In religion, fundamentalist views that insist on the literal truth of one scripture and encourage the use of violence to wipe out all competitors constitute a major threat to peace. The turn to antiscientific forms of religious belief and to forms of faith untouched by rational reflection and based on unquestioned authority is a major intellectual setback for the alleged progress of humanity.

The picture does not seem to be one of linear progress from religion through metaphysics to science. It is more like a picture of an undoubted growth in knowledge and understanding, in religion, morality, and science alike, alongside a misuse of that knowledge in the name of the naked will to power and world domination.

Science has enormously increased our understanding of nature, but it is not our liberator from hatred and greed. It can be used either for good or evil. It can increase human health and welfare, or it can destroy the world. So it is, one would think, with religion. It can be, and has been, used for evil, to oppress and destroy. Or it can be, and has been, used for good, to found orphanages, schools, hospitals, and hospices, to sponsor great works of art, and to motivate humans to excellence in science and philosophy.

Was there then, as the Comtean myth asserted, an "age of magic or religion" that was founded on false views of causality and false beliefs in supernatural spirit and that was rendered obsolete by science?

A study of human history suggests that religious beliefs, like scientific beliefs, were much more naive and mistaken in very early human history than they are now. And they probably shared the moral ambiguity of all human activities, being used both to bolster the authority of religious charlatans and to motivate heroically virtuous action in tribal societies. It is, however, prejudice to assert that religion properly belonged to that era, whereas science did not. A more reasonable view is that both religion (reverence for the spiritual world) and science (understanding of the natural world) were in a undeveloped state in prehistory and in need of much further development.

The Origins of Religion and Spiritual Sensibility

What form did religious beliefs take in prehistory? The disappointing, but important, answer is that we do not know. The anthropologist Edward Evans-Pritchard ridiculed a number of well-known attempts to get into the minds of early human beings and say how they invented religion in his classic book *Theories of Primitive Religion* (1965). The general technique he criticizes seems to have been to say, "If I had been an early human being living in a cave, I would probably have been a very fearful and superstitious individual; and so that is what they probably were."

The claims of some writers influenced by evolutionary biology are not much stronger. Scott Atran (2004, 6) writes that "religion is . . . a recurring cultural by-product of the complex evolutionary landscape. . . . [C]ore religious beliefs minimally violate ordinary human notions about how the world is . . . enabling people to imagine minimally impossible supernatural worlds that solve existential problems, including death and deception." His thesis is that religion is not adaptive as such, but the creation of imaginary worlds is a means of solving problems in the real world, at least psychologically.

How is Atran supposed to know this? He clearly has not observed early religion, since no one has. From the graves and statuettes and other artifacts we have, it is very hard to draw many positive conclusions. Atran seems to be imposing on the past what he feels to be true of the present, but in a more childish way.

I doubt if this can be considered serious science. Ironically, it is itself an imaginary story (he just made it up) that violates ordinary human notions about the existence of a Spiritual Reality (most people think there is such a reality), enabling the author to solve the problem of how religion could arise when there is no Spiritual Reality.

To say there is a Spiritual Reality is to say that, underlying the world of things perceived by the senses, there is a reality that is not bound by space and time and that has the nature of consciousness and value. That reality will be conceived in terms of the concepts available in specific societies—in that sense, it will be socially constructed—used in a metaphorical or symbolic way to evoke a sense of what cannot be straightforwardly described.

We know that many early societies worshipped many gods and that the gods were associated with natural phenomena, with significant historical events, and with human values and desirable or feared possibilities. But we do not know that the god of thunder, for example, was invented to explain why it thundered and so that he could be propitiated in order to control the weather. This is to see early religion as primitive (and useless) technology. An alternative account is that thunder might be perceived as a metaphor for the destructive power of God, rather than God being a quasiscientific inference from the occurrence of thunder.

Perhaps some evolutionary biologists simply lack a sense of poetry and metaphor and, therefore, cannot understand what it would be for thunder to be taken as a "sign" of God—not evidence for God but a sensory image of a reality that cannot be physically sensed but whose nature is expressed in some way in everything that is. Some symbols can be taken as especially appropriate and revelatory signs of that reality. For instance, the abode of the gods will be "above"—physical height is a natural sensory image for spiritual superiority. Thunder from the sky can be a sensory image for the fearful power of the source of all being.

On such an account, the "religious sense" would lie in a disposition to take finite things or events as signs, communications, or disclosures of an unseen deeper reality. It may be mistaken, but the mistake is not that of thinking the cause of thunder is an invisible man pushing the clouds together.

In early religions that we know about, there are often many gods, both good and bad. That reflects the sense that there are many aspects of Spiritual Reality, perhaps many consciousnesses and values and disvalues, both good and bad, and some of them may speak to particular individuals more than others. So we can choose our own God, our own symbol of Spirit. Or, more probably, our tribe may choose it for us, and we learn one set of symbols of Spirit as especially significant for our society. This may be for historical reasons, associated with major events in the past or for reasons of cultural custom, leading us to prefer some symbols of ultimate reality (say, kingship) to others (bananas, perhaps). Not many tribes think the Supreme Spirit is a banana—though some do. More tribes think there is a king of the gods. One of those tribes was an ancestor of the Abrahamic faiths.

Evolutionary psychologists are surely correct in thinking that religion must have originated in prerational rituals and beliefs that had some important function in their societies. They are correct in seeing that many early beliefs are clearly false, if taken literally, and are sometimes morally scary, involving human sacrifice and mutilation. But they often seem to imply that the only function of beliefs is survival value or at least some by-product of such a function.

Daniel Dennett says, "Mother Nature is a philistine accountant who cares only about the immediate payoff in terms of differential replication" (2006, 80). That may be so. But when human consciousness comes on the scene, other payoffs may become important. Whatever Mother Nature thinks, people (many people, anyway) care about beauty, truth, and goodness, about ideals that attract them because of their inherent value. They find intimations of beauty in their environment, and, in their dances, songs, and rituals, they create beautiful forms that mediate transcendent beauty. That transcendent beauty may be symbolized in many finite forms, and the "world of spirits" is an imaginative narrative that evokes such a sensibility.

Some writers have talked of "memes," which are supposed to be units of thought or belief that are successful replicators in human culture. It is difficult to think of any analogy that a thought has to the chemical structure of a gene—a piece of a DNA molecule—and equally difficult to think of a principle of natural selection that could select favored memes. For that reason, I regard "memetics" as a pseudoscience. It implies that beliefs get selected because they are easily replicated or psychologically memorable, rather than because they are thought to be true.

When a "memetic" account is given of why early humans believed that 2 + 2 = 4, the account is not that the sum is correct but that those who believed it survived better than those who thought that 2 + 2 = 22. But the reason they survived better is that 2 plus 2 really does equal 4. That is a piece of knowledge that is useful because it is true.

The same goes for religion. Some social anthropologists, beginning with Emile Durkheim, claim that religion has the function of promoting social solidarity. That may be one of its functions, though it is not likely to be the only one. But it will only have that function if people believe that some religious claims are true. Religion is truth-claiming, though the truth is particularly vague, polysemic, and hard to describe. It is because such a reality is believed to exist that belief in it promotes moral solidarity and enthusiasm among its devotees.

The reasons early humans gave for their beliefs may be, from our point of view, naive and often mistaken—just as alchemy was a naive and mistaken aim of early chemistry, in the sixteenth century. But it may have expressed a desire for truth and may well have been rooted in a discernment of truth, just as alchemy was, however partial and undeveloped.

Daniel Dennett locates the beginnings of religion in what the early anthropologist E. B. Tylor termed "animism"—"a hyperactive habit of finding agency wherever anything puzzles or frightens us" (2006, 123). This may be rather near the truth, though the way it is put is unduly dismissive. The formulation encourages us to think that religion is a childish attitude that sees little invisible men and women hiding in trees, sprinkling us with rain, and living in waterfalls. The implication is that there is little difference in kind between belief in fairies and belief in a Conscious Agency underlying the world of appearances that our senses present to us.

Perhaps belief in fairies is a degenerate and literalized form of belief in naturally beautiful objects as signs of Spiritual Presence. If so, we might look to the myths and rituals of early religion as poetic and dramatic means of expressing and evoking what Donald Hughes describes as "the mysterious interrelatedness of all that is" (quoted in Gottlieb 1996, 138). "Indians," he says, "regarded things in nature as spiritual beings, not because they were seeking some explanation for natural phenomena, but because human beings experience a spiritual resonance in nature" (quoted in Gottlieb 1996, 139). Evolutionary psychology must leave open the possibility that such a sense of spiritual resonance, the sense that humans participate in a spiritual universe and are not conscious, largely deluded freaks in an impersonal universe, is a natural human attitude that has survived primarily because it is believed to disclose truth.

The Development of Theism in Hebrew Thought

Religion has survived from the earliest recorded human history, but it has changed, just as a scientific attempt to understand the world has done. Local tribal cults widened and developed into four main streams of religious understanding. Bearing in mind that there are many overlaps between and variations within these streams of thought, they may be termed: theism, idealism, dualism, and monism. The first, the theistic, tradition was developed by the Hebrew prophets, in which the many gods, spirits, and ancestors who were symbols of transcendence were unified into the idea of one creator God of moral purpose. Within the Bible, this development can be seen particularly clearly, and it reaches a culminating point in the eighth to the sixth centuries BCE, with the idea of one ineffable God who interacts with humans as a morally commanding and supremely good personal reality.

In the Hebrew Bible, there are no "proofs of" or arguments for God. Indeed, in the book of Job, the three friends of Job who try to give philosophical explanations of the ways of God are characterized as "false friends." The general impression is that human reason is fickle and not wholly trustworthy. Reason is not bad—the wisdom of God is ultimately wholly reasonable—but human reason can be used for many different purposes, good and bad. It cannot in and of itself reveal truth, for its job is to draw reliable inferences and to make connections in thought from truths established in other ways.

The popular understanding of proofs of God implies that God is not immediately known but is a sort of inference from events in the world. That is foreign to the biblical outlook. Biblical belief in God is not a matter of just opting blindly for some idea without any evidence. It is a matter of encountering the power and glory of God, primarily in the demands of morality and in the events of life, seen as encounters with a personal reality that transcends all human concepts but is apprehended as just and merciful.

Rudolf Otto, in his 1917 work *The Idea of the Holy,* and Martin Buber, in *I and Thou,* first published in 1923, catch this sense perfectly. Otto called it the sense of the numinous, a sense of mystery, awesome power, and passionate attraction. The numinous can be sensed in nature, in moral claims, in aesthetic beauty, and in personal relationships. If reason is involved, its function is to construct an always partly inadequate conceptual description of this suprarational reality, to align it with our highest moral insights and our most adequate general description of the experienced world. That is an important function.

The basis of biblical faith is not inferential reason. It is personal encounter. God is the one who liberates us from evil (from slavery in Egypt) and who fills the heart with joy. To have faith is to entrust your life to God. But neither faith nor abstract argument establishes that God exists. Reason tries, often rather feebly, to make belief in God rational—self-consistent, coherent with other knowledge, and fruitful for understanding. Faith tries, equally feebly, to make the religious way of life a positive, personally and morally fulfilling relationship to God. But belief in the actuality of God, like belief in the actuality of anything real and vital, is rooted in encounter with a personal, moral, liberating, and transforming power and presence.

This is, as Tylor and Dennett suggest, seeing all things as mediating a personal reality or realities, but it is not helpfully called "animism." It is consciousness of the power and presence of absolute Goodness, mediated and yet partly concealed by our experience of living in a human world that is a complex interplay of beauty and intelligibility, of hatred and ignorance.

It is still possible, of course, to believe that there is no such objective personal reality, however sophisticated we try to be about it. So, appeal to "encounter" will hardly convince those who regard it as a sort of psychological illusion. Nevertheless, impartiality and honesty require us to concede that we cannot be certain religious believers are deluded, so we should try to approach their beliefs with an initial sensitivity. We may think this sort of "subjective" evidence is insufficient, but it seems unlikely that it is simply some form of irrational delusion.

Theism, Idealism, and Arguments for God

Belief in a Supreme Spiritual Reality is often developed in a philosophically profound way. This is clear in a second development of the basic idea of Spiritual Reality, idealism, which is characteristic of some major Indian traditions. The Supreme Lord is not a separate personal being but the inner nature of all reality, whose nature is consciousness, intelligence, and bliss, conscious union with which is the goal of the religious life.

As in the Hebrew tradition, this view begins with an analysis of the human condition and with the realization that there is something deeply unsatisfying about the way most humans live. For Hebrews, this was seen as "slavery to sin," a sort of rebellion against goodness for the sake of egoistic pride and self-will. In the Indian traditions, it is seen as "ignorance" (*avidya*), a failure to see that you are part of one all-encompassing Spiritual Reality and a bondage to the desires of the individual isolated ego.

For Indian idealism, liberation from egoism and the ignorance it brings is accomplished by a personal realization of the unity of all things in the universal Self. In this tradition, too, reason is not a reliable way to God because reason shares in the fundamental ignorance that is the bondage of the ego. Again, reason is very important, and argumentation and inference play a major part in Indian religious thinking. But, as David Hume said, "reason is the slave of the passions," and the fundamental orientation of reason is set by basic human desires and attitudes, operating at a sub- (or supra-) rational level. Where love of individual ego predominates, reason will only serve to make egoism more effective. But where love of the Supreme Self predominates, reason will help us to discern where true human liberation lies.

The idealist view differs from the theistic view, but they can be seen to be complementary perspectives on the relation between finite selves and the Supreme Self. In detail, they cannot both be true. But they can be seen as conceptual models drawn from different ways of interpreting experience, both fail to be wholly adequate and each stresses distinctive insights. As the basic models are elaborated by philosophers (like Sankara and Ramanuja in the Indian tradition or Maimonides, Aquinas, and Al Gazzali in the Abrahamic tradition), they generate inferences that can be checked against scientific knowledge, for example. In that way, reason helps to verify or disprove specific religious interpretations, though it rarely generates wholly conclusive or incontestable conclusions. Arguments for God can be seen as ways of showing the coherence of religious interpretations with scientific ones. That is exactly what Aquinas was doing when he wrote of the "five ways of demonstrating the existence of God." He was taking the best scientific thought of his day, based on Aristotle, and showing how the idea of God as the perfect, necessary, First Cause was a coherent and plausible corollary of Aristotelian theories of causality.

The price of this attempt was that, as Aristotelian notions of causality were dropped, Aquinas' specific arguments lost plausibility, and Kant was able to show how Newtonian physics no longer made the Aristotelian arguments seem plausible. Kant, in turn, took some of the leading basic beliefs of his own eighteenth-century Prussian culture—beliefs in human freedom, individual moral responsibility, and self-improvement—and made them into a model for conceiving God in a new way, as the reality that made free moral self-improvement obligatory and possible in a basically mechanistic universe.

It was not at all, as some mistakenly think, that Kant set out to destroy all metaphysical thinking and all belief in or rational "arguments for" God. On the contrary, he set out to place metaphysics on a firm basis for the first time. A crucial step in his philosophy was to distinguish "theoretical" from "practical" reason and to root moral and religious beliefs in the realm of practical reason. If you can follow him in making that distinction, then Kant's arguments for God consist in showing how God is not necessary for theoretical reason (i.e., for Newtonian physics) but is necessary for practical reason (for rational commitment to the absolute demands of universal morality).

This is not an argument from universally accepted morality to God, who suddenly pops out of the argument unexpectedly, like a rabbit out of a hat. It is an attempt to construct a conceptual model for Spirit (which Kant assumed to be the "noumenal" basis for the world of appearances) that would reinforce the new emphasis on human autonomy and moral freedom that was the focus of the revolutionary spirit of the eighteenth century. This model downgraded the "servile" obedience of worship but found the basis of moral autonomy in the self-legislation of practical reason, the practical will of the universe toward free self-improvement for all.

When so-called proofs of God are seen as attempts to construct a systematic conceptual scheme within which Spirit can have a coherent place, then we can better understand both their cultural and historical conditions and their real character as imaginative constructions of a worldview from a spiritual perspective.

It can also be seen that the worldview of atheistic materialism has precisely the same intellectual character, except that it is an imaginative construction that excludes Spirit from serious consideration. Sometimes—in the work of Richard Dawkins, for example—a neo-Darwinian model of adaptation through chance mutation and blind selection is taken as the key model for understanding the whole of reality. That model must then be rationally assessed in exactly the same way as theistic or idealist models will be assessed.

It can be said to be verified if it seems to be economical, fruitful, and comprehensive—if it requires few basic concepts and entities, if it motivates scientific inquiry, and if it can give a good explanation for all features of the humanly experienced world. It will be falsified if it fails to explain aesthetic, moral, or religious beliefs well, if it threatens human dignity and freedom, and if it omits many features of the experienced world.

But such verification and falsification are never conclusive. It is always a matter of finding a cumulative set of reasons that together point to a favored model and trying to show that apparent counterinstances are due to misunderstandings or oversimplifications. Both theism and materialism can be rationally held and argued for, but reason is never decisive in either case. The question of the sorts of experience you have, the importance you give to them, and the sorts of concepts you find most adequate to interpret them looks as though it will remain highly contested for the foreseeable future.

That is why there are no knock-down proofs of God and why there could never be. There are no knock-down proofs of materialism or atheism either. To say that there is evidence for materialism and not for God is to beg the question and use rhetoric instead of rational argument. For the sciences, which quite intentionally deal only with the material and which, therefore, insist on the need for material evidence, have no view on whether there is a nonmaterial reality for which one would need nonmaterial evidence. It is perfectly rational to hold that there is, but reason is not the final arbiter of the issue. As Blaise Pascal said, "The heart has its reasons, of which reason is unaware." God is not known by reason, though reason has an important part to play in constructing human ideas about God. God is known by the heart, by a passionate commitment to the ultimate authenticity of a specific sort of human awareness of truth. Materialism is also known by the heart, in just the same way. But, for the theist, it is God who is believed to grasp the heart and unite it to the Divine in such a way that to deny divine reality becomes a betrayal of the deepest personal commitment there could be.

Nontheistic Developments in Religion

Not all religions believe in God. A third main development of the idea of Spirit is nontheistic, but it is far from being materialist. Renouncing traditions like Buddhism developed a more impersonal notion of Spirit in terms of nirvana. This was also a reality of consciousness, intelligence, and bliss but was not conceived as a supreme personal Lord or as the Creator of the universe. It is, nevertheless, an underlying reality into which humans can enter, by overcoming the attachments of selfish desire and the illusion of the Ultimate Reality of the sensory world. In some ways, Buddhism represents the polar opposite of modern materialist views, which see Spiritual Reality as illusion and the material world as the only form of reality. Buddhism presents a different perspective—the material world is an illusion of fettered consciousness, and the only enduring reality is the calm and peace of unlimited and Pure Consciousness.

The Four Noble Truths of Buddhism form a very good antidote to a rationalist, deductive or inductive, understanding of proofs of God, and they help to reveal the real roots of such proofs. The first truth is that "all is unsatisfactory or has the nature of suffering." Reflection on human experience can bring a person to the point of seeing that everyday human life is filled with sorrow. If this is not seen, then Buddhism cannot even have initial appeal. So, the argument is not to an evaluatively neutral fact that anyone could see if he or she tried hard enough, whatever that person's own personal feelings and attitudes. It is precisely an attempt to get people to take up a specific attitude or feeling to the whole of their experience. It is essentially evaluative, and so it is more like art, prompting a perspective on life, than like science, establishing a fact that is true no matter you feel about it.

The second truth is that the cause of suffering is attachment, the sort of desire that makes a person possessive, envious, or anxious about possessions. This is, again, an evaluative diagnosis, and agreement with it requires not dispassionate inquiry but a hard-won insight into your own motives, desires, and state of mind.

The third truth is that there is a way to end suffering. And the fourth truth sets out the Eightfold Path as this way, a way of intellectual insight, moral training, and meditation. A person who adheres to Buddhism will find these truths verified in personal experience, as suffering decreases and liberation is found.

Arguments for the truth of Buddhism are attempts to evoke a specific perspective on human life, which will become corroborated by practice and commitment to a path of discipline and belief. This could be called faith, but it is not personal trust in a divine Lord. It is rather commitment to a practice in the belief that it will lead to liberation, even though, at the beginning, there is no theoretical certainty that it will do so.

The Buddhist way helps to clarify the nature of religious argument and of religious faith. Religious argument does not provide universal proofs, and religious faith does not call for blind acceptance. Argument seeks to evoke a set of attitudes toward experience, and faith is commitment to a practice that may resolve the problems highlighted by those attitudes—in other words, a practice that leads to liberation from greed, hatred, and ignorance.

Buddhist belief does not lead to a personal God or a Supreme Self. Its description of Spirit is a more impersonal idea of a state of supreme wisdom and bliss. So it may be seen not as a mere contradiction of theistic beliefs but as an alternative model for Spirit, based on a different set of cumulative reasons that pick out important human attitudes and practices.

A closely related model is found in the fourth major development of the idea of Spirit. Founded mostly in East Asia, it attempts to integrate the spiritual dimension—nirvana, or the Tao, or the Way of Heaven (*Tian*)—more closely with finite existence and human conduct. For this view, Spiritual Reality is identical with material reality. But when the one reality is seen truly, it can be seen that the spiritual is the primary effective causal and moral force and is not just a by-product or epiphenomenon of material causation.

Confucian ideas of the Way tend to stress the importance of society and civility, whereas Taoist ideas are more concerned with harmony with the flow of nature. Again, this difference can be seen as a result of attention to different aspects of experience—society and nature—which leads to the construction of differing trajectories of interpretation. The common element is a belief that there is an authentic or truly human way of life written into the natural order, that most human lives exhibit lack of harmony with that order, and that conformity to the Way leads to a more personally fulfilling and morally committed life.

These spiritual paths differ, but they are all reflective and systematic developments from earlier human beliefs about Transcendent Reality. They are all rooted in the teachings of major religious adepts, who are credited with an ability to discern the spiritual more deeply and whose views have become normative for various religious traditions. The differences between them more or less cover the spectrum of possible divergent interpretations, and each uses a different, but related, key model as the basis of its general interpretations.

Within those traditions, religious philosophers have developed sophisticated and complex conceptual schemes to systematize the original normative disclosures in ways that are rationally and morally acceptable. Such developments constitute a second phase in the development of religion, a stage of normative disclosures, systematically articulated by utilizing the best philosophical or scientific tools that were available at the time.

Most of these developments occurred before modern science had begun, but it is misleading to call them "prescientific," if that word implies they were less intellectually acceptable than scientific views. On the contrary, if anything, they were more advanced intellectually than the scientific views of their own day. It was not for nothing that theology was called "queen of the sciences" in medieval Europe, for theology was indeed the most systematically developed body of beliefs that was available, and the embryonic physics and chemistry that then existed (mostly dependent not on religion but on the thoughts of ancient Greeks like Aristotle) were almost wholly mistaken and unsystematized.

Post-Enlightenment Religion

Things were to change yet again, and, after the sixteenth century, what might be called the third phase of religious development, introducing recognizably modern interpretations of religion and of science, came into existence. In this third phase, the study of history became a more critical discipline, requiring close attention to available evidence and suspicion of heroic narratives with a moral message that had characterized much earlier history. The study of science introduced new technologies, like the telescope and microscope, that made experiment and observation much more reliable. There was also a revolution in mathematical thinking that made it possible to describe nature in precise quantitative terms. Human society itself became an object of scientific (in the sense of closely observed and dispassionate) study, and old systems of political absolutism were criticized in the name of human autonomy and democracy.

In this dramatic intellectual change, science was just one, though an important one, of the elements of new critical learning that could be called "evidentialism." That is the requirement that all factual assertions should be backed up by carefully recorded evidence, and all political and moral assertions call for justification in terms of what can be seen to contribute to universal human welfare.

If there was an intellectual war, it was a war between traditional religious and scientific authority and the new evidentialism, not a war between religion and science as such. Certainly, some people saw the situation as a war because the rise of biblical criticism seemed to suggest that religious belief was not based on firm historical evidence. The methods of science appeared, at least for a time, to support the belief that the universe was a closed causal mechanism that allowed no room for and required no reference to God. And religious morality was often seen as authoritarian and supportive of reactionary political institutions like absolute monarchy.

There was always another side to religion, however. Perhaps religious belief was primarily based on personal spiritual experience, rather than on poorly evidenced historical facts like the virgin birth. Perhaps science revealed the beauty and elegance of nature but left the realms of consciousness, value, and purpose untouched. Perhaps religious morality had a radical side that required consideration of all human beings as equal and even required special consideration for those disadvantaged by poverty and social oppression. Religious morality always had the potential to challenge the belief that all law is the positive law of particular nation states or political systems and that what humans decide is the only ultimate arbiter of what is right.

Indeed, it is not implausible to see the Enlightenment as a product in Europe of Christian thinking. The Christian claim that God had been revealed in a historical person led to a great interest in history. The claim that Jesus embodied the eternal *Logos*, or Wisdom of God, and that all things were destined to be "united in Christ" led to an interest in the structure of a rational universe patterned on divine wisdom and accessible to humans, who were made in the image of God. And the claim that God created all persons to live in fellowship and to fulfill their God-given talents led to doctrines of human rights and a search for a more cohesive idea of the common good.

These insights were slow in coming and were, to some extent, impeded by the alliance of Christianity with the Roman, Spanish, and British Empires, to name but three. But they were there in the scriptural sources from the first, and, when the time was right, they began to come to light.

The search for authentic history, for understanding of the laws of an intelligible cosmos, and for a moral and political law based on reason and not on the will to power is not an antireligious movement. Religious motives can and often did underpin these quests. The third stage of religion embodies critical study and analysis of history, of the cosmos, and of human morality. These things can plausibly be seen as expressing a deeper insight into the true nature of religious faith, just as the invention of calculus, the telescope, and the laws of nature made science in its modern sense possible for the first time.

In this way of seeing the history of the Enlightenment, far from supplanting religion, science helps religion to discover its own distinctive contribution to human knowledge. There may, as Comte suggested, be three major stages in human development, but religion is involved at every stage and is not confined to the first stage and destined to be left behind. In the third stage, which is not yet completed, religion is able to disentangle itself from reliance on uncertain historical claims, from competition with the factual observations of science, and from authoritarian forms of morality.

Yet, while there is no competition with science, it is not true that science has no impact on religion. On the contrary, we must, however cautiously, use the best science of our day, as Aquinas did in his, to refine the concepts of Spiritual Reality that history has bequeathed to us. There will be no "proofs" and no experimental and publicly available evidence. But there will be conceptual schemes that are more consilient with science and that show what sort of concept of Spirit is compatible with, and perhaps even enriches, the insights of science into the nature of the physical world.

God and the Multiverse

Possibly the first lesson that modern science teaches is that a spiritual dimension of reality, if there is one, is likely to be unitary and intelligible. Science sees the universe as one interconnected set of phenomena, bound together by mathematically intelligible laws. There is a unity about it that does not suggest a plurality of spiritual powers. If there is a Spiritual Reality, it will be a mathematically inclined, unitary intelligence—we might say, metaphorically, a God of wisdom.

Moreover, the cosmos orginated with a big bang. It had one common origin, and it developed in accordance with a set of complex laws (the laws of quantum cosmology) that, in some way, seem to precede the physical universe itself. That further suggests that Spirit is a creator, not just a designer, of independent matter. Matter itself originates from quantum fluctuations in a vacuum. It has an origin, and this origin is itself eternal (beyond time and space) and intelligible.

From all the possible universes there could be, one universe is selected for existence. This selection out of a vast realm of possibility suggests selection on a rational principle—again, in metaphorical terms, free choice by an Extracosmic Intelligence. That is creation, the bringing into being of a universe by an act of free choice. The scientific picture helps to make clear the metaphorical language of "action by a personal being" that theism uses and to free that language of undue literalism or anthropomorphism. But it is entirely in line with the classical theological definitions of God as given, for example, by Thomas Aquinas.

This should not be taken as an inferential proof of God. It is rather a demonstration of what view of Spirit the scientific view of the universe suggests. There is a good argument to the existence of one wise Creator from modern cosmology, but that is only the case if we accept the existence of Spiritual Reality in the first place and are wondering how to describe it and its probable relation to the cosmos. Such an acceptance is rooted in personal experience. So, the classical proofs of God might be better construed not as arguments to an otherwise unknown Spiritual Reality from material nature but as interpretations of an experienced Spiritual Reality in the light of the best available scientific knowledge. Naturally, if we reject all such experience or think that the idea of an unembodied Intelligence is incoherent or vacuous, these proofs will not be convincing.

Yet modern cosmology can be quite supportive of the idea that there is an underlying cosmic intelligence. Not many physicists would take seriously the opinion that the universe just exists by chance. As Martin Rees says (2001), that suggestion is giving up on the very basis of science, the basic principle that all things have a reason for existing. If that principle is accepted, the only real intellectually respectable alternatives, Rees says, are either creation by intelligence or the existence of a multiverse.

For those who posit a multiverse, this space/time in which we exist is only one of many. Other space/time universes, a great number of them, may bubble out from this one in black holes. Or they may continually split off from this one as alternative quantum states. Or—the most extreme possibility—every possible universe may actually exist, a view taken by Max Tegmark (2007).

On the one hand, this theory of a multiverse is a very controversial area of cosmology, and some scientists say that positing completely unobservable universes is not really science at all. On the other hand, string theory and some other cosmological theories posit fundamental equations for understanding the universe that certainly open up the possibility that there are other universes and even make it likely that there are. For instance, if this universe originates by a quantum fluctuation in a vacuum, there is reason to think that other universes, with different physical laws and constants, would originate in a similar way. This universe would only be one of many, and there would be many variations in the laws of nature and in the values taken by such constants as the cosmological constant, the gravitational constant, Planck's constant, and so on.

The reason that a multiverse might be taken as an alternative to an intelligent Creator is that, if this is the only universe there is, it is hugely improbable that it should have just the right set of laws to give rise to organized complexity and to intelligent life. But if there is a multiverse, then a huge number, perhaps an infinite number, of universes will exist, with just about every possible combination of laws. In that case, this universe would not be so improbable at all. It is bound to exist sooner or later, and there is nothing very special about it, even if it is the only possible universe that could contain carbon-based intelligent humanoid life in it.

So, instead of one intelligent Creator, who selects this universe out of the huge range of possible universes, we would have an immense number of different universes, and we would do away with the necessity of introducing a Selector, who would still stand in need of explanation anyway. We could just appeal to the basic laws of quantum physics and show that many diverse universes necessarily arise from them. That, it may be felt, is a simpler and more compelling hypothesis.

Some Problems with the Multiverse

But the more you look at the idea of the multiverse, the less it seems to present an acceptable alternative to God. Believers in God have no difficulty in accepting that there is a large number of possible universes. They will exist in the mind of God, but they will not be actual physical universes. They will include, for example, universes in which there is intolerable suffering for all sentient beings for no reason at all. There will be universes in which I, or someone exactly like me, exists but does the exact opposite of everything I do in this universe. If I decide not to steal a large sum of money in this universe, I will decide to steal it in some other universe.

In Tegmark's (2007) view, there will be universes in which pink elephants endlessly dance gavottes and other universes in which unicorns and mermaids really do exist. There will be universes in which there is a creator God but other universes in which there is not and some universes in which there are many gods. Everything will be true somewhere. To most people, this idea seems a more extravagant proposal than any known religious creed. Indeed, every system of religious belief will be true in some universe. That does not have much to offer in the way of economy, simplicity, or plausibility.

What makes the range of possible universes what they are? Is there an exhaustive realm of all possibilities? What principle could ensure that all of these possibilities actually exist? If the set of possibilities is infinite, could all of them actually exist—can one have an actual infinite number of universes (that is, a number that is always larger than any number you can think of)? The problems multiply on reflection. It is not that the proposal is silly, but to say that it is simpler than proposing an intelligent Creator is not convincing.

But the extreme proposal that all possible universes exist is the only one that makes the existence of this universe virtually certain. If you go for the less extravagant "bubble universe" view or the "splitting universe" view, you only get a limited number of universes. What number of universes is needed to make the existence of this universe less improbable? If the set of possible universes is infinite, we might have to say that the existence of any universe at all is hugely improbable. But the existence of a large number of universes would not be less improbable; if anything, it would be more improbable. For, if the existence of one universe is highly improbable, then the existence of 1 + n universes is even more improbable, by a factor of n. So, a limited multiverse would not really help to make this universe more likely. It would only compound the problem of why the precise number of universes, having the nature they do, exists.

It could be said that universes are generated by chance from quantum laws. But now the problem is that of where and in what sense the laws of quantum physics exist. And how does a set of laws produce actual physical universes? As Stephen Hawking has said, "What is it that breathes fire into the equations and makes a universe for them to describe?" (1998, 190). How can you get physical things out of sets of mathematical equations? That would indeed be the modern equivalent of the Philosophers' Stone, which was supposed to turn lead into gold. But it would be much more powerful, for it would turn nothing into everything.

We are back to the final question: if there is something that is ultimately self-existent, that logically precedes the existence of everything else, what is it? The multiverse theory, in at least some forms, seems to place that ultimate in a Platonic realm of mathematical truths. But in what sense does such a Platonic realm exist?

At just this point, theism offers what seems to be a wholly rational hypothesis.

First, mathematical equations are conceived by minds, so this ultimate existent is suspiciously mind-like—more like God than like matter. If possible universes are considered as mathematical structures, they will be necessary, and it is reasonable to postulate that there must be an actual necessary mind in which they subsist.

Second, there is no reason that God may not create many universes, so the multiverse theory does not compete as an alternative to God. It just extends the creative power of God further than we had thought.

Third, most people would think that there needs to be a selection principle, by which some universe or universes are selected to be actual out of the realm of possible universes. The quasi-Platonic mathematical realm, which is a realm of pure necessity, cannot itself account for the existence of contingent universes. You need an additional, non-mathematical principle that can account for the existence of contingent universes. As I suggested in chapter one, a good explanatory selection principle is that a universe is chosen for the sake of realizing some otherwise unobtainable value or worthwhile set of states and processes. But that implies that the Ultimate Reality has something analogous to purpose or intention—again, that it is mind-like.

Fourth, it seems plausible to suppose that values only exist as values if there is something like a consciousness that places a value on them, that recognizes and appreciates their value. The selection principle will operate only if there is a consciousness that can appreciate the possibility of value.

Fifth, only a Being with active causal power can bring physical universes into being. That causal power must be different from, and not part of, any universe that it brings into being. It must be sufficient to produce all the amazing complexity of physical universes. This suggests a reality of enormous power, existing beyond any particular physical or material universe. Further than that it is hard to go, but a Being that conceives, intends, and brings matter into existence is remarkably like the classical idea of God as the cause of all finite existence through knowledge and intention.

Of course, this does not prove God. But if your choices are between the existence of a huge number of universes, all of which exist for no particular reason, and a Supreme Intelligence, existing by necessity, that selects contingent universes from the realm of all possibilities for the sake of their value, anyone may be forgiven for thinking that God is the simpler and more rational hypothesis.

The problem of the multiverse is a complex and exciting one, and it places the hypothesis of God firmly on the intellectual agenda. The God hypothesis seems to be at least as good as the available alternatives, though this consideration alone will not intellectually compel anyone to believe there is a God. The whole issue is discussed from many different viewpoints, theistic and naturalistic, by Bernard Carr (2007), and his book, *Universe or Multiverse?*, provides a masterly discussion of state-of-the-art thinking at the time of its publication.

Fine-tuning Arguments

So far I have considered only what the reason could be for the existence of any universe at all. Refusing to look for a reason is giving up on the basic principle of all science—always seek a reason for everything. But that means you are looking for a self-explanatory Being that explains why everything, including itself, exists. Some philosophers reject the possibility of such a Being and say that we ultimately just have to accept that we cannot explain absolutely everything.

Some pure mathematicians, however, have suggested that the idea of a self-explanatory Being is coherent and that the set of all possible mathematical truths may be said to constitute such a being. Here we would have an uncausable, eternal, changeless reality, to the existence of which there is simply no alternative. Mathematicians do not usually think of this as God, but that may be because they are thinking of God as a rather arbitrary person who is not very reasonable at all. However, if you think of God—as Anselm and Aquinas, Leibniz and Hegel did—as a rational Mind with the creative power to actualize possible mathematical structures for the sake of consciously appreciable values, the postulate of God, as an ultimate reason for the existence of one or more universes, becomes both rational and plausible. If we turn to consider the nature of our universe in particular, the amazing fact is that this universe does possess a deep structure that seems supremely beautiful and intelligible—just what the hypothesis of God would imply.

In recent years, many cosmologists have pointed out further features of this universe that seem to make it particularly improbable that it should exist by chance. In 1974, Brandon Carter proposed the anthropic principle, stating that "our location in the universe is necessarily privileged to the extent of being compatible with our existence as observers" (291). Given that carbon-based intelligent life exists in this universe, the fundamental physical and cosmological quantities of the universe must be compatible with this fact. That may seem trivially true, but it assumes that we have come into existence in accordance with a set of general laws, and it suggests an incredibly precise set of values those laws need to follow in order to have produced us.

The anthropic principle in this "weak" form produces some surprising results. For instance, it explains why there is so much empty space by showing that an expanding universe with an upper bound on the rate of expansion would have to be just as large as it is, in order to have had the time for stars to form, explode, and seed planets with carbon. The laws of fundamental physics give a time span of about thirteen billion years for that process, and so the universe would have to be about thirteen billion light years in size. There has to be as much intergalactic space as there is in order for us to have come into existence in accordance with the general laws of physics.

The anthropic principle throws up many other curious correspondences that turn out to be necessary conditions of human existence, given that our existence is generated by the operation of basic laws and constants of physics. A very large set of quantities that need to be exactly what they are to produce intelligent life has been identified. They are usually referred to as "fine-tuned" values, since they need to be very precisely coordinated, just as old-fashioned radios used to have to be finely tuned by hand to get just the right wavelength for the desired program. The slightest deviation in the gravitational constant, for example, would result in the universe's being unable to produce the relatively stable atomic structures that are necessary for life to evolve.

Robin Collins presents what he calls "six solid cases of fine-tuning" in his paper "The Evidence for Fine-Tuning" (2003). First, the cosmological constant is a term in Einstein's equation that, if positive, leads the universe to expand and, if negative, leads it to contract. The existence of life requires this constant soon after the big bang to settle on a quantity very near zero and to be so precisely adjusted within a large range of possible values that it has to be fine-tuned to at least one part in 10^{53}.

Second, the strong force that binds neutrons and protons together in the nucleus of atoms also has to be precisely what it is in order to overcome the repulsion between the protons in the nucleus.

Third, the production of elements necessary for life requires an abundance of carbon and oxygen, but that requires a fairly precise adjustment of the strong nuclear force.

Fourth, the mass of protons and neutrons needs to be so adjusted that, if the mass of the neutron were increased by one part in seven hundred, then the formation of helium in stars could not occur.

Fifth, if the weak force were weaker than it is, stars would be composed almost entirely of helium, which is quick burning and would not allow time for life to develop on planets.

Sixth, gravitational forces need to be very close to what they are to enable atomic and planetary systems to form stable complexes. If the force of gravity were even slightly stronger, all stars would be blue giants; if even slightly weaker, all would be red dwarfs; in neither case could life have developed.

These are just six examples selected by Collins from a much larger set that can be found detailed, for example, in Michael Denton's *Nature's*

Destiny (1998). Modern physics has a quite new understanding of how precisely the various forces of nature need to be adjusted in order for a life-bearing universe to exist.

Stephen Hawking (1996) points out that the existence of life also seems to depend precisely upon the rate at which the universe is expanding. He suggests that a reduction in the rate of expansion by one part in 1,012 at the time when the temperature of the universe was 1010 K would have resulted in the universe's starting to recollapse when its radius was only 1/3,000 of the present value and the temperature was still 10,000 K.

Hawking concludes that life is possible only because the universe is expanding at just the rate required to avoid recollapse. In fact the balance between the force of expansion and of gravitational contraction would have prohibited a deviation in their ratio from unity by one part in 10^{60}.

But what is the significance of these insights? Some physicists, notably Steven Weinberg (1999) and Alan Guth (1997), are unimpressed. Others—Paul Davies (1982), John Barrow and Frank Tipler (1986), and Martin Rees (2001)—seem to be impressed. The unimpressed say that, of course, these forces need to be finely correlated to produce life, but since every possible universe is *a priori* equally improbable, this one is no more improbable than any other. It is hardly surprising that we find its conditions are just right for life because, after all, we are alive. While it is interesting to discover the complex set of correlations that are needed to produce life, this has no implication that anyone has planned things that way. If the forces had been even slightly different, we would not have been here, and no one would have been any the wiser. Fine-tuning is irrelevant to the existence of a designing God.

Those who are impressed, however, say, as Martin Rees does, "We should surely probe deeper, and ask why a unique recipe for the physical world should permit consequences as interesting as those we see around us" (2001, 163). Interesting consequences—that is the factor that makes all the difference. It is not just that this universe is very improbable. It is not even that human beings as a species are very important. It is that the existence of the kinds of intelligence, beauty, creativity, compassion, and friendship of which we are aware represent great values that could not have existed in the way they do in any other possible universe.

What fine-tuning arguments show is that states of great value have resulted from, *and could only have resulted from*, a set of laws that are precisely adjusted in a large number of unexpected and exceedingly improbable ways. When he introduced the weak anthropic principle, Brandon Carter also suggested a "strong" anthropic principle, which can be stated as follows: "the universe must have those properties which allow life to develop within it at some stage in its history." It is given this formulation in Barrow and Tipler (1986, 21). For many scientists, that is a step too far, and it suggests something very like a teleological explanation for the universe.

Unfortunately, Carter's formulation of the strong anthropic principle is ambiguous. It could mean merely that, given the existence of life, the universe must have the specific properties it has. But it could also be taken to mean that the fundamental laws of nature are as they are because the universe is and must be fitted for the generation of intelligent life.

The strong principle, unlike the weak principle, is controversial, and there is no compelling scientific reason to accept it. But it shows how natural and plausible it is, in the light of modern science, to see the universe as fine-tuned to generate intelligent life. The fact that the evolution of life generates brains from single-celled organisms and the amazingly intricate ordering of DNA into a complex and reproducible coding for the building of organisms strengthens the case for seeing purpose and direction in the basic structures of nature. It looks as though the whole process has been designed to produce the values that intelligent life make possible. And it looks as though those values could only be what they are because the process as a whole is what it is.

Science and Arguments for God

Some, like Richard Dawkins, argue that the Darwinian hypotheses of random mutation and natural selection have destroyed the design argument for a cosmic intelligence, God. For the appearance of design ("it looks as though") can be fully explained on strict Darwinian principles alone.

Even if that is true, however—and it seems unlikely that an explanation rooted in biology could be any sort of complete explanation for everything, biological and nonbiological—an explanation in terms of design by a creator God would still raise the probability of the existence of this universe considerably. The choice can be put fairly bluntly: either this universe is the result of a huge number of amazing coincidences that have progressively, but quite unexpectedly, led to states of great value. That is, the universe is incredibly improbable (though we may just have to put up with that and comfort ourselves with the thought that it is no more improbable than many other universes). Or the "coincidences" have all been superbly engineered so that the values that life makes possible would inevitably come into existence sooner or later. In the latter case, this universe would not be improbable at all (though it would still be just as amazing).

In general, it is a good scientific principle to accept a hypothesis that raises the probability of some phenomenon. Based on that principle, the hypothesis of God is vastly preferable to the postulate of pure chance, even if it is conceded that the universe could (exceedingly improbably) have come about by chance. If someone objects that this is a weak argument because God is just as improbable as the universe, he or she has missed the point. The point is that the probability of this universe is raised considerably by the existence of a rational God. For what we are talking about is the probability of many precisely correlated values, relative to a specific range of possible values that could have obtained, taking as given the general forces and constants of nature (weak and strong, electromagnetic and gravitational, and so on). Against that background of the given general laws of nature, an intelligent God raises the probability of this universe considerably.

It is quite a different question to ask whether the existence of God is probable or whether the existence of the set of physical laws we have is probable. In that case, there is no given finite set of possibilities against which we can measure the probability of the occurrence of some actuality. We have no way of even beginning to assess probabilities when there exists an unknown, possibly infinite, and wholly unspecifiable set of possibilities. Once we get into questions of truly ultimate existence, probability no longer has any purchase.

As I argued in chapter one, the question of what ultimately exists is not a matter of probability at all. It requires a decision about a general conceptual framework for interpreting the experienced world. In reflecting on such a general framework, a spiritual worldview may give fundamental importance to existential problems of suffering, guilt, anxiety, and egoism, leading to a diagnosis of the human condition that offers a way to relieve such problems and to the apprehension of signs of transcendent value that suggest the supremacy of a Higher Consciousness of wisdom, freedom, empathy, and universal compassion. A non-spiritual framework, on the other hand, may discount such considerations as unduly subjective and see the world as fundamentally impersonal, unconscious, deterministic, blind, and indifferent to human suffering and happiness.

"Proofs" of God neither establish the first set of attitudes nor undermine the second. "Evidence" for God is not a set of naturally inexplicable physical events that would, at best, demonstrate the existence of a superhuman magician. Proofs of God are uses of what John Wisdom (1963) called the "connecting technique," drawing analogies, picking out

patterns, connecting disparate kinds of data, and suggesting a key interpretative model for human experience as a whole. What might be called
evidence for God is, in fact, the evocation of a general perspective on the
world as the appearance of Transcendent Spirit.

The same sort of connecting technique and perspectival arguments
are also used to construct nontheistic and nonspiritual frameworks of
meaning. There are certainly a number of possible frameworks, and there
is no neutral way of deciding among them. Materialism is one of those
frameworks, and it rarely has a spiritual dimension. But there are other
frameworks that are religious but nontheistic.

Two of the great world spiritual traditions—Buddhism and East Asian
—would not be concerned with proofs of God at all. Largely bypassing
the idea of a Creator, they have an interest in positing a more impersonal yet immaterial basis of observed reality. Some scientists, like Fritjof Capra (1975), find such views more consilient with quantum physics,
with its ideas of entanglement and veiled reality. In them, there is a sense
that the observed material world is an appearance to human minds of
a deeper reality, and quantum physics may be felt to support such a
view.

The spiritual interest, however, is not in a purely speculative account
of the nature of ultimate reality. It is concerned with finding ways in
which the mind can access a deeper reality and be transformed by it.
So, nontheistic religious views express an interest and a corresponding
set of speculative considerations that wholly nonreligious views lack or
even oppose. The existence or nonexistence of such a "religious" interest
in self-transformation by conscious relationship to a Supreme Spiritual
Reality is a vitally important factor that underlies apparently speculative
arguments for the existence of God.

When this is taken into account, arguments for God can be seen as
attempts to show that the postulate of a Supreme Spiritual Reality is a
coherent and plausible one and that it can be adequately interpreted in
terms of one personal Creator.

Modern science can be used to show that the posulate of a Creator is
not necessary for a scientific understanding of the cosmos. The suggestion may be made that introducing a Creator is not helpful to science
since it threatens to put a stop to further investigation by just saying,
"God did it." Science is autonomous, and it does not need appeal to
any God.

On the other hand, modern science shows the cosmos to be awe-
inspiringly beautiful, complex, and mathematically elegant. Whether by
accident or design, it is precisely fine-tuned for the emergence of intelligence and moral consciousness. It can appear to be intelligently designed

for intelligent life, and it seems that the basis of the material universe is much stranger, much richer, and possibly more mind-like than the everyday world of material objects in four-dimensional space/time that we see around us.

In sum, it seems implausible to say that science has rendered religion obsolete. It has certainly helped to refine, and often reconstruct, religious interpretations of reality. But the belief that Ultimate Reality is fundamentally unconscious, deterministic, and indifferent is not a conclusion of modern science. It is a perspective as old as recorded human thought, and there are at least as many insights in modern science that count against it as there are in favor of it.

I have outlined some of these. But, in the end, as at the beginning, the religious believer can say that we know consciousness exists and that agents know, envisage, choose, enjoy, and have ideals, values, and purposes. Any adequate account of reality must include those as primary and irreducible facts. So, Ultimate Reality cannot be simply unconscious and indifferent. Somehow, the factors of consciousness and value must be included in any comprehensive account of Ultimate Reality. And this coheres well with the most basic religious belief that consciousness and value are at the heart of reality.

Science can show that some attempts to formulate religious views (like scriptural literalism) are blind alleys. It can help to provide more plausible and coherent accounts of religious beliefs. But science is not materialist by nature, and on the question of whether there is that of which science cannot directly speak, it is silent.

Comte may have been right in speaking of three great ages of human intellectual progress. But they were not ages of religion, metaphysics, and science, one after the other in sequential order. They were ages, in both religion and science, of local preliterate traditions, of classical and text-based reasoning, and of informed critical inquiry. It is just possible that we are at the beginning of a fourth stage, of a truly global consilience among many different cultures, and among religion, the humanities, and science.

Atheists may well think that the fourth stage is too long in coming or even that it is unlikely to come. The worst may happen. Religions may become more exclusive and intolerant. Science may become more subservient to state demands for bigger and more powerful weaponry and means of subjugation. Religion and science together may destroy the world. But it does not have to be like that. If religion is fully humanized and open to the critical methods and established truths of the sciences, and if science is used in the service of human welfare and the flourishing of all sentient beings, there can be a long and positive future for human life and for whatever forms of life may develop from it. That is only likely to occur if scientists and religious believers engage in a serious, sensitive, and inquiring conversation. For that to happen, both fundamentalist religion and fundamentalist atheism will have to be set aside, in favor of something more self-critical and humane. If that does happen, religion will not disappear, but it may, and it should, change.

10. Does Science Allow for Revelation and Divine Action?

(DOES QUANTUM PHYSICS PUT MATERIALISM IN QUESTION?)

The Possibility of Particular Divine Acts in the World

RELIGIONS DO NOT CONSIST solely of sophisticated beliefs about the ultimately spiritual nature of reality. At the level of everyday practice, there is a layer of beliefs about the actions of spirits, ancestors, or gods who listen to prayers, show concern with what is going on in the world, and give advice and practical help from time to time. Angels and demons and spiritual beings of various sorts are all parts of the ontology of religion.

This may be embarrassing to some theologians, who may wish to classify most of these beliefs as "superstition." But a theoretical line between superstition and religion is hard to draw, and while mystics may speak of wordless communion with an ineffable God, many religious practitioners will claim a much more direct and conversational relationship with a deity, a saint, or an ancestor, or will say that God speaks to them every day on very practical matters.

It is important to try to understand the sources of such beliefs. I think that they express a general, if vague and variously interpreted, sense that there is some sort of plan or destiny for our lives (perhaps the influence of the stars), and that there are active causal forces in nature that are nonmaterial and are closely related to human good and harm. I suspect that most of these beliefs are remnants of the first stage of religious life, the stage of local traditions, before close observations of nature or critical reflection on such observations had taken hold.

The major religious traditions either try to suppress such beliefs (as with most forms of Protestant Christianity) or incorporate them, appropriately modifed, into religious life as popular practices (as with many forms of Catholic Christianity). The main religions develop ideas of human destiny and objective spiritual causality so as to account for popular practices as ways of access to a Spiritual Reality that, in fact, has a deeper intellectual base. The problem for religions is to contain such popular beliefs and guard against the misunderstandings they may show, while encouraging the development of more complex understandings for those who are open to them.

It may be noted that, in science, similar problems exist. Fortunately, not many people need or want to know about quantum physics. But popular understandings (or misunderstandings) abound, and scientists may want to encourage attempts to understand, while accepting that it will not be possible to provide an accurate account of electrons, for example, if people cannot grasp what a probability wave is.

Unfortunately, in religion, many people who are unable to cope with the complexities of academic theology tend to think that they have a better grasp of spiritual realities than mere scholars. But that is rather like the thousands of people who think they can disprove Einstein's theory of relativity or Darwinian evolution, even though they cannot solve differential equations or do not know how to identify a gene.

The problem in religion is clearly shown in the development of the Hebrew religion, as illustrated in the Hebrew Bible. Many popular practices, like witchcraft, communication with the dead, and the use of fertility spells, are forbidden. They are taken to be attempts to use spiritual powers for immoral ends or by immoral means. On the other hand, prayers for healing, prophetic foretelling of the future, and the use of blessings and curses are legitimated because they can be positively related to Hebrew belief in one creator God who controls the future and acts in history to bless and judge the people of the twelve tribes.

The important element is the devotion of all life to God. Practices that ignore or impede this are forbidden. But it is not denied that there is a destiny, indeed a special calling or vocation, for the Jewish people and that there is a spiritual power, God, who acts to influence human good or ill. Spirits, angels, and demons continue to be part of the biblical worldview. They are increasingly seen in the Bible as aspects of the Divine Being itself, as it relates to the human world. Yet, most biblical writers, in both Old and New Testaments, continued to think there are many finite spiritual agencies, both good and bad, who act in the human world.

In the New Testament, if it is read literally, Jesus spoke with Moses and Elijah, long-dead prophets, was nourished by angels, exorcised demons, and spoke of Satan's "falling from heaven" or being defeated by the healing power of the Son of Man. These spiritual agents are parts of the second stage, the canonical, religious picture. Many believers in the third, critical, stage of religion banish all such agents as legendary, fictional, or purely symbolic characters. They may be figurative symbols for the corrupting force of human egoism and the integrating power of compassionate thought.

But is God, also, a figurative symbol? For some believers the answer is "yes." Certainly, the picture of God as a bearded father figure is such a symbol, one that fails to speak to many these days. But, for most believers, the symbol of the Father seated on a throne does symbolize an objective consciousness and will, however far beyond our imagining such a reality, in fact, is. It may be thought to do so more adequately than the symbols of many competing gods or spirits of nontheistic religion, though it should never be taken as a wholly adequate picture of the Ultimate Reality of perfect consciousness, wisdom, goodness, and beauty that underlies the visible universe.

If there is such a reality, God, it will affect the nature of the universe. But will God act in the human world to influence human good and ill? The Abrahamic religions seem to give an unequivocal "yes" to that question. The God of Abraham "speaks" to Abraham and the prophets, tells them to do specific things, delivers Israel from Egypt, judges their evil acts, and gives them a historical destiny to be the "priests of the earth."

Although the biblical God can and does act miraculously, in amazing ways that seem to transcend the regularities of nature, God usually acts in more normal ways that do not surpass nature's regularities. This difference between miraculous and ordinary divine action is confusingly put by saying that some divine acts "break the laws of nature" and others do not. That suggests the eighteenth-century picture that the laws of nature are universal and inflexible rules, which God would have to break in order to act.

What is needed is a different account of the laws of nature, as abstract mathematical descriptions or models of some artificially isolated aspects of physical phenomena. Such models are often stochastic or probabilistic, and, as discussed in chapter four, they are never exhaustive or complete, capable of providing full information about all aspects of phenomena and of predicting exactly how objects will behave in future.

For such an account, a miracle is defined in terms of its amazingness, its religious significance, and the impossibility of giving an account of it in terms of natural regularities, however mathematically modeled. Ordinary divine acts will lack these features, but they will still describe features of physical situations that are not fully accounted for by mathematically formulated laws of physical regularity alone. Natural regularities continue to obtain—we can give an account in terms of natural regularities. But such regularities allow for causal influences of a nonphysical sort. In fact, such influences are a normal part of any physical world in which persons exist.

Revelation As a Form of Divine Action

When I voluntarily raise my arm, this is a perfectly normal thing to do. No one would think it was an amazing miracle, of tremendous spiritual significance. But a mental feature, my intention and decision, was the main cause of my arm's going up. Lots of physical causes were also necessary; but, in the complex physical state constituted by my brain, body, and environment, intentional causes are also allowed to operate. At least in such complex highly organized states, the physical allows and invites mental influence. Such influence is part of the normal way of things.

There are many arguments about whether mental states are reducible to physical states, and, in chapter six, I have argued they are not. But, even if they were, there is no question that God, who by definition precedes all physical states, is not a physical being or state. So, in God's case, a purely mental (or spiritual) state is believed to cause physical states—most dramatically, God creates the universe.

It seems possible that God could create specific physical states not wholly accounted for by preceding physical states and general mathematical descriptions of such states (the laws of nature). Such causal influence would not "interfere in" or "break" laws of nature because such laws specifically allow, and in some circumstances, invite, the influence of nonphysical factors.

What is needed to make this picture seem plausible is a view of the physical cosmos as intrinsically oriented to a spiritual cause and goal. The cosmos not only springs from a Supreme Consciousness: it is destined to produce beings that will relate in knowledge and cooperative action to that Consciousness. After the example of the anthropic principle and following the lead of some early Christian writers, we might see believers in God as committed to a principle of theosis (*theopoiesis*, or *theosis* in shortened form, means "deification" and was used by the fourth-century Christian theologian Athanasius). This principle states that the cosmos must be such that it will produce beings of awareness, intention, a sense of transcendence, and the possibility of conscious union with God.

We can, then, say that the cosmos will be open to the particular actions of God wherever that is necessary to establish a unity of awareness and will with God. We can only say very generally when that will be. But it will entail occasions when God "speaks" or communicates with finite persons and actively unites them to the Divine Nature. If that did not happen, there would be little sense in speaking of conscious union with God as a goal of the religious life.

Revelation primarily consists in the communicative action of God, disclosing the reality and nature of God and, at least in general terms, the purpose and goal of the cosmos. If there is a God with a purpose for human lives, it is almost inconceivable that God should not communicate that purpose and the means to achieve it. And it is highly probable that God will do so through exceptional individuals of great wisdom, moral excellence, and mental stability, who have an especially clear and vivid awareness of God. So, for anyone who accepts the existence of a Supreme Transcendent Value, there is a high prior probability that there will exist divinely inspired prophets, who will become vehicles of divine communication.

It does not follow that religious doctrines are to be accepted without question on the authority of some ancient prophet. On the contrary, because of the developing and incremental nature of human knowledge and the frailty of human minds, it seems likely that what is felt to be divinely revealed at a particular time will be subject to much subsequent development and modification. It will be largely conditioned, and therefore limited, by the concepts and beliefs available in the cultural context of prophets. For anyone who accepts the importance of informed critical inquiry, revelation is likely to be seen as a divine communication that is received and interpreted by the very imperfect comprehension of human minds and cultures.

Particular persons have specific abilities and preferences and exist in specific historical and social contexts. Their perception of the supreme beauty and goodness that is God and of the moral goal of the cosmos will be partly dependent upon their current conceptions of beauty and goodness and upon their current ideas about the nature of the cosmos.

Reflecting upon the biblical record of divine revelation to the patriarchs and prophets over many centuries, we may hypothesize that God's revelatory actions consisted in raising up a succession of leaders and prophets to whom could be progressively communicated an objective vision of Supreme Goodness, a categorical moral demand for justice and mercy, and a promise of moral fulfillment in the future. The history of ancient Israel gave rise to a cumulative and historically unique tradition of conscious relationship between one group of nomadic tribes and a God who laid on them the vocation to become "the priests of the Lord" for all the earth (Isa. 61:6).

But, as is clear from the biblical account, this is complicated by the fact that human responses to divine initiatives are ambiguous and infected with the will to pleasure and power. The objective moral vision is almost always compromised. In the case of virtually all the patriarchs and prophets of Israel, the divine vocation was compromised, and there was no smooth progression toward a society of justice and peace or toward a finally perfect understanding of what God is and requires. For that reason, the understanding and reception of revelation require continual critical judgment and sensitive discrimination. That process will need to continue for as long as humans continue to exist.

Providence and History

For the Abrahamic religions, God does not just act to reveal the divine nature and purpose. God also actively works to ensure that the divine purpose is realized. This seems to be virtually an entailment of the belief that there is a divine goal. It is extremely unlikely that God should have a goal for the universe and do nothing in particular to bring it about.

But, if we look for the providential acts of God in history, we find no easy triumph of the good and elimination of the bad. In some of the tragic events of history, like the Lisbon earthquake or the Holocaust, human suffering is not prevented by God. Providence seems hard to find, and these events understandably seem to many to contradict any belief in divine providence.

The conclusion seems inevitable that the scope for providential divine action is severely limited—as I have suggested in chapters two and three —limited by the necessary outworking of the laws of nature and by the freely chosen acts of morally imperfect humanity. It follows that providential acts must be seen in terms of causal influence rather than in terms of determination. God is a causal influence for good and against evil. Because God is the creator and final goal of the universe, God can ensure that goodness will finally triumph, though perhaps not within human history in this space/time.

It could be that, as God experiences the tragic history of this world and as that history passes into the divine mind and memory, its evil is mitigated or transformed by being subordinated to the overall will to the triumph of the good that characterizes the divine purpose. The memory of evil may be muted and transformed by being placed within a wider pattern making for good and within the overwhelming goodness of the Divine Being.

If finite beings are given a share in the life to come, they will have greater knowledge of the Divine Mind, and this world's evil will be seen by them as it exists, redeemed, in the Divine Life. If this is the case, there will be no situation in this life without ultimate hope and without the obligation to work for good even in the midst of apparent despair and desolation. But the good will not be saved from all present evil, and there will be no inevitable progress toward greater goodness in the history of the earth.

There is always in this world the conflict of the divine call to goodness and the human fall toward self-will. There is objective demand and the enabling power of grace. But there is also the rejection of goodness and the self-destructive trajectory of evil. Divine grace will take the form of the opening up of positive possibilities for growth in knowledge of God and the finite mediation of divine power through cooperative personal agency (especially through the saints and prophets). But there will also be negative forces produced by the human will to egoistic power, and "divine judgment" will then impede human purposes and desires.

The acts of God in the biblical tradition are acts of judgment and of grace. This is not plausibly pictured as some extracosmic person issuing immediate statutory punishments for specific acts of rebellion and pleasant rewards for submissive obedience. It may perhaps be pictured as the general orientation of the cosmos toward God. The physical structure allows and requires God to exert causal influence to implement that orientation. There will in each situation be a positive possibility that may be communicated to persons—though even then the apprehension of it may be obscured by self-will and the social ambiguities it produces. If divine blessing can be seen as the opening up of positive possibilities, then divine judgment will consist in the narrowing of possibilities, so that self-regarding choices eventually result in destruction of the self.

If we ask where God's action is to be discerned in the world, the answer is that it is discerned in every impulse toward goodness and in every frustration of evil intent. If there is a "higher power making for righteousness," as Matthew Arnold put it, there is also a "higher power leading evil to destruction." In our human society, where good and evil are inextricably intertwined, there are virtually no instances of pure goodness or pure evil (for Jews and Muslims, some prophets may be such instances; for Christians, Jesus is an almost unique exception). Providence acts to disclose and encourage the good and to confuse and frustrate the evil. Yet, because good and evil lie within each of us, our perceptions of and relations to the Supreme Good carry all the ambiguity and imperfection of an estranged but redeemable human world.

What appears to us is a general tendency for goodness to conduce to flourishing and hatred to lead to destruction. Since our communities bind good and evil together in one common society, there is no easily discernible order of exact moral justice in our world. But God wills that persons should flourish and that evil should end in destruction and acts to influence human history accordingly.

If persons learn to be creative, empathetic, and compassionate, so they may learn to know God. Hatred, on the other hand, hides the divine being, and our involvement in the human community renders all our spiritual perceptions ambiguous. In our world, as Martin Luther said, God is hidden. But the active divine influence may be known and effective in those who truly turn to God—though we can never be sure who they may be or if we are truly among them!

In this ambiguous world, prayer will include the formulation of human wishes and requests for the future. This can be helpful both in making clear to ourselves what our deepest wishes are and in motivating us to act for good. But if God knows and responds to all things, then God will know and respond to human prayers. The forms of divine response will be limited by the constraints of nature and freedom. But it seems reasonable to think that our attempts to become more conscious of God, to discern the divine will, and to ask for divine help will open the world of which we are part to divine providential action in ways that might not otherwise have existed.

In that sense, believers may say that prayer will always be effective, though not necessarily in the direct ways we might imagine. They will be positive actions for good that may open the future more fully to forms of divine influence, prefiguring that perfect cooperation of human and Divine that is the ultimate goal for the future of the cosmos.

Process Philosophy

For many modern believers, Alfred North Whitehead's process philosophy provides an illuminating account of the providence of God (1978, see especially 79–89 and 342–351). Even where process philosophy is not accepted as a total system, Whitehead's influence on Christian theologians has been strong. It can be seen in the work of John Cobb Jr. and David Ray Griffin, and in William Vanstone's *Love's Endeavor, Love's Expense* (1977); each appropriate something of Whitehead's vision in their own ways.

For Whitehead, God experiences all the feelings of finite beings, including them in the Divine Being. And God is a constantly new creator, bringing new things into being, in a time that flows toward an open future but a future that is always governed by having its ultimate goal in God.

Whitehead also stresses that finite persons are responsible for the ways in which they take the influences of their environment and shape them in free and creative ways. God, the Supreme Good, formulates an "initial aim" for each new situation and communicates it to those receptive to divine influence (whether or not they consciously know it). But God does not compel them to act in a predetermined way. Each creature makes his or her own freely creative choices. God, thus, acts primarily as a "lure" or Ideal Goal, causally influencing but not determining things toward their ultimate goal of union with the Divine.

In Whitehead's philosophy, finite persons are societies of small events or "actual occasions," each one existing for a moment, integrating its direct past and projecting creatively into its immediate future. At this point, I wish to distinguish personal subjects more sharply from the pre- and subpersonal realities from which persons emerge, and I would give God a rather stronger causal role in the way things go. Yet, Whitehead's emphasis on the influencing and persuasive character of divine causality seems to me to fit the facts of experience and make possible a more satisfactory explanation of the presence of suffering and frustration in the world.

So, God will work cooperatively with wills that are open to divine direction and inspire them to new heights of insight and creativity. God will also act to frustrate destructive decisions, though not by some form of external and immediate punishment. Rather, God allows the self-destructive tendencies of the evil will to slowly work themselves out, and God will leave persons to the darkness of loveless lives or the flames of egoistic passion—the two main biblical images of hell.

In the prehuman world—and that is most of cosmic history so far—there is no possibility of free decision and cooperative response. But the laws of the cosmos will be intelligible (to provide the possibility of future understanding and control), open (to allow for alternative futures between which future free choices can be made), goal-directed (gradually building more complex structures that eventually allow consciousness and creativity to exist), and interconnected (so that persons will be integral parts of the cosmos, its destiny and theirs bound closely together).

This basic structure must be preserved by all particular divine actions. As I have argued in chapter four, miracles are possible rarely and for an overwhelmingly good reason. But God's normal actions work within the structure of intelligible regularity, limited openness, continuous teleological development, and the interconnectedness of objects in a cosmic totality. In such a worldview, the scope for divine action is limited, and necessarily so. But it is a real causal factor in the development of the cosmos and attains its consummation in that interpenetration of infinite and finite knowledge and will that can make the finite an authentic and unclouded image of the infinite. That probably lies beyond this physical cosmos, while nevertheless constituting its inner reality and goal.

For such a view, it is misleading to speak of God's interfering in a closed causal system. The system is not exhaustively described by the purely physical laws of nature, which are mathematical models of measurable physical regularities, taken in isolation from those unmeasurable causal factors that are characteristic of personal and spiritual causality and that are an important part of the world that we know and experience. God is better conceived as the perfect Intelligibility and Beauty that underlies the cosmos and that directs it toward a final goal, when the cosmos will be a clear visible image or manifestation of its own inner spiritual nature.

Indian Religious Traditions and Spiritual Causality

I have presented this account of divine action in terms of the Abrahamic religions, trying to show how the symbolic images used by those faiths represent the suffusion of the physical cosmos by the Spiritual Reality of God. God is a causal influence that makes a difference in how things are, even at the physical level.

The Indian religious traditions do not typically speak of a God who has the cosmic and historical purpose of deifying creation. Yet, Indian theistic traditions see the cosmos as a manifestation of Spirit and, thus, as dependent upon a Spiritual Reality of consciousness, intelligence, and bliss. Less stress is placed upon a historically specific moral demand for a society of justice and peace, or upon the real possibility of such a society. But there is a strong sense of spiritual causality and of human destiny as lying in release from the wheel of rebirth into a union with Spirit.

Talk of divine judgment and grace is often replaced by talk of the law of karma or moral desert. It is not that a personal Judge assigns rewards and punishments for human conduct, but that there is an impersonal law according to which bad deeds bring suffering and good deeds bring happiness. This is not a mathematically describable law. It expresses a moral ordering of the universe, such that over many lifetimes we reap the consequences of our actions. We make ourselves the sorts of persons whose lives are governed by our own past acts, for good or ill. If we seek power and pleasure, we will eventually become locked into personalities that are always unsatisfied and that will inevitably suffer the frustrations of failure and boredom and a sense of futility and emptiness. Only if we seek compassion and wisdom will we become persons who will attain lasting fulfillment and happiness.

This outlook is a useful corrective to the overly anthropomorphic imagery sometimes found in Abrahamic traditions. Indian views place responsibility squarely on us and on internal connections between virtue and happiness. Yet those connections are often said to be put in place by the creator Spirit and the possibility of forgiveness and of "assistance by the gods" mitigates the impersonality of karmic law and the extreme difficulty of achieving release by our own efforts alone.

Even Buddhist traditions, especially in the Mahayana schools, offer the possibility of help by compassionate bodhisattvas and of a blissful existence in a Pure Buddha Land. More typical of traditional Buddhism is the retention of karmic law, without the existence of any supernatural personal beings. However, there is still an attainable goal of wisdom and bliss—*nibbana*—and spiritual causality still obtains, as the determination of our own futures by moral and meditative practice.

In Buddhism, the cosmos as such may not have a goal. But each human person (each series of qualities in a personal life) has a goal, which is the cessation of suffering and rebirth. The ultimate determinant of what happens to us is our own intentions and mental states, not just the laws of physical nature. There is a supernatural reality, for *nibbana* is beyond the limitations of space and time.

There may be no supernatural God, but there is a causal determination of the future by intention and mental effort. So, there are laws other than physical laws that have a significant causal role. Insofar as persons exist between births and are part causes of their subsequent births, they exist beyond this space/time and, in that sense, are supernatural causes. It looks as though the truth of Buddhism entails the existence of nonphysical causality and of some form of supernatural reality and, thus, raises similar questions of compatibility with scientific explanations to those raised by theism.

East Asian religions like Confucianism are perhaps the least supernaturally oriented. At a popular level, ancestors, spirits, and hungry ghosts—all supernatural agents—play a part in religious practice. But at a more sophisticated level, Confucianism and some Chinese forms of Buddhism are very "this-worldly" in emphasis and focus on enlightened and harmonious living in the world.

Insofar as Confucianism is not just a humanistic moral code, it refers to a Way of Heaven (*Tian*) that insight is needed to discern and that constitutes an objective moral order. Conformity with it brings fulfillment, and straying from the Way brings chaos. The similarity with belief in divine providence is that there is an objective moral imperative, there is a causal law that egoism leads to destruction and harmonious living leads to fulfillment, and there is a close connection between morality and seeing the true nature of reality (doing what is right follows from seeing what reality is).

Some East Asian religions come closest to denying a separately existing supernatural reality. But they give a supernatural dimension to all existence. They see Spirit and matter as interfused aspects of a single reality. But the significant difference from naturalistic materialism is that they give causal priority to the spiritual aspect. The perception of truth and the determination to live in harmony with the truth are the primary causal factors in personal life. Moral conduct is not a by-product of material processes in the brain. There are nonphysical aspects of reality, and they play a decisive causal role in the human world.

At a popular level, then, religions generally invoke supernatural causality, positing gods or spirits or heavenly intermediaries who help humans achieve their goals in various ways—or darker forces that may lead humans astray. At a more sophisticated level, religions range from forms of what may be called transcendental humanism to supernatural theism. Transcendental humanism (e.g., Confucianism) stresses the importance of personal values in relation to a nonphysical and causally determining aspect of the natural world, an aspect that is not just a product of physical forces. Supernatural theism (e.g., Islam) thinks of a transcendent personal God who acts in the world to bring about some cosmic purpose.

Virtually all religions seem committed to the existence of nonphysical causes, and most religions assert the existence of at least one supernatural cause. So, it is important to ask whether science precludes such causes or, if it permits them, whether a scientific view of nature may offer insights into how such causes operate in the world.

Science and the End of Reductionism

It must be said that nothing is more calculated to enrage some scientists than the suggestion that there are supernatural causes. The whole of modern science, it may be said, rests on the axiom that every event has a cause, and all causes are to be found within the "natural" realm, that is, within observable space/time. There was even an infamous editorial in the British scientific journal *Nature* that declared that all supernatural causes were ruled out by science and, thus, were intrinsically anti-scientific (see issue of July 19, 1984).

On reflection, however, the whole topic of causality turns out to be full of unsolved problems. In some ways, it might even be said that modern science does not really deal in causes—in what ultimately makes things be what they are—at all. It deals in mathematical descriptions of observed relationships. Thus, Boyle's law of gases deals with the relationship between temperature, pressure, and volume in a gas. It gives an accurate mathematical description of the behavior of gases in a confined space, given that there are no external interferences.

It could be said that the initial state of the system, plus the formula of Boyle's law, "causes" subsequent states of the system. But it is hard to see how a physical state at a specific time plus a law of nature could bring about any future state. All we know is that gases behave in mathematically describable ways. We might assume that they do so because of some intrinsic properties ("powers"?) of the molecules making up the gas. But to say what those powers are just involves a restatement of the laws of behavior.

Modern science largely depends upon increasingly accurate observation, upon devising experimental methods for isolating various measurable properties, and upon inventing equations that describe the behavior of things with those properties. It is hugely illuminating to find that the behavior of gases is the result of the motion of normally imperceptible molecules, that these, in turn, result from the structure and behavior of their constituent atoms, and that subatomic particles cause atoms to behave in the ways they do.

When we say that subatomic particles cause the observable behavior of gases, we mean that the behavior of such particles (they may be waves at the quantum level) gives atoms a set of structures (an atomic weight, for example) that can be described more simply by the periodic table at the level of atoms and molecules. Then, the behavior of molecules can be described at the level of normal human perception as the observed behavior of a gas as it is bubbled through various pieces of apparatus (in Boyle's experiments).

These levels are differences of scale, and one of the major discoveries of modern science is that the observed world is a simpler redescription of a much smaller world of particles that can only be observed with special instruments.

This discovery initially gave rise to the project of reductionism, the proposal that all observable phenomena are simplifying redescriptions of the behavior of fundamental particles. A full and exhaustive description of the world would, thus, consist in specifying the behavior of all those particles.

It has now been discovered that the reductionist project cannot in practice be carried through since the fundamental particles that are the basis of the theory (quarks or something even smaller) can only be observed indirectly and very rarely under very special conditions, requiring closely controlled experiments in extremely expensive particle accelerators. There is at present no conceivable way of giving a full description of the behavior of all subatomic particles that obtains even when they are unobserved. Moreover, as noted in chapter four, the Heisenberg uncertainty principle prohibits a complete knowledge of all the properties of a particle (e.g., momentum and position) at the same time. So, it could never be shown that a full description of the quantum world would provide a correct and complete description of levels of greater scale.

Worse than that, fundamental particles in quantum physics turn out also to be probability waves in Hilbert space. There is no agreement on how to interpret this mathematical formalism in realistic terms. It seems as though there is not a level of fundamental particles at all, in any straightforward sense. We do not know what the most basic level of physical reality is, and perhaps we will never know. It is what the quantum physicist Bernard d'Espagnat has called a "veiled reality" (1990). So when we try to reduce all scientific explanations to a most basic level of physical reality, we find that level to be elusive, disputed, and hardly even imaginable.

Moreover, it may be impossible in principle to provide a reductionist explanation of a complex physical reality solely in terms of the behavior of its parts. In quantum mechanics, the property of nonlocality or entanglement, by which particles that have interacted continue to be correlated in their behavior even when separated by large distances, suggests that to describe the behavior of a complex physical structure requires reference to the structure as a whole, not just to the way particles behave when they are isolated in laboratory conditions. Perhaps it is even true that a complete description of the behavior of a particle would not be wholly adequate unless it included reference to the universe as a whole and to all the possible forms of interaction that might obtain within its parts. As John Polkinghorne puts it, the outcome of the behavior of a collection of many billiard ball–like objects, after only 10^{-10} seconds, "would be affected by the variation in the gravitational field due to an extra electron on the other side of the universe" (1989, 28). This obviously means that it would be wholly unpredictable.

A further complicating factor, as if we needed any more, is that, if the universe as a whole is an evolving entity, conditions in the real universe will never be exactly similar at two different times. Predictions will only be accurate in regions where very similar conditions obtain and where interaction with remote regions of the universe is negligible. Fortunately, that is quite good enough for most of the time. But it is a long way from the assertion that all behavior can be completely explained, in principle, by a description of some fundamental physical level. It may turn out that a complete description of that basic level would require reference to the whole state of the universe, if that state modifies the behavior of all its parts.

Quantum theory has wholly undermined the belief that it is possible to determine exactly some initial state of the universe and predict exactly what will happen thereafter. It does not strictly disprove determinism— there are still determined quantum determinists who believe in "hidden variables"—but it disproves the belief that we could know some initial state completely and that we could predict its subsequent behavior with certainty. Thus, even for a wholly naturalistic theory, the reductionist belief that we can determine some lowest level of physical reality and explain all subsequent events in terms of that looks very flimsy.

Reductionism is, thus, an expression of pure faith, grounded in the elegance of mathematical descriptions and a belief that all physical behavior is wholly determined by the behavior of matter's smallest constituents. There is little empirical evidence for it and much empirical evidence against it, even though there are features of classical scientific methodology that made the faith seem a desirable and reasonable one.

Whole–Part Causation

Most contemporary scientists believe that the behavior of fundamental particles is modifed by the wider physical systems of which they can form a part. This can be most easily imagined by thinking of cells in an organic body, all of which contain the same DNA. Yet, depending on where in an organism the cells are, they develop in different ways, to perform different functions. The only way to account for this is to say that the behavior of the DNA molecules and their constituent atoms is modified by the wider organic system of which they are part.

In a similar way, an organism's behavior patterns and its interactions with its environment over time can help to influence the DNA sequences that are switched on in the organism. Such environmental influence on smaller structures was termed "downward causation" or "top-down causation" by Donald Campbell (1974).

This idea was adopted by the physical biochemist Arthur Peacocke in a number of works, and he uses the related term *whole–part influence* "to represent the net effect of all those ways in which a system as a whole . . . is a determining factor in what happens to its parts" (2007, 16). As a scientist, Peacocke feels committed to naturalism, which he defines as the view that there are "no 'supernatural' entities, no 'miracles' that break the laws or regularities of nature discovered by science, no dualisms within the natural world" (2007, 9). All is explicable by the natural sciences, though the sciences must accept the fact of emergence in the natural world—that is, the existence of whole–part causation.

For Peacocke, complex physical systems affect the behavior of their constituent parts, but no new "extra forces or entities" are introduced. "All concrete particulars in the world (including human beings)—with all of their properties—are constituted only of fundamental physical entities of matter/energy" (2007, 12). The terms of higher-level descriptions cannot be reduced to terms of the lowest level, though all the entities there are can be found exhaustively specified at the lowest level.

Thus, we may say that particles behave differently when they are parts of a larger organic whole. To that extent, mathematical descriptions of particle behavior must include reference to whole systems as well as individual particles. But there is no reference to extra, much less immaterial, entities. The only substances (entities) that exist are physical substances, while such substances in suitably complex arrays have emergent properties and powers.

For this sort of nonreductive materialism, the nature of matter cannot be ascertained until all its potentialities, within the total structure of the physical universe, have been unfolded. That is, at least, a different sort of materialism than the classical reductionist theory. But is it really a sort of materialism at all? Peacocke accepts the existence of God, a purely immaterial consciousness, whose particular intentions influence events in the world, so that "they would not otherwise have happened had God not specifically intended them" (2007, 45). If immaterial intentions cause some material events to be as they are, when they could have been otherwise, then it looks very much as though there are material events that have an immaterial, supernatural cause after all. And purely material explanations will not, in fact, provide a fully adequate account of why things are as they are in the cosmos. A full explanation will require reference to the intentions of an immaterial Conscious Being.

Peacocke pictures this by thinking of God as "containing" the cosmos within the Divine Being (that is what *panentheism* means). God is, thus, the total environment within which the cosmos exists, and whole–part causation obtains not only in complex structures within the cosmos but between God and the cosmos. God is a real causal influence on events in the universe, though "without abrogating natural regularities" (2007, 46).

The fact remains that the Ultimate Reality, God, cannot be explained as a very complex arrangement of simple elementary particles. Ontological primacy must be given to consciousness and its contents. The consciousness of God exists whether or not the universe exists, so there is, at least, one supernatural cause, and a full explanation of many physical events requires reference to its intentions since those events would not have happened if those intentions had not existed. All this means that the regularities of nature must be compatible with some form of supernatural causality. And it means that there are, after all, supernatural causes—not all causes exist within the natural realm.

The theory is not quite as naturalistic as we might think. It involves the existence of quite a lot of supernatural causality and a fundamental dualism between God and the physical cosmos. What, then, is the force of talking about emergence and whole–part causation?

It is, I think, to stress that there is a continuous development in the cosmos from simple elements to complex structures and that human consciousness is the result of a gradual unfolding of the potentialities of matter. New properties and causal powers come into existence that are natural developments of matter and yet are similar in kind to the nature of the Ultimate Spiritual Reality that has initiated and sustains the whole process.

Thus, the basic nature of matter, at the most fundamental level, is what it is in order that finite embodied consciousnesses should develop. The ultimate form of explanation is teleological, the intentions of the Creator being the "whole" that influences the nature of the elementary material parts. That influence is not all-determining. It lays down natural regularities and principles of emergence, so that the cosmos has its own relative autonomy—but an autonomy intrinsically open to divine influence toward the emergence of consciousness and value.

Divine action is, thus, not occasional interference in the laws of nature. It is continuous with natural processes, present throughout the whole cosmos and entirely compatible with our mathematical descriptions of physical behavior—which, accordingly, must be rather looser and more flexible than some Newtonian physicists thought.

Are There Causes outside the Domain of Science?

It is a remarkable fact that we can provide mathematical descriptions of physical behavior and that there are various levels of description (subatomic, atomic, molecular, macromolecular, and cosmic) that provide simplifying and elegant descriptions that enable us to understand physical phenomena much better. But there is little justification for supposing that our descriptions exactly mirror every way in which everything in the whole universe behaves.

Does every event in the physical universe fall under some mathematical description of a general sort? There is no *a priori* reason that should be so, and it is not a condition of scientific success that it should be so. Science will proceed much as it does if most events that are observed in controlled experimental conditions fall under such descriptions ("laws") and if the descriptions thus generated prove useful guides to how things happen in the real world outside the laboratory. But surprises are the heart of scientific progress, and while scientists will look for elegant mathematical descriptions, they may fail to find them, except in rather general terms.

In quantum theory, there is no way of telling exactly when or how an atomic particle will change its quantum state, though the probability of its doing so at a specific time can be mathematically assigned. Paul Dirac says, "Questions about what decides whether the photon is to go through [a crystal of tourmaline, which only allows photons of a specific polarization to go through] or not and how it changes its direction of polarization when it does go through cannot be investigated by experiment and should be regarded as outside the domain of science" (1958, 6).

Here are millions of specific events (changes of quantum state) that do not fall under any general descriptions, though classes of such events do fall under general probabilistic descriptions (given by the Schrödinger equations, which assign roughly classical properties to wave packets). These "laws" permit alternatives, and the laws assign a range of possible alternatives, no known reason being assignable for which one is actually taken. This does not cause science to collapse, for the existence of such alternatives (present in unmeasured particles as superpositions) is allowed, or even entailed, by the formalism, and their range is limited in precisely specifiable ways.

What that shows is that laws (mathematical descriptions of behavior) can allow elements of flexibility or openness in the phenomena they describe. To put it another way, mathematical descriptions can select the data on which they operate, ignoring other data for the moment, and proceed in a probabilistic way. Dirac says, "The limitation in the power of observation puts a limitation on the number of data that can be assigned to a state. Thus a state of an atomic system must be specified by fewer or more indefinite data than a complete set of numerical values for all the coordinates and velocities at some instant of time" (1958, 11).

Dirac writes that "quantum mechanics may be defined as the application of equations of motion to atomic particles" (1958, 312). But he holds, for instance, that "quantum electrodynamics does not provide a complete description of nature" (1958, 307) and that there may be much that lies, in principle, beyond our capacity to observe it, for instance, because of its extreme smallness and its consequent perturbation by our techniques of observation. It, thus, seems that a complete account of the basic level of nature is certainly beyond us at present, and perhaps that it is likely to remain so.

That must throw doubt on any claim that we know that this basic level completely explains all higher levels of nature. There seem to be many events and states that escape the possibility of precise mathematical formalization. And when we consider the considerable effort and expense that is required to isolate systems in order to obtain experimental data, we might begin to suspect that where, in the real world, systems are not isolated but are entangled with many other systems, some of which we know little about, the picture of a closed deterministic web of causality has lost its appeal. There may be many causal influences on the physical world that do not fall under mathematical equations. And the most obvious of these influences is the influence of conscious intentions and decisions on the bodily states of intelligent organic life forms.

Conscious intentions do not break the laws of nature, but, at least for common sense, they introduce new causal factors that supplement a purely physical account of human or animal behavior. The laws of nature seem to function more-or-less deterministically when there is no personal influence involved, but they leave room for personal influence in specific highly complex physical contexts (that is, in brains). This need not be a matter of there being "gaps" in causality in brains, where persons could insert themselves. It might be more a case of different sorts of causal factors operating more clearly when the physical substratum creates the right conditions for such factors to operate.

A major objection to this theory is that it can sound very much like the "God of the gaps," an expression coined by the Methodist mathematician A. C. Coulson in 1958. This is a God who is introduced in order to fill in a gap in a scientific explanation. The classical example is Newton's postulate that God would have to adjust the laws of gravity occasionally to keep the planets in their orbits.

If you say that physical laws do not explain everything, are you saying that there are gaps in scientific explanation? The "gap" image makes you think of a seamless web of deterministic causality that needs to be tweaked at various points to make things go the way God wants. But suppose there is not such a seamless web at all. The fundamental laws of nature are probabilistic. There is nothing wrong with laws of nature, no deficiency that can be filled by the introduction of God as part of a scientific explanation, but there are some states that those laws do not cover. It is not that there are gaps in the theory that God could satisfactorily fill. Rather, there are limits to the range and applicability of the laws of nature. Law-like causality may be a pervasive feature of the universe. But so may be creative, non-law-like causality.

God could never enter into a scientific theory, any more than a physicist's love of Beethoven would have any place in the laws of fluid mechanics. But that does not mean that the love of Beethoven does not exist or that it is wholly explained by fluid mechanics. It is just something that does not enter into a scientific law-like, mathematically expressible theory.

When we consider the social and psychological sciences, sciences that deal with persons in their full social reality, it is obvious that very few accurate mathematical descriptions of human behavior have been discovered. The range of alternatives for human action is just too great to permit the formulation of any but the most highly general laws, like "people will do what benefits them." Even such a law will not operate all the time and is, in any case, highly disputed. Some would say that "people will do what benefits their genes (unknown to them)," and some might hold that many people are quite genuinely altruistic. In any case, these laws cannot be expressed in differential equations, so they fail a primary test of hard science.

In economics, there are many mathematical formulae that are very useful to investment analysts, for example. But they are rather like average rules of thumb, and particular circumstances may overturn them—otherwise, every good mathematician would be very rich!

So, it may not be true that every event has a physical cause, or a specific set of such causes, that completely and exhaustively explains the occurrence of the event. It is enough if general mathematical descriptions fit the facts well enough to be immensely useful. Such descriptions operate with total accuracy only in closely controlled conditions. And, even then, in the quantum world that is the lowest base of physical reality, they seem to operate only probabilistically. The proposal that all events are determined at a basic physical level by a set of unchangeable and completely specific set of laws does not seem to fit the facts of modern science.

The End of the Closed Causal Web?

John Polkinghorne points out that "the predictable systems, studied by Newton and his successors, are exceptional in their simplicity" (1989, 2). "Recent advances in science," he says, "point to an openness and flexibility within physical processes" (13). This is most obvious at the quantum level, but Polkinghorne argues that, because of the nature of complex dynamic systems, "even at those macrocosmic levels where classical physics gives an adequate account, there is an openness to the future which relaxes the unrelenting grip of mechanical determinism" (130). In the real world, where delicate systems are never truly isolated but often have an infinitesimally balanced sensitivity to events far away in the universe, Newton's laws give "no more than an approximation to a more supple reality." Such an ontological openness allows the operation of further causal principles, active in bringing about the future.

Polkinghorne proposes the concept of "information" or pattern-forming influence as a model for divine action. This is, in effect, an appeal to teleology, a purposeful ordering of nature that leaves mathematical descriptions of nature as complete as they can be, yet still gives an intelligible place to nonphysical causal influences that cannot be brought under and do not compete with the general regularities described by the equations of physics.

It might prove helpful to reformulate talk of "laws of nature," with its implication that such laws actually exist before or outside the physical universe, as talk of mathematical descriptions of behavior. Then, it will be no surprise that the laws of nature deal only with "natural" causes. That is only saying that the variables of our mathematical equations must be filled with precisely measurable and observable values, if the equations are to work. There is no known way of measuring intentions, feelings, or thoughts. So, there are no equations that include them.

That does not mean they do not exist or that they have no influence. It just means, for example, that we cannot formulate a law for the creation of a universe by the intention of God, for there is no general mathematical description of the creation of universes. If there were, that really would be the ultimate equation to explain the universe. But it is highly unlikely to exist.

In the same way, if God changes some physical state, that change will not fall under any mathematical description, for precisely the same reason—God's acts fall under no general law. That is the reason God is not part of science. God just does not fit into our equations. God is not the observable and measurable value of a variable.

Why, then, should some scientists get so upset at the thought of God's changing some physical state? Presumably because then there would be some event that did not fall under a general mathematical description. But there are millions of such events anyway—including the change in quantum states of atoms and the free actions of human persons. Such events are not meaningless or wholly random. In both cases, there is a selection from a limited range of alternatives. In the case of persons, this selection is made for a reason, consciously entertained by the person. In the case of electrons, no consciousness is involved, but there may well be underlying constraints that weight the probabilities in ways not yet obvious to us and not capable of being framed in precise and universal mathematical descriptions. These might include teleological considerations concerning what is required for the successive emergence of stable atoms, replicating molecules, central nervous systems, and a conscious neocortex. No one has devised a mathematical formalism that can measure and correlate the formation and implementation of goals precisely. So such considerations will, as Dirac puts it, lie outside the boundaries of science.

Laws of nature are humanly constructed mathematical descriptions of the behavior of objects with a set of relevant denumerable properties. But what the hidden causes of that behavior are we have no idea, and how far our descriptions mirror their true nature we cannot know. We can only say that our descriptions work well enough—in fact, with supreme accuracy in relatively closed or controlled conditions—but not that there is nothing else to be described, or perhaps even, as Dirac and d'Espagnat suggest, beyond description.

Quantum Physics and Consciousness

Quantum physics helps to demolish the picture of laws of nature as wholly objective, all-determining forces, weaving a closed and inflexible causal web that none can escape. The interpretation of quantum physics is very controversial, but virtually all agree that electrons are probability waves in a multidimensional abstract "space" that take precise position only when experimentally constrained and measured.

The "measurement problem" is a wholly unresolved area of quantum interpretation, but it establishes that the world of specifically locatable point particles with rigidly designatable properties that we used to postulate in physics has disappeared. The real world, as it exists unobserved, or at least unmeasured by our apparatus, does not consist of such particles. It seems to consist of smeared-out, wave-like entities that half-exist in a number of different states (superpositions).

Furthermore, those waves are entangled in complex ways, which we can express mathematically but can hardly begin to imagine. There is a reality that mathematics represents without picturing. As to what really exists, we do not know. But our mathematical models work. "Description" has now been pressed to its furthest extent. The quantum physicist is not describing in the sense that a painter copies what he sees. The physicist is constructing elegant mathematical relationships, using numbers that do not correspond one-to-one with objective entities but that provide a nonpicturing model of a hidden but real world of fields and forces.

Mathematical description has passed into mathematical modeling, rooted in and confirmed by experimental observations but no longer simply setting down what is weighed and counted. In the strange quantum world, mathematics has the form of description, but exactly how the mathematics is to be interpreted—what its terms correspond to in reality—remains hidden.

The laws of nature do not make things happen. They describe the regularities of events, but they do not "make" or bring into existence anything. In quantum physics, they construct models of an intelligible world of supreme intellectual beauty but remain agnostic about the precise nature of the objective reality that lies veiled and always beyond their formulae.

A Creative Power brings things into being. Why should this power always conform to our mathematical descriptions or be forced to travel always on the railway lines of enforced regularity? There is a place for regularity. Our world would be incomprehensible and unlivable without it. But there is also a place for creativity, for the new and unexpected, for what goes beyond all the descriptions of what has gone before. Quantum physics suggests a model of the cosmos as a probabilistic, holistic, entangled, flexible reality that is far from the predesignated tram lines of the Newtonian model.

But what has all this to do with supernatural causes? Well, it may put the supernatural in a rather different light. God need not be conceived as a pure spirit quite outside the physical world, having to interfere with its mechanism from time to time. The cosmos itself may have a form of intelligibility that is intrinsically open to the creative influence of a more-than-physical reality. Isaac Newton believed that space and time were the "sensoria" of God. Quantum physics makes even more plausible the supposition that our physical reality, replete with intellectual beauty and intelligibility, with both mathematical regularity and emergent creativity, is one finite expression of a supreme underlying Spiritual Reality.

I do not think there is any question of quantum physics' "proving" God. It can be given a perfectly naturalistic interpretation—or it need not be interpreted at all! But it does raise deep and unresolved questions about the ultimate nature of physical reality. It puts a question mark against the belief that there is one solid physical reality of more-or-less ordinary but very small objects and that, in this reality, consciousness, value, and purpose are problematic and causally irrelevant ideas that need to be explained away.

According to the most widely accepted interpretation of quantum physics, the Copenhagen interpretation, what we know of fundamental physical reality is the relation between elementary particles, a specific measuring apparatus devised by an observer, and an observing consciousness. The dynamic properties of electrons, such as position and direction of travel, do not exist until they are produced by what Niels Bohr called "the entire measurement situation." No doubt something exists, but it is consciousness of the everyday phenomenal world that gives electrons precise position and momentum.

Consciousness changes reality, and, for some quantum theorists, like

Henry Stapp, Eugene Wigner, and John von Neumann, it creates reality or, at least, some of the important properties of reality. In such a mysterious field as quantum physics, it would be unwise to pick out one interpretation as the correct one, when theories will probably change very rapidly. Nevertheless, for a quantum physicist it is hard to dismiss the possibility that, as Eugene Wigner put it, "The content of consciousness is an ultimate reality" (1983, 181).

In some way, the world of which we are ordinarily conscious, which includes seeing electrons as specks on a screen, is different in kind from the unobserved world represented by wave functions and Schrödinger equations. We might say that the quantum world does not really exist (one version of the Copenhagen interpretation) or that it exists as a world of "potencies" (to use Heisenberg's term), or that it exists as a superposition of all possible states (the Hugh Everett many-worlds theory) or that it exists as an undivided whole (David Bohm's "implicate-order" theory). In any case, it seems to be human consciousness that is a constituent and fundamental element of the world as we see it. Without consciousness, the perceived world would not exist as it does. This implies that consciousness is not just a by-product of matter as we perceive it. The material world as it appears to us is, at least in part, a product of consciousness.

No one (or, to be careful, I should say virtually no one) denies that human consciousness has a neural substratum that is the causal basis of its existence. No one denies that human consciousness is a very late arrival on the cosmic scene. But quantum theory suggests that human consciousness is a genuinely new and distinct reality, which gives a radically new character to observed physical reality.

The world as it appears to consciousness is not reducible to some basic level of purely material reality. Reductionism is not just wrong; it contradicts the best scientific evidence. Furthermore, the world as it appears to human consciousness is a world in which persons conceive and evaluate possibilities, make free and creative decisions, and primarily relate to their environment and to others in positive or negative affective ways.

The world in which humans exist is not a world solely of measurable and mathematically describable regularities. It is a world of evaluations, decisions, and purposes that are not precisely measurable or regular but that are explicable in terms of selection from a range of possibilities for the sake of enjoying some perceived value. It is, in short, a personal world, a world in which nonphysical causality (causality in terms of value and purpose, not in terms of quantity and regularity) plays a major role.

Any adequate account of causality must give an account of the laws of nature that permits nonphysical causality to play a positive role. If that is so, then the question of whether there is nonhuman, nonphysical causality is a question of fact (though not of scientific fact, if science is strictly defined in terms of publicly observable and repeatable data).

If consciousness is a basic and irreducible element of reality, then a Cosmic Consciousness—conceiving possibles, evaluating and selecting actual states for the sake of value, and not being causally dependent on any physical substratum—becomes a more plausible and attractive idea. It is an extrapolation from personal causality, but that does not make it unduly anthropomorphic since humans do not exhibit such a non-embodied, all-inclusive, and purely rational form of consciousness. The thought that human consciousness is not just a by-product of material processes suggests the possibility that some form of consciousness may be fundamental to the existence of matter itself.

Science makes a difference to how such a possible Cosmic Consciousness is conceived. The picture of an extracosmic person who could do absolutely anything must be replaced by the model of a perfectly realized consciousness, the acts of which are constrained by the laws of regularity and freedom that enable a cosmos of physically embodied and emergent persons to exist.

A supernatural cause acts wherever some human mind is brought to know the nature or purpose of a more-than-human Spiritual Reality or to feel guidance to a specific course of action and is helped to pursue that course. Despite the fact that there are many errors and misperceptions in religion, as in every area of human knowledge, it is reasonable for a person who guards against such errors as carefully as possible to believe that there is a form of Objective Spiritual Causality or that there is divine guidance and inspiration in the universe.

Science may lead someone to think that there is a vast Intelligence underlying the universe. It will be personal experience that leads someone to think there is a personal God or a spiritual law of cosmic justice. Science can help to construct a reasonable and coherent account of such a Spiritual Reality. But it will probably be an acceptance of the existence of consciousness and personal causality as an irreducible element of reality and of a belief that such a personal causality, which is not just that of other finite persons, has been experienced that opens the way to thinking of a personal God.

Science and Religious Belief: An Inconclusive Conclusion

When people claim to know God, they rarely claim to have come across an infinite Cosmic Consciousness that contains all possible states and that acts on purely rational principles. The major philosophers of most world faiths all distinguish between the ultimate essence of God, which is beyond the grasp of the human mind, and the appearances of God to human beings. Maimonides in Judaism, Al Gazzali in Islam, Sankara in Hinduism, Aquinas and Gregory Palamas in Christianity—all stress the unknowability of the Divine Essence, as the infinite reality underlying all the appearances of finite worlds. This is not some modern revisionist idea of God. It is the classical idea, which is as far from any anthropomorphic conception as you could get.

But once you have posited Consciousness as the ultimate basis of reality, it is natural to think that Consciousness should have some purpose in creating a universe. Part of that purpose is simply the beauty and elegance of the universe that can be enjoyed by God. But it could also be the creation of finite persons who can share that enjoyment and cooperate in fashioning new forms of beauty. Such finite persons might be able to know God and to cooperate with God in realizing a cosmic purpose. If so, the Infinite Source of all Being must find some way of revealing its nature, its purpose, and some way of helping finite persons to implement that purpose.

Religions are based on some originative revelation, some disclosure of the divine nature and purpose that has occurred in history. Even Buddhism, with no interest in a creator God, is based on a disclosure of the way to liberation that occurred in the teaching of Siddartha Gautama, the Buddha for our age.

So God, or Spiritual Reality, is claimed to disclose itself in finite events or persons and in ways suited to human understanding. The God of revealed religion is not a tyrant who orders people to keep telling him how wonderful he is and who helps the people he likes to find parking spaces. The God of revealed religion is the infinite source of being, making itself known to humans, for the sake of their well-being, in forms they can grasp. In and through the prophets of the Semitic traditions, the teachers of the Indian traditions, and the sages of the East Asian traditions, Infinite Spirit is disclosed in various ways through finite words and images.

This cuts little ice with the skeptic, who will point out the contradictions between the teachings of different prophets and religions and who will see personal experience as always prone to delusion and uncheckable fantasy. People may claim to experience God. But why do their experiences of the Divine differ so much? And how do they know it is God they experience? What possible tests are there for genuineness and truth?

Still, at least religious believers can say they are not just relying on a very abstract hypothesis. There are experiences that have the power to change the way they see things and to raise them to a new quality of life, to liberate them from egoism, hatred, and selfish desire and give them a sense of joy, significance, moral renewal, and freedom. These are personally important and vital experiences that change lives.

These experiences are not publicly checkable, and many people think they are delusions. There is no way of independently testing the truth of such claims. So, for some people, they will never be convincing. Yet this is not a matter that science can resolve.

Science concerns itself precisely with the publicly testable, measurable, and repeatable. Religion claims that there is another way of access to truth. There is a Spiritual Reality, a Supreme Objective Consciousness. Obviously, it cannot be publicly observed since only physical things can be publicly observed. It cannot be measured, and it cannot be subjected to laboratory experiments. If there is any way of access to it, it must be by direct mental apprehension. Even if that apprehension is mediated through some physical event, Spirit cannot itself be physically observed.

Millions of people claim such apprehension of Spirit. Their accounts differ—as to whether it is one reality or many, personal or impersonal, transcendent or immanent, omnipotent or limited in power. But they differ in ways that correlate with different fundamental descriptions of the nature of reality, different metaphysical conceptual schemes. Some differences reflect historical, cultural, and psychological factors that give rise to different ways of describing human experiences and differing ideas on the sorts of experiences that are rationally desirable.

Diversity is not really surprising. It exists in morality, in art, in philosophy, in history, in law, and in approaches to science, too. It is part of the nature of human experience, embodied, historical, and person-relative as it is. So, the believer may say, we should expect diversity in claims to apprehend Spirit. But what is fundamental is the claim to apprehend a nonmaterial reality of consciousness and great value, knowledge of which can liberate human lives from evil and lead them to inner fulfillment.

Claims to apprehend Spirit may be beyond the scope of the physical sciences. It is the philosophy of materialism that denies the reality of Spirit and the reliability of spiritual experience. The natural sciences are concerned only with the physical. On the question of whether there are nonphysical, spiritual realities that can be known by direct apprehension, the natural sciences have little to say, and, at that point, the claims of particular religious traditions need to be patiently investigated.

Religions are based on the fundamental axiom of the ontological primacy of Spirit. Without such an axiom, religion cannot get started. Science can live with that axiom but will not provide or prove it. But with such an axiom, it is much more probable that the natural order will exhibit the intellectual beauty, the integrated complexity, and the awe-inspiring sublimity that is revealed ever more fully by the natural sciences.

Are there supernatural causes? Science, properly concerned as it is with the natural world, does not deal with them. But if the physical cosmos is essentially open to creative and holistic influences, to a pattern-forming purpose tending to the emergence of many forms of distinctive value, and if its goal is unity of being with Spirit, then it seems entirely plausible and in accordance with the deepest insights of natural science to affirm that there are. The creative mathematical Intelligence that natural scientists can readily understand can also be seen as the basis of the moral order of the cosmos or as the active personal God of religious devotion. To see Spirit thus is the role of religion, and, in that sense, religion and science are, as Stephen Gould said in *Rock of Ages* (1977), distinct intellectual magisteria. But they overlap and influence one another more closely than Gould allowed. For religious believers, at least, they describe complementary aspects of a cosmos in which both physical and conscious entities exist. But for the religious believer, consciousness must be regarded as more fundamental.

Religions claim to offer ways in which a Supreme Consciousness can be known in personal experience. The natural sciences are primarily concerned with natural, nonconscious facts. For some, the findings of science point toward a Primordial Consciousness as the source and foundation of all things. For others, science promises to explain the cosmos completely in material terms, without any reference to such a Primordial Consciousness. One of these views is correct. Which one? That remains the biggest question of all.

References

Anderson, S. W., et al. 1999. Impairment of social and moral behavior related to early damage in human prefrontal cortex. *Nature Neuroscience* 2: 1032–37.

Argyle, Michael. 1958. *Religious behaviour*. London: Routledge.

Atkins, Peter. 1994. *Creation revisited*. New York: Penguin.

Atran, Scott. 2004. Religion's evolutionary landscape. *Behavioural and Brain Sciences* 27: 713–70.

Augustine. 1991. *De Trinitate*. Trans. Edmund Hill. New York: New City Press.

Ayala, Francisco. 2004. Design without designer. In *Debating design*, eds. William Dembski and Michael Ruse, 55–80. Cambridge: Cambridge University Press.

Ayer, A. J. 1936. *Language, truth and logic*. London: Victor Gollancz.

Barrow, John, and Frank Tipler. 1986. *The anthropic cosmological principle*. Oxford: Oxford University Press.

Boethius. 1969. *The consolation of philosophy*. Trans. V. E. Watts. Harmondsworth, UK: Penguin.

Brown, Warren. 2004. Neurobiological embodiment of spirituality and soul. In *From cells to souls*, ed. Malcolm Jeeves, 58–76. Grand Rapids, MI: Wm. B. Eerdmans.

Brown, Warren, Nancey Murphy, and Newton Malony. 1998. *Whatever happened to the soul?* Minneapolis: Fortress Press.

Buber, Martin. 1958. *I and thou*. Trans. Ronald Gregor Smith. Edinburgh: T. and T. Clark.

Burkhardt, T. H., F. Bowers, and I. Skrupskelis. 1978. *Essays in philosophy*. Cambridge, MA: Harvard University Press.

Calvin, John. 1989. *Institutes of the Christian religion*. Trans. Henry Beveridge. Grand Rapids, MI: Wm. B. Eerdmans.

Campbell, Donald. 1974. Downward causation in hierarchically organized systems. In *Studies in the philosophy of biology*, eds. F. Ayala and F. Dobhzhansky, 179–86. London: Macmillan.

Capra, Fritjof. 1975. *The tao of physics*. Berkeley, CA: Shambhala.

Carr, Bernard. 2004. Mind and the cosmos. In *Science, consciousness and ultimate reality*, ed. David Lorimer, 33–64. Charlottesville, VA: Imprint Academic.

———. 2007. *Universe or multiverse?* Cambridge: Cambridge University Press.

Carter, Brandon. 1974. Large number coincidences and the anthropic principle in cosmology. In *Confrontation of cosmological theories with observation*, ed. M. S. Longair. Dordrecht, Holland: Reidel.

Collins, Robin. 2003. The evidence for fine-tuning. In *God and design: The teleological argument and modern science*, ed. Neil Manson. New York: Routledge.

Conway Morris, Simon. 2002. Does biology have an eschatology? In *The far-future universe*, ed. George Ellis, 158–76. Philadelphia: Templeton Foundation Press.

———. 2003. *Life's solution*. Cambridge: Cambridge University Press.

Crick, Francis. 1994. *The astonishing hypothesis*. New York: Simon and Schuster.

Damasio, Antonio R. 1994. *Descartes' error: Emotion, reason and the human brain*. New York: Crosset Putnam.

Darwin, Charles. 1859. *On the origin of opecies*. London: John Murray.

———. 1871. *On the origin of opecies*. 6th ed. Oxford: Oxford University Press.

———. 1968. *On the origin of opecies*. Ed. J. W. Burrow. Harmondsworth, UK: Penguin.

———. 1985. *The correspondence of Charles Darwin*, vol. 8. Ed. Frederick Burkhardt and Sydney Smith. Cambridge: Cambridge University Press.

Davies, Paul. 1982. *The accidental universe*. Cambridge: Cambridge University Press.

Dawkins, Richard. 1978. *The selfish gene*. St. Albans, UK: Granada Publishing.

———. 2006. *The God delusion*. London: Bantam.

Dennett, Daniel. 1992. *Consciousness explained*. New York: Penguin.

———. 2006. *Breaking the spell*. New York: Viking.

Denton, Michael. 1998. *Nature's destiny*. New York: Free Press.

Descartes, René. 1960. *Meditations*. Trans. Arthur Wollaston. Harmondsworth: Penguin.

Dirac, Paul. 1958. *The principles of quantum mechanics*, 4th ed. Oxford: Oxford University Press.

Durkheim, Emile. 1963. *The elementary forms of religious life*. Trans. J. Swain. New York: Macmillan.

Dyson, Freeman. 2002. Life in the universe: Is life digital or analogue?" In *The far-future universe*, ed. George Ellis, 140–57. Philadelphia: Templeton Foundation Press.

Edelman, Gerald. 1992. *Bright air, brilliant fire*. New York: Penguin.

Einstein, Albert. 1929. *Festschrift für Aunel Stadola*. Zurich: Orell Fussli.

———. 1970. *Out of my later years*. Westport, CT: Greenwood Press.

Espagant, Bernard d'. 1990. *Reality and the physicist*. Cambridge: Cambridge University Press.

———. 1995. *Veiled reality*. Reading, MA: Addison-Wesley Pub.

Evans-Pritchard, Edward. 1965. *Theories of primitive religion*. Oxford, UK: Clarendon Press.

Farrell, B. A. 1970. On the design of a conscious device. *Mind* (July).

Gale, Richard. 1991. *On the nature and existence of God*. Cambridge: Cambridge University Press.

Gingerich, Owen. 2002. Cosmic eschatology versus human eschatology. In *The far-future universe*, ed. George Ellis, 225–34. Philadelphia: Templeton Foundation Press.

Glock, Charles Y., and Rodney Stark. 1965. *Religion and society in tension*. Chicago: Rand McNally.

Goodwin, Brian. 1994. *How the leopard changed its spots*. London: Weidenfeld and Nicolson.

Gottlieb, Roger, ed. 1996. *This sacred earth*. New York: Routledge.

Gould, Stephen J. 1989. *Wonderful life*. New York: W. W. Norton.

———. 1999. *Rock of ages*. New York: Ballantine Publishing Group.

Greeley, A. M. 1974. *Ecstasy: A way of knowing*. Englewood Cliffs, NJ: Prentice-Hall.

Gregory, Richard L., ed. 1987. *The Oxford companion to the mind*. Oxford: Oxford University Press.

Guth, Alan. 1997. *The inflationary universe*. New York: Helix Books.

Hay, David. 1990. *Religious experience today*. London: Mowbray.

Hawking, Stephen. Quantum cosmology. 1996. In *The nature of space and time*, eds. Stephen Hawking and Roger Penrose. Princeton, NJ: Princeton University Press.

———. 1998. *A brief history of time*, 10th anniv. ed. New York: Bantam.

Hindu scriptures. 1966. Trans. R. C. Zaehner. London: Dent.

Hume, David. 1955. *An inquiry concerning human understanding*. Ed. Charles W. Handel. New York: Liberal Arts Press.

Huxley, T. H. 1947. *Evolution and ethics*. London: Pilot Press.

Isham, Chris. 1993. God, time, and the creation of the universe. In *Explorations in science and theology*, 55–60. London: Royal Society of Arts.

James, William. 1968. *Varieties of religious experience*. London: Fontana.

Jeeves, Malcolm. 2006. Linking mind and brain. In *Human nature*, ed. Malcolm Jeeves, 181–97. Edinburgh: Royal Society of Edinburgh.

Johnson, Phillip. 2000. *The wedge of truth*. Downers Grove, IL: InterVarsity Press.

Jung, Carl. 1963. *Memories, dreams, reflections*. London: Fontana.

Kim, Jaegwon. 1994. The myth of nonreductive materialism. In *The mind–body problem*, ed. Richard Warren and Tadeusz Szubka, 242–60. Oxford, UK: Basil Blackwell.

Koenig, Harold, et al., eds. 2000. *The handbook of religion and health*. Oxford: Oxford University Press.

Leslie, John. 2001. *Infinite minds*. Oxford: Oxford University Press.

Leuba, James Henry. 1925. *The psychology of religious mysticism*. London: Kegan Paul.

Longair, M. 1984. *Theoretical concepts in physics*. Cambridge: Cambridge University Press.

Mackie, J. L. 1977. *Ethics: Inventing right and wrong*. New York: Penguin.

Maguire, E. A., et al. 2000. Navigation related structural change in the hippocampi of taxi-drivers. *Proceedings of the National Academy of Science of the USA* 97: 4398–4403.

Maslow, Abraham. 1964. *Religions, values and peak experiences*. New York: Viking.

Miller, Kenneth. 2004. The flagellum unspun. In *Debating design*, eds. William Dembski and Michael Ruse, 81–98. Cambridge: Cambridge University Press.

Milner, David. 2006. Visual awareness and the primate brain. In *Human nature*, ed. Malcolm Jeeves, 138–54. Edinburgh: Royal Society of Edinburgh.

Moltmann, Jurgen. 2002. Cosmos and theosis. In *The far-future universe*, ed. George Ellis, 249–65. Philadelphia: Templeton Foundation Press.

O'Craven, Kathleen M., and Nancy Kanwisher. 2006. Mental imagery of faces and places activates corresponding stimulus-specific brain regions. *Journal of Cognitive Neuroscience* 12: 1013–23.

Otto, Rudolf. 1959. *The idea of the holy*. Trans. John W. Harvey. New York: Penguin.

Peacocke, Arthur. 2001. *Paths from science towards God*. Oxford, UK: Oneworld Press.

———. 2007. *All that is*. Minneapolis: Fortress Press.

Penrose, Roger. 1997. *The large, the small and the human mind*. Cambridge: Cambridge University Press.

Plantinga, Alvin. 1983. Reason and belief in God. In *Faith and rationality*, eds. Alvin Plantinga and Nicholas Wolterstorff, 16–93. South Bend, IN: University of Notre Dame.

Polkinghorne, John. 1989. *Science and providence*. London: SPCK.

———. 2005. *Exploring reality*. London: SPCK.

Popper, Karl. 1972. *Objective knowledge: An evolutionary approach*. Oxford, UK: Clarendon Press.

Rees, Martin. 2001. *Our cosmic habitat*. Princeton, NJ: Princeton University Press.

———. 2002. Living in a multiverse. In *The far-future universe*, ed. George Ellis, 65–85. Philadelphia: Templeton Foundation Press.

Ridley, Matt. 1996. *The origins of virtue*. New York: Viking.

Ruse, Michael. 1995. *Evolutionary naturalism*. London: Routledge.

Ryle, Gilbert. 1949. *The concept of mind*. London: Hutchinson's University Library.

Sadato, N. et al. 1996. Activation of the primary visual cortex by Braille reading in blind subjects. *Nature* 380: 526–28.

Searle, John. 1980. Minds, brains, and programs. *Behavioural and Brain Sciences* 3 (1980): 417–58.

Smart, Ninian. 1997. *Dimensions of the sacred*. London: Fontana.

Starbuck, Edwin Diller. 1899. *The psychology of religion*. London: Walter Scott.

Swinburne, Richard. 1970. *The concept of miracles*. London: Macmillan.

———. 2004. *The existence of God*. Oxford: Oxford University Press.

Taliaferro, Charles. 1994. *Consciousness and the mind of God*. Cambridge: Cambridge University Press.

Taylor, Richard. 1966. *Action and purpose*. Englewood Cliffs, NJ: Prentice-Hall.

Tegmark, Max. 2007. The multiverse hierarchy. In *Universe or multiverse?* ed. Bernard Carr, 99–125. Cambridge: Cambridge University Press.

Teilhard de Chardin, Pierre. 1959. *The phenomenon of man*. Trans. Bernard Wall. London: Collins.

Tipler, Frank J. 1994. *The physics of immortality*. New York: Doubleday.

Trivers, Robert. 1971. The evolution of reciprocal altruism. *Quarterly Review of Biology* 46: 35–57.

Tugwell, Simon. 1990. *Human immortality and the redemption of death*. London: Darton, Longman and Todd.

Vanstone, William. 1977. *Love's endeavour, love's expense*. London: Darton, Longman and Todd.

The Vedanta sutras. 1962. Trans. George Thibaut. In vol. 34, *Sacred books of the East*, ed. Max Muller. Delhi, India: Motilal Banarsidass.

Ward, Keith. 2007. *Is religious dangerous?* London: Lion/Hudson.

Weinberg, Steven. 1993. *Dreams of a final theory*. London: Vintage.

———. 1999. A designer universe? *The New York Review of Books* 46, no. 14) (October).

Whitehead, Alfred North. 1978. *Process and reality*. Ed. David Ray Griffin and Donald W. Sherburne. New York: Macmillan.

Wigner, Eugene. 1960. The unreasonable effectiveness of mathematics in natural sciences. *Communications in Pure and Applied Mathematics* 13, no. 1) (February 1960).

———. 1983. Remarks on the mind–body question. In *Quantum theory and measurement*, eds. J. A. Wheeler and W. H. Zurek, 168–81. Princeton, NJ: Princeton University Press.

Wilson, E. O. 1975. *Sociobiology: The new synthesis*. Cambridge, MA: Harvard University Press.

———. 1998. *Consilience*. London: Little, Brown.

Wisdom, John. 1963. Gods. In *Logic and language*, ed. A. G. N. Flew, Oxford, UK: Basil Blackwell.

Index